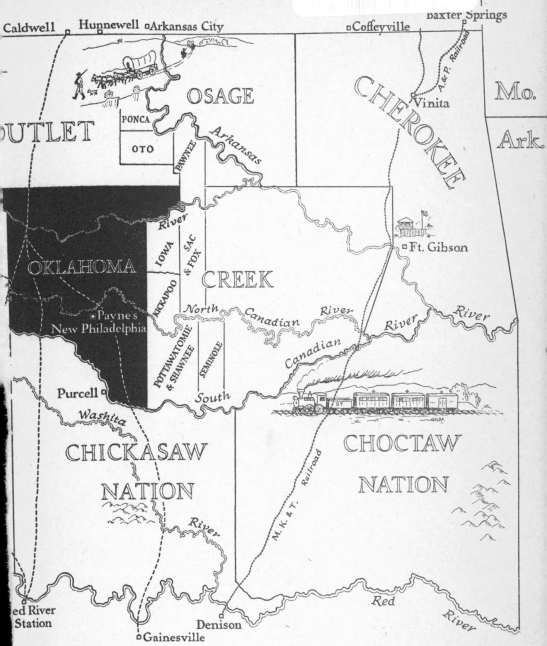

s a s

Caldwell Hunnewell □Arkansas City

OSAGE

□Coffeyville Baxter Springs

CHEROKEE

Mo.

OUTLET

PONCA

OTO

A. & P. Railroad

Vinita

Arkansas

Ark.

PAWNEE

River

OKLAHOMA

IOWA

SAC & FOX

KICKAPOO

CREEK

□Payne's
New Philadelphia

POTTAWATOMIE & SHAWNEE

SEMINOLE

North Canadian River

Ft. Gibson

River

River

Canadian

Purcell □

South

Washita

CHICKASAW

NATION

River

M. K. & T. Railroad

CHOCTAW

NATION

97

ed River
Station

Denison

□Gainesville

Red

River

T e x a s

Land Hunger

By Carl Coke Rister

PUBLISHED BY THE UNIVERSITY OF OKLAHOMA PRESS
NORMAN, OKLAHOMA

Southern Plainsmen, 1938

Border Captives, 1940

Land Hunger, 1942

The Southwestern Frontier, 1865–1881
CLEVELAND, 1928

The Greater Southwest
(*with* R. N. Richardson)
GLENDALE, 1934

Western America
(*with* LeRoy R. Hafen)
NEW YORK, 1941

DAVID L. PAYNE

Land Hunger:

David L. Payne
and the Oklahoma Boomers

By CARL COKE RISTER

NORMAN
UNIVERSITY OF OKLAHOMA PRESS
1942

To Ollie and Tommie Carson

Preface

The restless land hunger which drew thousands of men into the Boomer Movement to open the "Oklahoma" district of the Indian Territory to settlement is a phenomenon of power and of human determination. It is personified in the character of David L. Payne, the Oklahoma Boomer, a border adventurer of much the same mold as Buffalo Bill Cody, Kit Carson, Ewing Young, and Sam Houston. Like these others, Payne was not content to settle down to the tedium of a sedentary life, to be hedged about by long-established social conventions. He was essentially a border leader, seeking those fields of activity in which his bold, restless spirit could meet the challenge of a hazardous life. In a never-ending effort to enter and settle Oklahoma he found such a field. The Indians of the Five Civilized Tribes, the cattlemen, and even the federal government offered strong opposition, but this seemed only to stimulate him to greater effort to force the opening of the unassigned lands to white settlement.

The narrative in the following pages, then, is more than a biography, for Payne's life from 1879 to 1884 was so dedicated to the Boomer cause that its portrayal also depicts the movement. In the first three chapters the author presents Payne during his years in Indiana and Kansas when he was being conditioned in mind and body to meet the hard experiences of Oklahoma invasions. There is in Chapter IV a sketch of the Indian settlements after the Civil War incident to Indian Territory reservation assignments and to the origin of the Boomer Movement. The next eleven chapters are devoted to the high tide of the Boomer Movement while Payne was its leader, a period of field operations. Payne's death in 1884 brought to the front his able friend William L. Couch, who was leader of the Boomers until the final success of their movement.

Although Payne was dead, his spirit now, as a "pillar of fire," furnished Couch and other Boomer leaders the inspiration to carry on to ultimate success. For this reason the last two chapters constitute a fitting climax—in a sense, Payne's posthumous victory.

In this great border movement, the author has sought to portray Payne, the principal actor, objectively, and not to condemn or condone his many acts and motives. He must be judged in the light of his times. At best, the frontier was raw, and men's virtues were not polished by education and traditional influences. The prairie frontier was cruelly exacting of body, mind and soul, and only the strongest personalities could finally emerge unblemished. It so resulted, paradoxical as it may seem, that the average leader revealed striking qualities of strength and conspicuous elements of weakness, as was the case with Payne.

CARL COKE RISTER

Norman, Oklahoma
July 16, 1942

Acknowledgments

My task in preparing this study for publication was made easier than it otherwise would have been because of the many courtesies extended by others. The University of Oklahoma Faculty Research Committee awarded me a grant-in-aid with which to buy microfilms and maps. The National Archives made available manuscripts for microfilming from the files of the Department of Justice, the Department of Interior, and the Department of War. Also the staffs of the Library of Congress, the University of Oklahoma Library, the Phillips Collection (University of Oklahoma), the Oklahoma State Historical Library and Indian Archives at Oklahoma City, the Missouri State Historical Library and the University of Missouri Library at Columbia, the Wichita University Library at Wichita, Kansas, the University of Colorado Library at Boulder, and the Kansas State Historical Library at Topeka were unfailingly obliging and helpful.

I am particularly indebted to my friends for services rendered. To Gaston L. Litton, who listed materials for microfilming in the National Archives; to Niles Miller, Research Director, Kansas State Historical Library, for many different favors; and to my colleague, Professor E. E. Dale, for reading the manuscript, I owe my thanks. Then, Eugene Couch, son of W. L. Couch, the Boomer leader, assisted by reading the manuscript, and in identifying Oklahoma landmarks and in making available valuable materials. And Miss Mary Thoburn permitted me to use William M. Bloss's manuscript biography of David L. Payne, which was of great value. Finally, my wife, Mattie May Rister, rendered valuable assistance in copying materials, in compiling bibliographies, and in many other ways. For all these courtesies and services I am grateful. But any errors that may be found in the book are my own.

C. C. R.

The Chapters

The Illustrations

Land Hunger

1 : *From Indiana to Kansas*

*T*HE *QUEST* for free land has ever been the major driving force in the westward march of the American frontier. It was a factor when John Sevier and James Robertson led Virginia and North Carolina settlers along Piedmont trails to occupy the Holston and Watauga valleys; and it caused Daniel Boone to carve the Wilderness Trail from Watauga to Kentucky. Following the enactment of the land law of 1820, it led thousands of settlers to the tangled wilderness between Louisiana and Missouri, from which, sixteen years later, the state of Arkansas was shaped. Stephen F. Austin traveled the Camino Real of Texas in 1821, bringing colonists to develop his Brazos land grant, and by 1836 other thousands of immigrants had arrived. In the spring of this year Santa Anna sought to drive these land-hungry Anglo-Americans back across the Sabine, and he was in a fair way to succeed until Sam Houston and his buckskin-clad colonists charged the Mexican camp at San Jacinto on April 21 with the battle cry, "Remember the Alamo! Remember Goliad!" And the star of a young republic rose over the Texas plains. About the same time Marcus Whitman and H. H. Spaulding started with their young wives from Liberty, Missouri, for distant Oregon, paving the way for Anglo-American homes in this remote western land.

Hard times in those states immediately east of the Mississippi River drove many homeseekers westward. Land exploiters

3

and frenzied speculators had precipitated a panic, which President Andrew Jackson sought to arrest by his Specie Circular of July 10, 1836, but to no avail. Low income and high taxes afflicted the people like a scourge of locusts. Many a settler loaded his family into a covered wagon, abandoned his small claim, and crossed the Mississippi in search of untaxed land. It was these migrants who broke the barrier of stratified Indian reservations west of Arkansas and Missouri and finally forced the opening of the Great Plains for homestead entry.

But along the California coast, San Francisco, Los Angeles, and Monterey were yet sleepy Spanish-American villages, little knowing that before the passing of another decade and a half they were to become the pulsating centers of a thriving Pacific commonwealth. Between these towns and St. Louis was a vast, lonely, arid and semiarid waste with only occasional oases of white occupation, such as Fort Laramie and Bent's Trading Post.

Nevertheless, by 1836 the West had begun to feel its growing pains. Caravans were moving over the Santa Fe Trail and northwestward toward Oregon. The trans-Mississippi West had become a stage for robust action on which many characters had already played colorful roles. Robert Gray, a young New England mariner, had dropped anchor at a great Oregon river which he named the Columbia, after his flagship, establishing thereby the first claim of the United States to the fertile acres of this region. Philip Nolan had led his horse-hunters from Natchez to the Trinity River of Texas and there met his death, but the memoirs of Ellis P. Bean, a survivor, were later read and discussed by many prospective immigrants. Then later Jedediah Smith, Jim Bridger, and other mountain men explored the hidden parks and canyons of the Rockies and relayed their descriptions back to waiting adventurers and homeseekers.

And now was to appear another who was to help shape government policy relating to free land on part of the last American frontier. On a cold winter day, December 30, 1836, in a farmhouse about four miles east of the Indiana village of Fairmount, William Payne bent over the bed of his wife, Celia, and gazed with fond regard into the tiny red face of a newborn son, the fifth to be presented him since he had moved to Grant County. One could well believe that he offered a prayer of thanksgiving, for William was a devout man. And it might well be that this prayer was also for his son's future usefulness, a hope that was fulfilled in more ways than one. The boy indeed became a homesteader, hunter, scout, Indian fighter, legislator, and the invader of our last American frontier, the spiritual heir of all our trail blazers.

William and Celia named him David. Some thought that Celia wished to honor her brother; others were quite sure it was in memory of her famous cousin, Davy Crockett, who had recently fallen at the Alamo. But who can say? It might have been that Celia, with prophetic vision, had thought of the Biblical David who had slain Goliath, for certainly there were giants in the West to be slain before ambitious homeseekers could claim its far-flung acres.

Little is known about Dave's early childhood. He grew into a strapping, awkward country boy, the idol of his parents and the envy of his older brothers. His pattern of life was much like that of his associates. Since he was reared on a farm, he worked in the fields, milked the cows, shucked and shelled corn for the mill, split rails to mend the farm fences, tended his father's oxen, and occasionally drove into Fairmount with his father and mother and other members of the family. Even as a small boy he evinced much interest in the West. During the spring and summer Fairmount was visited by movers, some on their way to Missouri or Texas and others traveling back "to God's country," after having encountered adventure and hard experience in an untamed West. Often young Dave loitered about the blacksmith shop, the general merchandise store, or the post office, where strangers were wont to swap stories of travel. Here he learned of the countless herds of buffalo, deer, and antelope ranging the Great Plains, of the hazards of travel through western wilds, of Indian battles, of outlaw escapades, and of hidden treasures. All these stories he pigeonholed in his young mind as memoranda for the future, for he early resolved to join this restless host of movers one day and learn firsthand what the West had to offer.

Dave's father and mother had other plans. Their son must be educated, brought up in the Church, and trained to take his place as a Christian leader in the Fairmount community. They were handicapped, however, for schools were indifferent and teachers few. Community pride in education did not exist, and funds for buildings, equipment, and teachers' salaries were not to be had. No doubt the five-month term of 1851–52, when young Dave joined other local lads in a quest of "readin', 'ritin', and 'rithmetic," was like many another of the Middle West at this early date. The boys gathered in the kitchen of John Brewer's farmhouse, since it was the most centrally located; and here about the open hearth they studied whatever book each chanced to have: a dictionary, a speller, a grammar, or an arithmetic. William A. Ruder, who had been reared under the uncomfortable admonition of "Spare the rod and spoil the child," was the teacher, who kept "one jump ahead of his pupils" in lesson assignments. One is not told what record young Payne made in deportment, but judging from his propensity for practical jokes in later life, one may infer that he shared with his fellows in testing the fiber of Schoolmaster Ruder's hickory switch. Still, he made progress. One of his boyhood friends, Gabrille Havens, later said that Dave was an eager reader and developed into more than an average student. Both in the schoolroom and on the playground he was "precocious, witty," and exemplified an "abundance of initiative."

Nor was Dave's spiritual bringing-up neglected. On Sundays his father and mother loaded their ten children (Jack, Morgan, James, Wesley, David, John, Allen, Margaret, William, and Jennie) into a commodious wagon and drove to the Sugar Grove Methodist Church. Here Dave is pictured as a lad of sixteen, strong, restless, eager to learn, and not entirely averse to religious impressions. He became a great friend of the Reverend Bowers, the minister, obviously to the great pleasure of William and Celia Payne. Mrs. Bowers, a well-educated "city" girl, was equally interested in the lad. As a consequence, Dave spent much time in the Bowers' home, and quite often was hired to do the chores about the place while the preacher and his wife were away on "appointment."

In the Bowers home Dave found an unexpected boon—a library—and under the direction of Mrs. Bowers he studied literature and oratory, thus in part fitting himself for future leadership. The branches of study found here were mastered in the intervals between farm work. Dave was studious and ambitious, and as he advanced in years the minister's library became increasingly valuable in adding to his mental equipment. It is probable that the Bowers thought of a ministerial career for their young friend, for already he was known as an "exhorter."

Grant County could furnish no finer specimen of vigorous, budding manhood than this young Hoosier. He was "straight as an arrow, fleet as a deer, and supple as a cat, in all athletic sports he was the acknowledged champion." In later years old settlers of Fairmount remembered the marvelous exploits of "Oklahoma Payne" at village tournaments and country "raisings." While in school, he had taken part in games—jumping, running, wrestling—and perhaps hunting after school hours. And at the age of twenty-one he had grown into a young giant. He was now ready to measure his strength with other youths and seek adventure beyond the Mississippi.

Land Hunger

The year 1857 marked a definite turning point in Dave's life. National events of momentous consequence were looming large on the horizon. James Buchanan, the Pennsylvania "Doughface," had been elevated to the presidency of the United States, much to the dislike of free-soilers; the Dred Scott decision, permitting slaveholders to enter federal territories with their property, had deeply angered Abolitionists and had caused them to organize Emigrant Aid societies to take control of Kansas; the refusal of Brigham Young and his Mormon settlers of the Great Basin to recognize the primacy of the federal courts had caused Colonel Albert Sidney Johnston to march westward with his army of invasion. The solution of problems incident to these events greatly influenced not only the life of David L. Payne but also that of many another.

Upon the outbreak of the "Mormon War," Dave and his older brother, Jack, rode away from their Indiana home to join the army of Johnston. But when they arrived on the border they found that the troops had already marched away. It was just as well, for additional recruits were not needed. Johnston occupied Utah without bloodshed and brought the Mormons to terms. Meanwhile Dave and Jack traveled on to Fort Leavenworth, Kansas, and thence on over to Doniphan, a neighboring county, where they visited a cousin, Mrs. Jenkins.

Here at last was the West! Only a few cabins dotted the Kansas prairies. There was yet much to remind the visitors that this was frontier country. Stretching in a limitless expanse westward were the silent prairies billowing in buffalo grass and tall bluestem like a vast sea of green. The rivers and creeks were well timbered with walnut, cottonwood, hickory, and other kinds of trees. And what was still more interesting to the delighted boys was the great abundance of wild game. Startled deer and antelope bounded away before them, and peacefully grazing buffalo were everywhere. Coyotes skulked by the trail and made anxious mo-

8

ments for the youths at night by their constant yowling and snarling.

Dave and Jack were told that there was yet much unclaimed land in Doniphan County. It was natural, therefore, that they should become homesteaders. Dave established claim to a quarter-section tract in Burr Oak Township, about a mile from the Missouri River, a property of rich bottom land; and Jack settled on a similar claim near by. Having established homesteads, the boys now found that their funds were exhausted and that they must seek employment. But work was in great plenty; immigrants soon moved in all about them and offered good wages for plowing, splitting rails, fencing, and other work. Dave and Jack took a contract to fence a farm and went to work splitting rails. Dave was not long content with such backbreaking toil, however, and erected a sawmill. In this venture he was unsuccessful and presently was without funds again.

It is not clear just how Dave acquired possession of his homestead. The free-homestead law was yet a part of the future, but an enactment of 1841 permitted a pre-emptor to acquire title to 160 acres by paying the minimum price of one dollar per acre. Under this law the monetary consideration was not large and it is supposed that Dave had pretty well cleared his title by 1861, at the outbreak of the Civil War.

On June 30, 1858, a general land office was located in Doniphan County. Towns where supplies could be purchased were at considerable distances and as a consequence the settlers were often short of food. Dave now saw another opportunity. For weeks past, during slack hours, he and Jack had hunted wild turkey in the Missouri bottoms and deer and antelope on the prairie. They had met with great success and had feasted to their hearts' content on wild game in wide variety. The settlers needed wild game too, thought Dave, and would pay good prices. Why should he not become a professional hunter? In this pursuit he could find both pleasure and profit. So now the rail-splitter became a hunter. In his new employment he came to fear little the stampede of the buffalo herd, the buzz of the rattlesnake, the howl of the wolf, or the scream of the panther. All were regarded as the fitting accompaniment of border life and must be experienced.

But he did not long follow the trade of a hunter. Regions farther west wooed him. He sought and found employment as a guide and scout, both for private parties and for the government. During this period he traveled rather extensively over the southern Plains and southern Rockies, at one time visiting the gold fields of Colorado. He also explored the Cimarron country, a region of near-desert aridity dreaded by early travelers and one in which more than one adventurer lost his life. Subsequently he was called "the Cimarron Scout," and was regarded by his fellows as worthy to associate with Kit Carson and Buffalo Bill, whom he knew personally.

By 1861 Payne was a man whom frontiersmen could understand and admire. Now grown to the height of six feet and four inches and weighing more than two hundred pounds, he had reached his full physical growth. He bore himself as a seasoned westerner, was broad-shouldered, square-chested, and strong. His physiognomy was striking and prepossessing. He had a large, well-shaped head, a broad, prominent forehead, steel-gray eyes, a well-shaped nose, an oval face, and a firmly set jaw, indicating tenacity of purpose and great will power. In manners, he was easy, fluent in conversation, agreeable, and quick in repartee. He had been bronzed by the sun, adapted to the ways of the plains, inured to hardships and dangers, and reconditioned in mind to meet the strenuous life ahead. In short, he had graduated into a plainsman, bold and resourceful.

2 : "Old Ox-Heart"

WAR DRUMS and bugle notes were heard throughout Kansas in the spring of 1861, and long lines of dust-covered troops were seen on well-traveled roads. Fort Sumter had been fired upon by Beauregard's Confederates. President Abraham Lincoln had sent out a call for volunteers and Kansas youths had given enthusiastic response. The New England Emigrant Aid Society had won its struggle with the Missouri "border ruffians" for the control of Kansas and a new free-soil state was added to the Union. Everywhere, in towns and villages, men in blue were soon engaged in the strenuous task of training, and companies and regiments were taking form to join the forces of Phillips, Lyons, and others.

David Lewis Payne's Civil War experiences are briefly recorded in relation to the Kansas organizations with which he served. In 1861 he enlisted in the Fourth Regiment of Kansas Volunteers, which was presently merged with the Third Infantry; still later, he joined the Tenth Regiment of Kansas Volunteers, in which he served the full time of three years. He was in Company F, first commanded by John J. Boyd and later by Nathan Price.

During the first part of the war Dave's regiment operated in Kansas, Missouri, and Arkansas; and in December, 1862, with other Union troops, it hotly engaged the Confederates in the battle of Prairie Grove, Arkansas. At one stage of the battle Lieutenant Cyrus Leland, of Dave's company, was wounded. Dave saw the officer lying on the ground exposed to Confederate fire and directly in the line of their advance. Without thinking of danger to himself, Private Payne dashed back to the stricken officer, picked him up, and carried him to a first-aid station, half a mile back of the lines. By this act of gallantry he gained the undying friendship of Leland, who was later to rise to high political position in Kansas.

Dave made a good soldier and more than once was offered a commission, but he was content to serve in a more humble role, although he did accept the noncommissioned rank of sergeant. His services with the Tenth Regiment of Volunteers expired in August, 1864, and he returned to his Doniphan County farm, where he was welcomed by neighbors and friends. Bronzed by life in the open and hardened by grueling experiences, he appeared every inch a soldier. His services had seemingly given him manly poise and confidence. To soldiers and neighbors alike he was genial, conversant of army life and border problems, and he was held in high esteem.

Friends of General Tom Ewing noticed these qualities, too, and sought Dave's support for Ewing's election to the United States Senate over Senator James H. Lane. He accepted their overtures with enthusiasm, for Ewing had more than once befriended him. Dave, as well as others of the Tenth Regiment, was to stand for election to the legislature. Evidently he had no sound convictions as to party principles and was ready to follow his own personal inclinations. The *Kansas Chief* (Troy, Kansas) of April 25, 1889, stated that he ran as a Republican although in Indiana he had voted as a Democrat, and that in subsequent years he had "lapses" of this kind.

Although Ewing was defeated for the senatorship, Dave was elected to the Kansas House of Representatives. As an agitator, he had a confident, man-to-man air and talked glibly of political problems as though he had been long in the service of the state. Moreover, he resorted to other familiar political stratagems. Whenever the occasion afforded, he spoke to religious congregations with all the fervor of his earlier years. He interested himself in any newborn babies of the county and spent generously of his slender means to buy them presents, thus winning the hearts of fond mothers and fathers. Although Dave seemed more interested in the political fortunes of his friend than in his own, he found himself elected to the legislature from the second district of Doniphan County, consisting of Wolf River and Burr Oak townships.

But before the beginning of the legislative session, General Sterling Price moved northward through Missouri with his fast-traveling Confederate army. Payne was now called upon to accept a captaincy in the Kansas militia which was to expel the invader; and this, it seems, he did with a great deal of reluctance. He shared in the battle of Westport in September, 1864. Price withdrew, however, almost as quickly as he had advanced, and once more Dave turned his attention to his new political job. Yet he had tasted the rewards of military authority, and his appetite called for more; after this he was more inclined to accept such offers, as will be shown.

Dave felt keenly his lack of political experience, once he had arrived in Topeka, and was generally quiet and watchful in the session that followed, although constant in attendance. Only once did he "speak out of turn" as a first-session man. When a special bounty act was up for discussion, he opposed it vigorously. His colleagues overlooked his indiscretion, for they recognized his unselfish sincerity, knowing that he would share in the benefits of the law. Payne's opposition was based upon the fact that Kansas had exceeded her quota under all requisitions and could meet additional demands without bribing her volunteers. Besides, the granting of bounties to future volunteers was an unjust discrimination against the soldiers in the field who had freely enlisted, accepting the hazards and enduring the hardships of campaigning. Kansas, Payne urged, had furnished more men in proportion to population than any other state and was able to replenish her ranks without a bounty stimulus. "I have served three years as a private soldier without bounty," he said, "and am ready to re-enlist upon the same terms as soon as the legislature adjourns." The bill was defeated by an overwhelming vote.

After the adjournment of the legislature, Dave re-enlisted in the army as he had promised, this time in the Eighth Regiment of the United States Volunteers, Company G. Here again he was generous to a fault. The *Kansas Chief* of June 13, 1867, says that he refused a bounty of a thousand dollars which was offered if he would allow himself to be credited to St. Joseph to make up its quota, and instead substituted for a friend and neighbor who had a large family. As a member of Hancock's corps he served in the Army of the Potomac, and came to be regarded as one of the hardiest and pluckiest men of the corps. Secretary of War E. M. Stanton learned something of his record through a mutual Kansas friend and offered him a commission, but it was respectfully declined. "There are only a few Kansas boys here," Payne replied, "and I wish to stay with them. All the loyal states will be represented at Richmond, and the highest favor you can do our Kansas company is to give them a place in the advance as we move on the last stronghold of the Rebellion." This was his last Civil War service. On April 6, 1865, he was present at Appomattox, when Lee surrendered to Grant, and in March, 1866, he was discharged.

Having been mustered out of the army, Dave again sought out his political friends, and was named Sergeant-at-Arms in the Kansas Senate during the sessions of 1866 and 1867, after which, as a Johnson Democrat, on March 18, 1867, he was appointed Postmaster at Leavenworth, Governor Crawford becoming his bondsman.

Dave had emerged from his border and Civil War experiences with traits which were to characterize him in later years. Stirring days in the field had left him restless and intolerant of humdrum life, not content to settle down to the quiet ways of peace. Gradually, too, he had drifted away from his early religious convictions, although up to the early 1870's he occasionally attended church services. For many years he had been associated with rough, untamed characters who were accustomed to pillage, bloodshed, and war, and he had gradually taken up their habits of drinking, cursing, and gambling. He had also evinced an amazing disregard for money. He was careless not only with his own money but also with that of his friends. One who knew him said: "If there was a man among his contemporaries from whom he did not borrow, or to whom he did not lend, it would be interesting to know what character of man he was. He did not borrow because he loved money. On the contrary, he hated it."

When Dave was in the Kansas Legislature his borrowing habit was well known. On one occasion a few members of the legislature were discussing him, and a wager was made that while he would borrow money from everyone, he would lend what he had just as readily. It was known that he was about to receive a post-office order for a considerable amount, and one of his friends wagered that he could borrow every dollar of it. The post office was watched and it was soon known that Dave had received the money. Then his friend approached him, told his story of need, and was able to borrow the entire amount!

The ringing call for border service against hostile Indians on the frontier now caused Payne to forget the responsibilities of his official position. Caravans on the Santa Fe Trail had been plundered, and workmen on the Kansas Pacific Railroad nearing Fort Hays were being harassed. The Eighteenth Regiment of

Kansas Volunteers was thrown in the field and Crawford offered Dave the captaincy of Company D. He accepted with alacrity and with his company joined the Volunteers on the Smoky Hill River, near Fort Harker. Before accepting Crawford's proffer, he applied through Senator Ross for a leave of absence, accompanying the application with his resignation as Postmaster, the latter to be presented in the event the former was not granted. But the leave was granted. The regiment was immediately ordered to the front under the command of Colonel H. L. Moore, of Lawrence. Its term of hard riding (but little fighting) lasted for only four months. Meanwhile the Leavenworth post office was left to the care of a deputy. During this period an inspector found Payne's accounts sadly in arrears. But Payne would not allow his bondsman, Governor Crawford, to suffer, and deeded to him the Doniphan County farm.

Dave lost his job, of course, but the loyal governor sought to have him reinstated. On February 20, 1868, while Payne was yet in the field, Crawford wrote J. S. Beard, United States Mail Agent: "Captain D. L. Payne's services were of incalculable value to the State last summer. He left the post office at Leavenworth and answered his Country's call. It would be a source of much pleasure to me as well as to all the friends of good soldiers in Kansas if he could be re-instated in the office. Cannot this be done?" But Uncle Sam was not so accommodating. Michael L. Dunn was appointed to succeed Payne on July 20, 1868.

Dave had already tired of his Leavenworth toy anyway, and was ready to turn his steps toward a more active field. He did not even return to champion his own cause. Eight months later at Atchison he wired Crawford: "Have Company here. Will leave here seven A.M. tomorrow." And when his company was disbanded, Dave was without both home and employment.

While in the field, Dave had demonstrated marked qualities of leadership, although in the beginning one of his fellow officers was not greatly impressed by his company. Writing later, Captain George B. Jenness said, "They [Payne's men] had no uniforms and all had worn their least valuable clothes." Payne was mounted on a large, rawboned horse, as the men straggled up from the cars in which they had ridden. He had a habit of "scrouching down in his saddle that made him anything but a pleasing military figure. . . . The Company reminded one of Jack Falstaff's rag-muffins, yet Payne was as proud as a prince of his following!"

A malignant type of Asiatic cholera was raging among the regulars at Fort Harker, and shortly after the arrival of the Kansans it broke out in a virulent form. The Eighteenth Volunteers were poorly equipped, new to camp life, and without a medical officer or medical supplies; consequently the men suffered more severely than did the regulars, losing twenty enlisted men and one officer within a week's time. Payne himself suffered a severe attack but was one of those who recovered.

The captain more than measured up to this occasion. To the enduring gratitude of his men, he scorned personal danger in waiting on those stricken. He was indefatigable, caring for the sick with parental solicitude, paying for medicines from his own purse, and helping to dig the graves of those who died. The severest cases were taken to his own tent. When three or four of his men were down at once, he divided his attention among them. When the troops were ordered from the fort on active duty, two of the sick men of Company D were left behind in tents outside the post. Payne visited them and found one suffering from lack of clothing. He pulled off his own flannels and stockings and gently placed them on the sick and dying soldier, saying, "Cheer up, my boy. Don't get discouraged. I hope to see you again soon, and there'll be oceans of fun ahead on the Plains." In another instance, on a severely cold day, he gave his own coat to a sick man who lay shivering on the ground. He was also mindful of the sick men's families. "Take good care of them," he is reported to have admonished the men's attendants. "Pay strict attention to their wants and note all they say. If they have any word for friends at home, be sure and get the name and place and remember their last requests." Thus in tribulation there was welded a bond of friendship which was to hold firm in years to follow. "Old Ox Heart," his men affectionately dubbed him during these severe trials.

But there was sunshine along with the shadow. After some weeks of active scouting and Indian-hunting, the Kansas volunteers came to Fort Larned. Here Dave's carelessness about military regulations revealed itself in a rather humorous manner. Along with other equipment issued to the command, Payne's men had been given sabers, or "toad-stickers," as they had laughingly called them. While on the march, the men complained that these weapons caused them much discomfort by jouncing about and banging them on shins and legs. So, in one way or another, the swords were soon disposed of. Then when the campaign was ended, Captain Payne was asked to account for all equipment issued his men. This troubled him greatly, for he knew that the missing sabers would be charged to his account, at the rate of eight dollars apiece. But he remembered that during the past campaign his mules had stampeded and had lost some of their supplies. Why not blame the loss of the sabers on this stampede? The indulgent quartermaster, who knew of Payne's carelessness, approved his accounting and on the returned document drew a picture of the head and tail of a mule protruding from a pile of sabers!

Custer thought much of Payne's qualities as a scout and, meeting him in Washington just before his (Custer's) last and fatal campaign, offered Dave a handsome salary to accompany him on the expedition against Sitting Bull.

"Old Ox-Heart" was always a subject of conversation around the soldiers' campfires and at mess. As an officer he had little in common with West Pointers. But there was no lack of discipline about him. When elected captain he declared that he would enforce a strict, soldierly discipline and that unruly conduct would be punished. "But," he said, "there will be no guard house, no bucking and gagging, or toting bags of sand; but I shall execute the penalty in person, and if I go for any man a second time he will think a mule factory has struck him, wrong end foremost. And if any man gets the best of me, I shall promote him on the spot." One instance of the latter sort occurred, and Payne proved as good as his word. When he attempted, "mule-factory" fashion, to make an example of a stalwart private named Henderson, the soldier retaliated in the same way, "kicking" the captain in the jaw and also giving him a black eye. The next morning Payne sent for the offender and, after gravely lecturing him on his offense, gave him a sergeant's warrant and two quart cans of fruit to treat his mess. "I believe," said he, "you are the best man in the company and the best men belong at the front."

Payne's favorite in the company was nicknamed "Man Friday" by his comrades. Friday seldom missed an opportunity to play a practical joke. On one occasion Payne found Friday in the officers' saloon, hobnobbing with the post commander and other officers. Upon seeing Payne enter, Friday advanced and handed him a glass of whiskey, saying, "Orderly, don't you want a drink?" Payne relished the joke as well as the liquor, and then asked if the commanding officer was present. "Yes, sir," replied the major in charge. Payne handed him a requisition for forage and requested his signature. The officer signed it and Payne then attached his own name. "What!" exclaimed the major, "Does your captain here allow you to sign his name?" Oh, yes," responded Friday, "that is all right; he acts as my clerk and private secretary."

In the spring of 1868, Kansas settlers had great cause to rejoice. For years the fierce Cheyennes had been devastating their isolated settlements, killing men, women, and children, stealing their horses and mules, and plundering and burning their homes. Now all this was to cease. A stocky, fiery little man, wearing on either shoulder the two stars of a major-general, had come to Fort Hays to set up headquarters. This was "Little Phil" Sheridan, hero of Winchester and the Shenandoah Valley, and campaigner of the Rio Grande.

When both red men and white sought him out to inquire what his policy would be, he gave them much food for thought by saying: "My policy is that punishment must follow crime. It is ridiculous to believe that savages will be content to follow the mild admonitions of the Peace Commission which Congress has sent out to the Great Plains, when we must hedge about civilized men with laws, courts and peace officers." All who heard him went away pondering these words. Did this mean that he was to hold the red man amenable to the white man's courts? Was the red raider to be punished for his crimes?

The general did not leave them long in doubt. Presently he began preparations for a winter campaign against the wild Cheyennes, Arapahoes, Comanches, and Kiowas. But his troops were inadequate for such a move and he could not draw others from neighboring departments. General W. T. Sherman, Sheridan's superior, asked Governor Crawford if he would not furnish state troops. The governor replied in the affirmative. In fact, he resigned his governorship to lead the Nineteenth Kansas Volunteers south to the scene of the campaign.

Sheridan had chosen the winter season to strike because he believed that the Indians would be in their camps, unable to escape his troops. Their horses would be too poor to match the stamina of cavalry horses.

On October 29, 1868, Payne was chosen captain of Company H, Nineteenth Regiment of Kansas Volunteers. As soon as the recruits had been organized into companies and hastily drilled, they took up their march for the south toward Beaver Creek, Indian Territory, a point fixed by General Sheridan to rendezvous the combined forces. But hardly had the march of the volunteers begun before they encountered a severe blizzard with the temperature hovering about zero. Moreover, "Apache Bill" and Crawford's other scouts knew little about the country through which the Kansans must travel, and for five days they were lost in deep snow. They wandered southward without food, except for buffalo meat. And before they had reached Sheridan's camp they had marched 205 miles in fourteen days on five days' rations and three days' forage for their horses. Yet they arrived at the rendezvous camp without material loss of men or horses.

It would be purposeless here to discuss the battle of the Washita, in November, 1868, in which Lieutenant Colonel George A. Custer and his Seventh Cavalry destroyed Black Kettle's camp of Cheyennes on the Washita, for the Kansas Volunteers did not share in it. But accompanying Sheridan's troops a few days later they visited the site and helped to bury Major Elliott and his detail of men, who had been surrounded and killed by the Indians. Then Sheridan marched on to Fort Cobb for the winter.

In the early part of the next year Sheridan established a new post, Fort Sill, near the eastern base of the Wichita Mountains, so that his troops could be stationed nearer the center of the country in which they were to operate. During the winter Payne conducted hazardous scouts from the new post through the Wichita Mountains, accompanied by "Wild Bill" and "California Joe," thus familiarizing himself with mineral-bearing soil and taking observations for future reference. "Occasionally," says a contemporary, "conflicts were had with small roving bands, and in one instance seven Indians were killed without the loss of a man in Payne's command." Payne later said that it was while stationed at Fort Sill that he first heard of "Oklahoma," an irregular, heart-shaped area near the center of the Indian Territory. It was a region of almost two million acres of land, surrendered to the federal government by the Creek and Seminole Indians in the treaties of 1866 in order to aid the government in settling thereon freedmen and other Indians. It was reported to be a region of rich bottom land; rippling streams filled with fish; prairies covered with grama, mesquite and bluestem grasses; and forests of walnut, pecan, elm, and oak.

But the Kansans had little time to think of future homesteads. On the Washita they had found the mangled corpses of Mrs. Clara Blinn and her child, and there were yet in the hands of the Cheyennes other captives, among whom were a Mrs. Morgan, a bride of only one month, and a Miss White, both of whom were on their way to southern Colorado when captured. In the spring of 1869, after General Sheridan had returned to Fort Hays, Custer undertook a campaign of thirty-one days against the guilty Cheyennes reported to be in the broken country of the foothills of the Staked Plains. The expedition was successful and the two women who had been in captivity nine months were recovered, although in the meantime they had suffered many indignities at the hands of their captors.

A part of the Cheyennes escaped and made off in a direction which caused Custer to fear that they planned to unite with other hostile warriors, says J. W. Buel, writing at a later date. He therefore sent Captain Payne with Jack Corwin and Charley Pickard back to Fort Hays for re-enforcements. The journey was made in four days and nights, the couriers changing mounts only twice and skirmishing with the Indians en route for nine hours. They first encountered more than one hundred Kiowa warriors, but by careful maneuvering managed to slip around them without being seen. Farther along the trail they encountered another band of Kiowas, but in a fight of nearly two hours the Indians were finally driven off.

Payne and his comrades had no further adventure until the

following day, when, on the Santa Fe Trail, they were set upon by a war party of Cheyennes. The scouts engaged the Indians in a running fight and finally reached Bob Wright's corral, near the Santa Fe Trail, where they were re-enforced by twelve men. Then the combined party drove the Indians away.

"On the Fourth day out," says Buel, "Payne reached Fort Hays, having performed the journey of three hundred and sixty five miles in one hundred hours, one of the swiftest rides, considering the obstacles and delays encountered, ever made on the plains." Before reaching the post, the riders had to rub tobacco in their eyes to keep from falling asleep on the way. A relief party was immediately sent southward, but it was not needed, for Custer's command returned to its Kansas post without mishap.

Thus were the curtains rung down on Payne's military career. His actual term of service as a volunteer soldier during the Civil War was longer than that of any other Kansas veteran, and then his subsequent border campaigns gave him broad experience. After he was mustered out of the army, Payne applied to the War Department for a record certificate. In reply, the Assistant Adjutant General wrote: "It is proper to add that the records of this office show that you served as an enlisted man in Company F, Tenth Kansas Volunteers, from August, 1861, to August, 1864; in Company G, Eighth United States Volunteers, from March, 1865, to March, 1866; as Captain, Company D, Eighteenth Kansas Cavalry, from July, 1867, to November, 1867; and as Captain, Company H, Nineteenth Kansas Cavalry, from October, 1868, to October, 1869." This comprised a total period of five years and six months. But it was not quite all. As previously stated, Payne also commanded a company of Kansas militia and participated in the battle of Westport, in September, 1864.

3 : From Pillar to Post

*D*URING the late sixties emigrant wagons traveled every road pointing toward western Kansas. This movement, indeed, had been one of the causes of the Indian outbreak during 1868 and 1869. Westward migrations had been accelerated by the federal Homestead Law of May 20, 1862, which provided that any head of a family or person twenty-one years of age, who was an American citizen and who had not borne arms against the United States government or given aid and comfort to its enemies, was entitled to homestead, after January 1 of the next year, 160 acres of the public domain. Hardly was Sheridan's winter campaign at an end before the resistless surge of homeseekers had pushed beyond what was considered legitimate public domain into Indian country about the headwaters of the Solomon and Republican rivers. And within the next twenty years, from 1870 to 1890, the population of Kansas increased from 364,000 to 1,-427,000; of Texas, from 818,000 to 2,235,000; and of Nebraska, from 122,000 to 1,058,000. Ex-soldiers who had only recently been mustered out of military service, fearless of Indian dangers and indifferent to border hardships, were largely responsible for the increase of population in frontier states.

Captain David L. Payne's six months of service with Custer had ended his military career, and he could now join this ex-soldier movement of border occupation. Governor Crawford had conferred on him the brevet rank of Major of Volunteers, but Payne had little thought of re-entering the army. Serving with the expeditions against the Indians in recent months, he had been given opportunity to appraise the possibilities of southwestern Kansas. It was a fine region of broad, sweeping prairies, grazed by countless herds of buffalo, deer, and antelope, and traversed by numerous streams, along the banks of which stood hedgelike borders of cottonwood, ash, walnut, and elm. Only here and there a sod house or dugout marked the habitation of pioneers.

In April, 1871, Payne traveled by train westward toward Emporia, and from there walked on to Towanda. Arriving in Sedgwick County, he examined at some length the unoccupied public lands and finally settled upon 160 acres in what later came to be known as Section 16 of Payne Township, on the road between Towanda and Wichita and about seven miles east of North Wichita.

"Payne's Ranch," as his homestead was called, was a stopping place for the stagecoach which ran from Humboldt and Emporia to the border town of Wichita. Here travelers had an opportunity to procure staple supplies. "Payne's Ranch" has been described as a dugout in the bank of Dry Creek with a board addition and a shed for horses. "The store," says a contemporary, "consisted of a bale of hay, a box of crackers, and a keg of whiskey," although it probably carried other things needed by immigrants. Here visitors could enjoy liquid refreshments all the time and strength-giving food a part of the time. The *Oklahoma War Chief* of January 19, 1883, says that Payne fed and clothed every starved immigrant, gave him "whiskey and ammunition or anything else he had, and in addition, a shake of the hand and 'God Bless you, old boy.'" In this primitive abode Dave was a Don Quixote whose Sancho Panza was a certain "Uncle Ned," a bald-headed darky of northern Kansas. Uncle Ned was steward, cook, bartender, servant, and financial manager. To Uncle Ned, Dave was of the same mold as Abe Lincoln and George Washington. Victor Murdock says that it was the prevailing opinion among the pioneers thereabouts that had it not been for Uncle Ned, "the larder would have been leaner than the law of livelihood allows." But Dave did much hunting, both to replenish his "larder" and to recruit his purse. He cured buffalo meat by hanging it in his dugout, which attracted the wolves at night. They scrambled over the roof attempting to get at the meat inside and greatly disturbed Uncle Ned's peace of mind.

It would seem from early records that Payne's dugout was also visited by other kinds of "wolves": drifters of the border, looking for a place to hang their hats; Bohemian story-tellers; and a varied assortment of ne'er-do-wells and poker players who came to loaf and to partake of "Old Ox-Heart's 'good cheer,' " which was dispensed liberally.

The succeeding year brought many homesteaders to Sedgwick County; and every man, woman, and child came to know the man after whom Payne Township was named. In each dugout Dave was a familiar and welcome visitor. He complimented the housewives on their good cooking, assured hopeful homesteaders that they had chosen wisely in coming to Sedgwick County, and gained the friendship of impressionable children by telling border stories and giving them small gifts. His neighbors often referred to him as the Davy Crockett of southern Kansas. William W. Bloss, who shared with Payne the hardships of the first invasions of Oklahoma, wrote in 1885 that the Sedgwick settlers told him of Payne's many acts of kindness. "There never was a time," said one, "when Dave would not divide his last side of bacon or pound of flour, and I never yet heard any man in Payne township breathe a word against him. If he should, there would be a fight or a foot-race, you bet."

But one should not infer that Dave was without fault; he was a conspicuous product of his environment. He enjoyed risqué stories, played poker with indifferent success, swore on equal terms with border bullwhackers and stage drivers, and drank as much "red likker" as any man.

Nor were his associates wisely chosen—if, indeed, they were chosen at all. One early pioneer remembers that some of the visitors at "Payne's Ranch" were border toughs who, although they might not pick one's pocket, would not be safe traveling companions after dark. In fact, about the time of their ranch visitations the corn at the near-by stage station was stolen and it was never known whether Payne or the toughs, or both, took it. Yet his neighbors were not greatly concerned, for it was during one of the hard years of grasshopper invasion and they had been the beneficiaries of Payne's gifts.

At this time, too, Rachel Anna Haines started housekeeping at the "Ranch." She later said that she and Payne had always been sweethearts; it is believed, however, that they had not become attached to each other until shortly before Payne's departure from Doniphan County. In subsequent years "Mrs. Haines" was closely identified with Payne's fortunes, and was affectionately referred to by the Oklahoma Boomers as "Ma Haines." No one seemed to know just why she was addressed as "Mrs. Haines," for according to her own narrative she was never married. Shortly after coming to "Payne's Ranch," Anna, as we shall frequently refer to her hereafter, became Dave's common-law wife. Both friends and foes of Payne saw little in this attachment to shock their sense of moral decency. The *Indian Chieftain* (Vinita, Indian Territory) of December 18, 1884, gave this explanation: "Years ago Payne and Anna formed a mutual attachment, swore eternal fidelity, and though without the sanction of the law have since lived as man and wife and as a fruit of such an alliance a son was born who is now fourteen years old." There is no doubt that Anna's support was at times decisive. Subsequently she wrote that first and last she spent more than fifteen

27

hundred dollars of her own money on Payne's Boomer Movement.

Dave was soon identified with Sedgwick County politics, although, writes Marjorie Aikman Coyne, his first interests were slightly irregular. William Shaefer, an early friend of Dave's, told her that shortly after Payne's coming an election was to be held in Sedgwick District to vote bonds to build a bridge. The bridge was badly needed, but there were voters who did not wish to increase the tax rates. As a consequence they invited Dave to come over and vote against the proposal. "Not only did he come," Shaefer is reported to have said, "but he brought along a wagon load of men from his 'ranch' and this turned the balance so that the bridge measure was defeated."

Yet this in no wise lessened Payne's popularity. On November 7, 1871, he was again candidate for election to the Kansas House of Representatives, and by eighteen votes defeated H. C. Sluss, a leading Republican lawyer of Wichita, in a district that was overwhelmingly Republican. Wichita citizens charged, however, that he was elected as a result of a "plot" to dismember Sedgwick County to the advantage of neighboring communities and towns. The Wichita *Eagle* of February 7, 1879, spiritedly condemned this eight-year-old "injustice." Prior to the legislative session of 1871–72, Sedgwick County contained forty-two townships and was one of the best settled counties along the border. At this time the Atchison, Topeka and Santa Fe Railroad was building through its northern townships. And towns within this area (Newton, Sedgwick City, and Park City), together with the neighboring counties of Reno, McPherson, Rice, and Marion, thought it to their advantage to reduce the size of Sedgwick County.

A "scheme" was devised, the *Eagle* believed, whereby all were to profit. Newton had grown because it had become the terminus of the Wichita and Southwestern Railroad, and now proposed, with the support of its fellow plotters, to vote for a county bond issue of $200,000 for an extension of the railroad on to Wichita, if in turn Wichita would vote for the establishment of Harvey County in part from fourteen districts of Sedgwick County. "The proposition was carried by a large majority vote," remembered the *Eagle,* "being supported by Mr. Congdon, the present Representative of Harvey, Mr. Hurd, Dr. Floyd and many others of Sedgwick City, and by all the leading men of Newton. For a truth, as the records will show, Sedgwick City and her interests, and Newton and her interests, were practically unanimous for the bonds." The "plotters" now sought to carry out their purpose by supporting "one Captain Dave Payne for the legislature against Mr. Sluss, of this city, the regular nominee. To the more surely fix Payne's interest and to command his hearty support for the scheme, he was given a piece of land at Newton, upon which a house was erected by his disinterested(?) admirers. Mr. Sluss was elected, but under a constitutional quibble, which Sluss would not contest, Payne was admitted to a seat in the legislature."

It was affirmed that the work planned was prosecuted with vigor and untiring energy, for upon its success hung the destinies of Newton, Hutchison, and other incipient towns, and that Payne, backed by a lobby consisting of "Mr. Bentley, a County Commissioner of Sedgwick residing at Newton, Captain Spicey, Judge Muse, Captain Sebastian and many others" from the present county of Harvey, was its principal proponent. The bill for the creation of Harvey County and for the adjustment of the boundaries of the others was passed, although Payne was marked as "present but not voting." He did later, however, propose a measure (and it was carried) which distributed the burden of the past indebtedness of the old county between Harvey and Sedgwick.

Thus, in the creation of Harvey County, Sedgwick lost fourteen townships of territory, over 250,000 acres of taxable land, two towns, and virtually thirty-three miles of railroad, worth over $250,000 for taxable purposes. The new county also took three townships from McPherson County and three from Marion. The Santa Fe Railroad guaranteed the future of Newton. Indeed, the town became a junction of two important railroads and the division point for the Santa Fe, with its roundhouse, officials, buildings, and hundreds of employees. "What would have proved only a mere 'whistling station,' had the road been built from Peabody as at first projected, became an important commercial center second only to Wichita."

Payne was an active and hard-working member of the legislature at this session. He proposed House Bill No. 1, which engendered the most exciting moments of the session. The measure provided for the removal of disabilities of Confederate soldiers in the state. Payne argued that as Kansas was the most radical and patriotic state during the war, she should now take the lead as the most liberal and progressive, proving to the South that she cherished no animosities against the latter's people, and that having fought for a principle and conquered, she could now afford to extend the hand of friendship. The legislature was overwhelmingly Republican, but the bill lacked only seven votes of the two-thirds necessary to pass.

Payne would not accept defeat. He believed that if he could rally soldier support for his proposal the legislature would not dare to continue its opposition. His Republican colleagues had been fearful of the ex-soldiers' displeasure if the resolution were passed. In order to prove to them that Kansas soldiers were tolerantly disposed toward Confederates, Payne issued a call, on his own authority, for a reunion of the Kansas Volunteers at Topeka on February 22. The veterans responded in large numbers. Already Payne had made arrangements for hotel accommodations and had assumed the responsibility of engaging public halls.

Payne had prepared a resolution which he first presented to all whom he met. To each man he explained that the war was over and that it was the duty of Kansans to lead in the work of restoring confidence to all sections by inaugurating an era of good feeling throughout the entire country. The Confederates had been worthy foes and had offered stubborn opposition while in the field. They had surrendered to their conquerors, who could now do no less than make it possible for Southerners to realign themselves with the nation.

At the opera house and elsewhere Dave read his resolution and then spoke briefly and eloquently to densely packed audiences. He charged that leadership of the opposition came largely from those who were "hell on dress parade" but had not fought in a single battle. And in each instance, when called upon to do so, the soldiers shouted their approval of the resolution. The opposing members of the legislature watched the soldier reaction carefully and were duly impressed. So on the following day, as soon as the routine of business was ended, Payne rose in his seat and moved to reconsider the amnesty bill. He remarked that he had nothing more to say than he had already said, but that he had sent his resolution to the clerk's desk to be read. When it was re-read by the clerk it was quickly carried, and a bill incorporating its proposal was likewise passed.

During this session Dave also served on the Committee of Railroads and Accounts and proposed sundry amendments relating to hedge and fence laws and local matters. Moreover, he presently gave evidence of departure from his earlier temperance views. Temperance workers in Kansas had sought a bill to regulate the sale of intoxicating liquors. Such a measure was finally introduced, but it was repeatedly tabled, largely because of Dave's opposition. At one time a resolution was under consideration to allow Topeka antisaloonists to assemble in the House of Representatives; but Payne proposed an amendment to provide that the anti-temperance society be accorded the same privilege.

In 1872 Dave was tendered the nomination for state senator by the Democratic district convention, representing seven counties. The district was overwhelmingly Republican, and he saw that defeat was inevitable. Besides, he had neither time nor money to devote to a campaign, and positively refused to make the race. The convention, however, would accept no refusal. His friends declared that there was no earthly chance of success for any other candidate. He was accordingly chosen, and then called upon for a speech. He responded, an intimate friend wrote later, substantially as follows:

Mr. Chairman and Gentlemen:—I crave your pardon, but I must depart from the generally accepted rule which requires a candidate to return thanks for the honor conferred. In all candor, you do me no favor, for while I do not doubt the sincerity of your motives or your friendship, I am too well aware that no member of our party—no matter whom—can overcome the Republican majority in this Senatorial district. I consider defeat inevitable. You had just as well envelop me in a soldier's overcoat and a pair of stoga boots and expect me to fly heavenward as to suppose that I can reach the State Senate in the approaching canvass, as a candidate of the Democratic convention. But I will do my best.

Of course Payne was defeated, but he made a most remarkable race. He ran ahead of his ticket in every voting precinct in the seven counties, excepting one. One township gave him every vote with the exception of three, and Payne Township, Sedgwick, gave him a solid vote of 366, the Republicans endorsing him to a man.

Once more Dave's homesteading venture came to grief. In July of 1871 he needed money and mortgaged his "ranch" for $750, and the mortgage instrument was then sold to Patterson Taylor. While thus encumbered, Payne was sued by M. M. Fechminer, to whom he owed $100, and a judgment against him was rendered by the court. Then to escape both horns of his dilemma he resorted to a questionable venture. He sold his homestead to his cousin, Jonathan Osburn, of Indiana, for $296. But Osburn did not have the cash and in November, 1872, gave Payne a note for the amount. Payne then endorsed and sold the note, and it finally passed through several hands before it was found that Osburn could not pay, and, indeed, that he had returned to Indiana without recording the deed. Creditors, therefore, then came to Payne and asked him to make good his endorsement. Taylor also became alarmed at this turn of events and sued Payne for a judgment on the mortgage which he held. Since Payne could not satisfy any of these demands, the court allowed Taylor, in the fall of 1874, to buy in his homestead for $500.

Dave now decided to move to Newton and turn over a new leaf. In the Harvey County campaign, the Newton Town Company had favored him with a grant of two lots. According to Judge John C. Nicholson, Payne was the temporary possessor of Lot 28 and Lot 32 in Block 33, where the Newton auditorium now stands. Nominally, the Town Company (of which the leading spirits were prominent Santa Fe officials) had sold him the lots for $100, but he kept them for only four days and resold them for the same price. It is alleged that the proceeds of these lots were finally used to defray the expenses of passing the Harvey County bill.

But Dave was by no means through with Newton. In November, 1872, he filed claim on a 160-acre tract of land, southeast quarter of Section 6, Newton Township, about half a mile west of the present Bethel College campus and crossed diagonally by United States Highway 81. His action was made possible by the Soldiers and Sailors Act passed by the federal Congress, which allowed homesteaders to count their time of service as part of the five-year period of residence required.

Dave was well liked and respected by Newton citizens, and for a few months his hopes were high. On July 7, 1872, the First

Presbyterian Church of Newton was organized with Payne as one of its charter members and chairman of the board of trustees, another instance of a departure from childhood traditions. But at the same time he did not depart entirely from his postwar habits. He was employed to dig two wells for the city, one at the present intersection of Fifth Street and Main Street and one at Sixth and Main, for which he was paid two dollars and a pint of whiskey a day. An early resident later asserted that he prized the whiskey more than his cash award! But on December 23, 1900, the editor of the Wichita *Eagle* said that Payne dug the wells "not because he wanted money as much as he thought the town wanted water."

Certain it is that Dave was careless in money matters here also. In desperate need of funds, he once more mortgaged his farm, in March, 1873, for $450, and once again when the loan fell due he was penniless. In order to escape the mortgage-holder this time, he sold twenty acres for $240 and borrowed the same amount, giving as security an additional forty acres. But he had jumped from the frying pan into the fire, for hardly was he free from the first mortgage when Abel Bent sued to recover $600 which Payne had borrowed from him. The court rendered judgment in Bent's favor, but again Payne was unable to meet such a financial obligation and his property was sold. Dave secured a temporary injunction to prevent its sale, but he could not renew the injunction and in March, 1875, he was again homeless.

A short time later Payne visited his old Indiana home. While he was there his father died and the family estate was divided among the surviving heirs. Thus Dave again had sufficient funds to plan a new life. In the early part of 1876 he turned his eyes toward Washington. He had returned to Kansas and secured testimonials and recommendations from such powerful politicians as General Tom Ewing, J. J. Ingalls, and Preston B. Plumb. As a consequence he secured a position in the folding room of the House of Representatives, where he worked from July, 1876, to January, 1877, receiving $662.40 as compensation.

Next, J. W. Polk, Doorkeeper of the House of Representatives, employed Dave as his assistant. Dave spent several months in Washington working up his chances, during which time he borrowed small amounts of money from various members of Congress. When the time came to elect a doorkeeper he received a majority of the votes, the members feeling that he would pay back what he had borrowed. But he never had sufficient funds to meet these obligations. His tenure was of short duration. Polk's removal from office on charges of official misconduct also caused the removal of all his subordinates. Payne shared the fate of his associates. Yet it seems that his services had been satisfactory, for on March 6, 1879, W. C. Langan, Clerk of Invalid Pensions, addressed a letter to D. W. Vorhees in which he said that Payne had been the "most faithful and willing employee on this side of the Capitol."

4 : The Forbidden Land

*W*HILE *PAYNE* was in search of Washington political plums, events were so developing in the Indian Territory and along the southern Kansas boundary as to provide opportunities better suited to his talents. It is necessary at this point, therefore, to give them summary treatment, for they constitute a background for all his later activities.

With the exception of the California gold rush of 1849, a similar stampede to the Pike's Peak country ten years later, and the pell-mell hegira to the Black Hills in 1875, no other area of the United States aroused such a spirit of adventure and competitive effort as did that part of the Indian Territory known as Oklahoma during the 1870's and 1880's. Within this new land, neither gold nor silver was the loadstone; it was free land. Frederick Jackson Turner has well said that the frontier, the greatest formative force in American life, was the "hither edge of free land." Yet during the early 1880's there was little free land of an arable sort left. Since the enactment of the Homestead Law, settlers had crowded onto the borders of Nebraska, Kansas, and Texas so that a decade and a half later they had occupied not only the arable lands of the Great Plains but also a part of the submarginal area. In this last move, they had encountered the opposition of cattlemen who argued that the "nesters" would ruin good cow ranges to little purpose. This was in part true, and they soon realized that drought was their greatest enemy. Again and again it drove them back to more humid regions, aided and abetted by its confreres, hot wind, sandstorm, and grasshopper.

To the landless citizens of the West, it was unthinkable that the Indian Territory should continue to remain wholly in the hands of some 75,000 semicivilized and wild Indians. Here was a region of 68,000 square miles, larger than the state of Missouri, with deep, rich soils, with lovely landscapes dotted with broad prairies and fine timber, and with rich coal, lead, and other mineral deposits. The region abounded in wild game and birds, and the clear, swift-running streams were filled with fish. To the occupants of the sun-scorched, submarginal Kansas and Texas plains, and to the homeless movers from Arkansas and Missouri, this was the promised but forbidden land. In the past, however, American pioneers had not been restrained in their efforts to occupy the public domain; nor should they be now!

During the Civil War the Five Civilized Tribes had supported the Confederacy, and at its close they were forced by the federal government to surrender a part of their land holdings. The Cherokees had tribally renounced their support of the South at Cowskin Prairie, in February, 1863, and for this reason the federal government treated them more leniently. They were allowed to retain control of the "Cherokee Strip,"* but were required to permit its settlement by other friendly Indians. The Creeks were forced to sell the western half of their claims for thirty cents an acre (3,250,560 acres for $975,168); the Seminoles had to give up their entire reservation of 2,169,080 acres for fifteen cents an acre ($325,362) and buy another, at fifty cents an acre, from the land taken from the Creeks. The Choctaws and Chickasaws sold the "Leased District," approximately

---

*Actually the Cherokee Outlet but more often referred to as the Cherokee Strip, this was an area extending from the ninety-sixth meridian west to the hundredth meridian and from the Kansas line south nearly sixty miles.

7,000,000 acres, between the ninety-eighth and hundredth meridians, for $300,000.

Federal commissioners then negotiated treaties with small tribal bands whereby the latter were given greatly reduced holdings along the eastern border of the lands surrendered by the Five Civilized Tribes, although the Osages were given a more princely estate. Then east of the hundredth meridian, from the Red River to the Cherokee Strip, the Comanches, Kiowas, and Katakas (Kiowa-Apaches), as one group of wild Indians, and the Cheyennes and Arapahoes as another, were given large holdings. After all reservation assignments had been made there was still left a roughly heart-shaped area of more than two million acres, bordered on the east by the Pawnee, Iowa, Kickapoo and Shawnee, and Potawatomi lands, on the south by the South Canadian River, on the west by the Cheyenne and Arapaho reservation, and on the north by the Strip. This was from the Creek and Seminole cessions, upon which federal commissioners had promised to settle other Indians and freedmen (Negroes and, presumably, former Indian slaves.)*

Not only was this the very heart of the Indian Territory, but the settlers demanding its opening considered it the most valuable part. And they believed that the government could ill afford to deny them entry. By the Fourteenth and Fifteenth amendments to the Constitution, Negroes were declared to be citizens of the United States; by Representative R. Q. Mills's amendment to the Indian Appropriation Bill of 1877, the Sioux Indians were prohibited from removing to Oklahoma; and by an enactment in the next year, Colorado, New Mexico, and Arizona tribes were also barred. Thus, complained a prospective homesteader, "the freedman and Indian are prevented from entering

---

*The term "Oklahoma" was applied by border settlers to this part of the Creek and Seminole cessions and will be so used hereafter in this study. But it should not be confused with the Territory of Oklahoma and the state of Oklahoma created later.

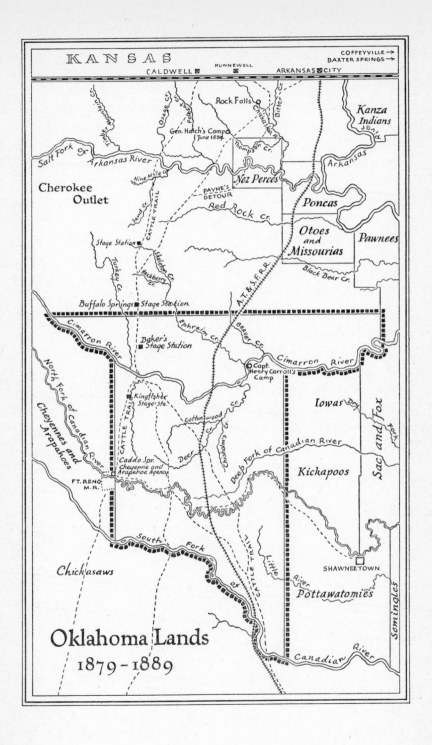

the ceded lands because they are forbidden by act of Congress; and the white settler is debarred by executive proclamation!"

More than one effort had been made to open the entire Indian Territory to settlement. During the early 1860's Senator Johnson offered, at the request of Indian Territory authorities, a bill to divide Indian lands in severalty, to grant the Indians citizenship, and to pave the way for statehood; but the bill was defeated, says William W. Bloss, "by the 'Indian ring,'" interested in exploiting the tribesmen. Again in the session of 1866–67, Representative R. T. Van Horn, of Kansas City, supported by Senator Pomeroy, of Missouri, and Representative Sidney Clark, of Kansas, offered a similar bill, but it died in the committee room. Then in the session of 1875–76, Representative B. J. Franklin, of Missouri, resurrected the bill and sought its enactment, but again it was buried in the tomb of forgotten measures. Yet it would not remain buried. Senator George G. Vest and Representative R. Graham Frost, of Missouri, subsequently sought its passage. But New England sentimentalists joined hands with the "Indian ring," sustained by a powerful lobby, to defeat it. In referring to those who opposed the bill, the Kansas City *Times* of April 29, 1879, charged that "All the opposition comes from this ring of Indian sharpers admitted to have spent over $300,-000 in Washington during the last two years, of money sacredly designed for schools and other territorial purposes, simply to defeat any legislation which by opening the Territory would end their pelf and power." The *Times* identified the "ring" as the "chiefs and leaders of the Indians" who handled tribal annuities.

Bloss stated in 1885 that as early as 1870 Dave Payne and W. B. Hutchison had set up at Wichita a colonization society with the object of opening the ceded lands to settlement, and that prospectors were sent to explore the region. They penetrated the Wichita Mountains and carefully examined canyons, bluffs, and eroded terrain for precious ores, but without sufficient results to justify mining operations. Discovery of mineral deposits in Colorado overshadowed the Indian Territory movement, and after one year's existence the colonization society lapsed.

But by 1878 the colonization idea was revived. The Black Hills invasion led by Charles C. Carpenter had shown how the Oklahoma impasse could be overcome. Cattle drovers passing up the Chisholm and Western trails had kept alive interest in the "forbidden land" by their frequent accounts of its availability for ranching and farming. Indeed, some of these, in spite of official frowns, had grazed the Comanche-Kiowa and Cheyenne-Arapaho reservations, although they were expelled by troops. Movers, on their way to Texas or traveling northward to Kansas, noticed, too, that here was a virgin wilderness of prairie and timber lands as rich as could be found in the West. Western newspapers joined the chorus of praise and asked how long the government would retain the land as a home for indolent Indians.

On February 15, 1879, Elias C. Boudinot, a clerk of the House Committee on Private Land Claims in Washington, published in the Chicago *Times* a lengthy article on the unoccupied lands in the Indian Territory, which in turn was copied extensively by other newspapers. In the article he maintained that there were fourteen million acres of unoccupied public land in the Indian Territory remaining from the Creek, Seminole, Choctaw, and Chickasaw cessions after other Indian assignments had been made. For those interested in establishing homesteads there, he had also prepared a letter of additional information and a map of the Indian Territory.

There were probably two reasons why Boudinot was interested in these unoccupied lands. First, he was a member of a prominent Cherokee family. During the Civil War he had served the tribe in two capacities, as a staff officer to Brigadier General Stand Watie and as a representative of the Cherokees to the Confederate Congress in Richmond. But now his pro-Southern attitude found no favor with Cherokee officials and it was only in the setting up of a new political and economic regime that he had hopes of regaining his lost influence.

Then, too, he was in the employ (or worked with officials) of the Missouri, Kansas and Texas Railroad, and perhaps other interests. In 1878 Judge T. C. Sears, of Sedalia, Missouri, an attorney for the Missouri, Kansas and Texas, admitted that he (as a lobbyist) had been in Washington helping to organize the Senate and House committees on Indian Affairs and Territories. "Colonel Boudinot and myself," he added, "have received within the last few weeks, scores of letters from all sections of the country making inquiries as to the status of the lands of the Indian Territory and the prospect of opening them for occupation."

The railroads would profit materially by having the country thrown open to settlement, in that their land grants would become available for sale and the roads could be better supported by running through a well-settled country. Moreover, merchants and business men of southwestern cities were also interested in settling the country. Editor Marshall M. Murdock of the Wichita *Eagle*, on February 13, 1879, stated that for years the Missouri, Kansas and Texas and the Atlantic and Pacific railroad projectors, backed by Kansas City and St. Louis commercial interests, had been pressing the Cherokees, Creeks, and Choctaws to throw open their country to settlement. They had used large sums of money in this endeavor and had brought much pressure to bear, but the Indians had stubbornly refused. "Time and again," wrote Murdock, "during the years the writer served in the State Senate, were efforts made to gain the consent of Kansas to the scheme. Stevens [a railroad lobbyist] at one time took the whole State government, by special train into the heart of the Territory where he feasted and wined the members in a manner nothing short of royal." Murdock was opposed to opening Indian Territory to settlement, for he argued that it would depopulate Kansas of its finest people. But if it succeeded, he reasoned practically, Wichita and Sedgwick County should profit from the enormous trade that would pass southward.

On April 28, 1879, another Wichitan stated that he had learned of a large and well-organized body of men, under the leadership of J. R. Boyd, former mayor of Baxter Springs, who had gone "right into the heart of the 14,000,000 acre tract of Government land, and had laid out the 'City of Oklahoma.' " "Claims are being staked out in every direction over the beautiful prairies," he gleefully affirmed, "and cabins are being built just as fast as teams can haul the materials." But there was no truth in his report, for it was some time yet before cabins were to be erected within the "forbidden land." Still his description of the country was much like that of subsequent invaders. "It lies in a most beautiful and fertile country between the Cimarron and Canadian rivers," he said, "and has every advantage for a great city.... There is no country in the world half so beautiful. Clear running streams of water; rich, rolling prairies, sweeping as far as the eye can reach; and better than all, and something that Kansas never had, grand old forests of trees along every stream."

There is little doubt that this and similar descriptions caused a settler stampede toward the towns near the Indian Territory—Chetopa, Baxter Springs, Caldwell, Wichita, Independence, and Coffeyville. One vied with another for homesteader favor, and all were to profit from emigrant trade. In southern Kansas, Wichita was boosted as the nearest outfitting point, which claim was energetically disputed by Caldwell and Hunnewell. Likewise Chetopa, Baxter Springs, Independence, and Coffeyville each claimed nearest proximity rights for Arkansas and Missouri homesteaders. An Independence champion wrote that his town was "the great outfitting point, and headquarters for immigrants." But a Coffeyville citizen heatedly denied this. "Now the facts are," he said, "this place is the very nearest railroad terminus from which to reach the public lands in the Territory. It is the point from which the government road runs to the Osage and Sac and Fox agencies."

The Coffeyville claimant failed to say that there were also other towns near the Indian Territory with railroad facilities. Wichita was one terminus of a branch of the Atchison, Topeka and Santa Fe, with Eldorado as the other. Chetopa was on the Missouri, Kansas and Texas, which at that time was built through the eastern part of the Indian Territory; and Baxter Springs, its near neighbor, was the southern terminus of the Missouri River, Fort Scott and Gulf. Moreover, the Atlantic and Pacific was completed as far as Vinita, Indian Territory, where it crossed the Missouri, Kansas and Texas.

By early May, 1879, homesteader movements had sprung up like mushrooms. Several thousand emigrants were moving toward the Indian Territory, and their trains of white-topped wagons in broken lines along the roadways appeared in the distance like patches of snow. The streets of Baxter Springs and Chetopa were generally thronged with anxious, bearded Missourians and Arkansans buying flour, bacon, coffee, and dry goods, or lined up at the post office asking for forwarded mail. By May 5, a number of those at Baxter Springs had crossed over to the Quapaw reservation in what is now northeastern Oklahoma and begun the staking of claims and erecting temporary huts. One reporter observed that "over 50,000 acres are already taken by squatters and hundreds are pouring in in wagons, on horseback and in every conceivable manner."

A similar scene was observed at Vinita. Here a Captain Seayrs sought to set up a company to colonize the Creek and Seminole cessions, and a party was sent out to mark a wagon road to the colonial site. But for some reason the movement collapsed.

News of another fiasco had come to discourage further activity at Baxter Springs. J. M. Bell, a prominent Cherokee attorney and a relation of Boudinot's, had marched from Vinita with a hundred Cherokee families, some of whom reached the Chikaskia River, thirty-five miles south of Arkansas City. They had been sent out by the Indian Territory Colonization Society, which had its headquarters at Chetopa. But they were presently rounded up and expelled by the military. They had made considerable preparations to stay. Large quantities of supplies had been purchased, a stage route between Chetopa and the colony site had been marked out, and a printing press and sawmill had been sent forward.

But the most formidable of these abortive movements was that headed by Charles C. Carpenter. He was described by a contemporary as a striking character who had long curls and who wore a fancy velvet vest and a beaver hat—in short, a man who would have a large following among the border drifters. The editor of the Topeka *Commonwealth,* however, saw him only as an adventurer. He was a "scalawag of the worst type, a burly, swaggering, reckless character who would have been lynched by the men he fooled in the Black Hills if they could have caught him." And Inspector John McNeal, of the Indian Service, described him as the "same bragging, lying nuisance" who had plagued General Fremont's camp in the Black Hills.

At least Carpenter was energetic. He and his wife came from Kansas City to Independence and set up headquarters late in April, 1879, he organizing the movers and she asking donations of the merchants. Carpenter announced that "All parties and colonists wishing to join my expedition to the Indian Territory will concentrate at Independence, Kansas, between May 5th and 7th, instead of Coffeyville, Kansas, as outfits in the way of mules, horses, harness, wagons, etc. can be bought cheaper at Independence than at any other point." The fact that Mrs. Carpenter had received large donations from Independence merchants and public-spirited men, with promises of more, might have been a determining factor in her husband's selection of Independence as headquarters. Indeed, the town's businessmen had promised to donate five hundred dollars when the first party of colonists arrived in town and a thousand dollars more when the colony was established on the Canadian.

Judson Learned, traveling passenger agent of the La Fayette, Muncie and Bloomington Railroad and formerly connected with the Land Department of the Santa Fe, heard of the movement headed by the boastful Carpenter and wrote him that he (Learned) could send to Independence "hundreds of our best citizens, and I may safely say thousands, when it is demonstrated that they can go there with safety." He said that his office had been crowded all day with parties desirous of learning something of the colonization movement.

Excitement now gripped the frontier. "Still they come," wrote a citizen of Coffeyville on April 23. "Thousands are moving southward," added another at Emporia. At Fort Scott, on May 2, an Indian Territory colony was generally talked of and John Forbes was organizing and locating soldiers and others holding land warrants, although one would wonder what kind of warrant would be valid in the "forbidden land."

In these border towns, one caravan of movers was much like another. The average homeseeker was poor. His wagon was pulled by sore-backed, gaunt horses and mules, and sometimes oxen, hardly able to move their cumbrous load. On the wagon's coupling pole there were likely to be sections of stovepipe, on its side a Georgia Stock or turning plow, and fastened to the endgate a coop of squawking chickens. Inside the wagon was a varied assortment of household effects—a battered trunk or two, a bedstead, mattresses, a grub box (sometimes attached to the endgate), then quilts, chairs, and other things. Everything bespoke poverty and want, even to the scantily clad bodies and hunger-pinched faces of the emigrant's wife and children.

Before the Indian Territory movement had reached its flood-tide, the Cherokees and Creeks had become gravely alarmed lest it also engulf their lands. On April 19, W. P. Adair and Daniel H. Ross (Cherokees), G. W. Stidham and Pleasant Porter (Creeks), delegates in Washington, addressed a letter to Commissioner E. A. Hayt, asking that the homesteaders be turned back and angrily charging that "railroad corporations and squatters" had laid plans to take forcible possession of their country.

As a consequence Hayt appealed to Secretary of the Interior Carl Schurz for support. But this was hardly necessary, since for several weeks Schurz had been uneasily watching the situation and had determined on a course of action. He presently called on President Rutherford B. Hayes to warn all prospective intruders that the Indian Territory was for Indians only, and the President promptly called a meeting of his cabinet to consider the matter. His secretaries advised prompt and vigorous action. Accordingly, on April 26, 1879, Hayes issued a proclamation that the lands taken from the Creeks, Seminoles, Choctaws, and Chickasaws were not open to homestead entry, and warning that invaders would be expelled by force.

The homesteaders manifested great disappointment. Carpenter was scornful. "If the administration attempts to 'stamp out' the invasion by military force," he declaimed noisily, "we shall appeal to the God of Battles and the United States Congress to protect us, the invaders, in our constitutional rights." He cared not a "fig" for "General Bull Run Pope," and challenged him to settle by "the Western Code" the differences between them. "If he will do this," he said, "we can end the controversy in five minutes." He regarded his threatened arrest by Pope as an insult. "He can arrest me and be damned," he bragged, "but unless he cuts a better figure on the frontier than

47

he did at Bull Run there will be a hellitisplit retreat, and it won't be Carpenter's expedition."

The fact that Carpenter's warlike utterances were approved by many of his adventurous followers impressed no end the businessmen of the town. And shortly after this tirade was delivered against the government, the Independence Arms Company distributed handbills on the streets advertising for sale 1,400 secondhand six-shooters, 1,000 Winchester rifles, 1,100 double-barreled shotguns, and an extensive array of scalping knives!

The bombast and heroic gesture to which Carpenter had given expression seemed to appeal to the adventurous homeseekers elsewhere, for they gathered at border towns in ever-increasing numbers. A Chetopa observer wrote a short time later that the Oklahoma movement bade fair to depopulate southwestern Missouri, western Arkansas, and southern Kansas. From Chetopa the Colonization Society was to send out each week a party under the guidance of George W. McFarlin. Undoubtedly it had some success, for presently Commissioner Hayt reported that there were 1,776 intruders on all the Indian reservations.

On May 6 Carpenter sent out his "Order Number 2," addressed "to all parties on their way to the Canadian River, Indian Territory." Emigrants east of the Missouri, Kansas and Texas Railroad should go by way of Chetopa, thence to the iron bridge across the Verdigris River, near Coffeyville, and on to the main trail to the Sac and Fox Agency. Those traveling west of the Leavenworth, Lawrence and Galveston Railroad should keep on down the track to Coffeyville. Parties west of this line, as far as Wichita, should go by way of Independence, thence on the government road to his general headquarters at Carpenter's City, eighteen miles west of the Sac and Fox Agency, "where the general headquarters of the Governor of the Territory will be established." He left his followers to infer that he was to be the future governor.

The Kansas City Times.

XVIII.   KANSAS CITY, MO., SUNDAY, MAY 4, 1879—SIXTEEN PAGES.   NO. 107.

OKLAHOMA ON TOAST.

The "Times" Expedition Halts at the Prospective Capital of the Virgin Empire.

A Land Not Flowing With Milk and Honey, But Adorned With Natural Products as the Original Paradise.

A Heaven-Kissed Country in its Bewildering Beauty and Perfumed Like Araby the Blest.

Full Description of the Magnificent Public Domain Traversed by the "Times" Expedition.

Various Other Dispatches From Strategic Points on the Frontier.

Eastern Kansas Wild with the Oklahoma Excitement.

A Stage Line Established at Chetopa by the New Colonization Society.

Information of Great Importance to Intending Immigrants.

An Expedition from Fort Scott will Cross the Borders Early this Week.

Letter from Hon. Sidney Clarke, Speaker of the Kansas House of Representatives.

The President May be Technically Right, but is Wrong in Policy and Unjust to the People.

The Government May Embarrass but it Cannot Stop the Rush to Oklahoma.

Very Latest Dispatches Announce the Discovery of Gold and Silver.

Specimen Ores to be Sent at Once to Kansas City for Assay.

The Editor of the Memphis "Journal" to be Put Out of Misery Without Benefit of Clergy.

The Universal Peace Association Congratulates Hayes on His Quaker Policy.

[By special Courier to Independence, Kan., and Special Telegram from Independence, May 2, to Kansas City Times.]

NORTH FORK OF THE CANADIAN, Indian Territory, May 1.—After rather rapid marches we reached the central of the new empire of OKLAHOMA...

The Kansas City Times.

VOL. XVIII. KANSAS CITY, MO., SUNDAY, MAY 18, 1879 —SIXTEEN PAGES. NO. 119.

JEFFERSON CITY.

The Governor Takes the "Times" "Taffy" and Wishes There Was More of It.

Dissolving Views of the Idiotic General Assembly.

The Auditor Caroms on the Treasurer, and Pockets the Balls, as Usual.

A Statement of What Missouri Owes, and Only the Devil to Pay.

"AN OLD FOOL FOR GETTING MAD."

[Special Dispatch to the Kansas City Times.]

JEFFERSON CITY, May 17.—When asked at noon to-day whether the interview published in the TIMES of this morning, relating to an extra session of the Legislature was correctly reported, the Governor replied: "Yes; but I'm an old fool for getting angry when the reporter wanted to interview me. The TIMES man made me angry for the purpose of getting me to say what I didn't want anybody to know at present." "Whom the Gods," etc., but this don't apply to the Governor. Your correspondent likes the old man, and hence does not seek his destruction.

REVISION.

The amendments which the House tacked on to the Senate bill authorizing four of the High Joints on revision to remain at the Capital and complete the work, will in all probability defeat the bill.

THAT DEFICIT.

As many as eight different official statements have been made in relation to the revenue fund. No two they have conflicted with each other. Of the three Auditor's statements published, they have never differed with each other more than $307 000. There is no other basis in the world upon which to estimate the receipts and expenditures for 1879 80, but by comparison with the receipts and expenditures for 1877 78, and the appropriations for the present and next years. I have no desire to criticise the Auditor's statements. His reports do not place the financial condition in a proper light before the money markets of the world; and while they are perhaps not intended to affect the credit of the State, they have nevertheless had a depreciating effect upon its bonds.

THE AUDITOR REVIEWED.

It will be observed that the Auditor, in his communication of May 16th, in comparing the probable expenditures of 1879 and 1880 with those of 1877 and 1878, does not include the transfer of one-fourth of the revenue to school moneys, but in his third table he places the amount at $328 255 18 per annum. There may be a reason for this omission since it would not verify the Auditor's statement of the condition of the finances. The actual sum transferred in 1877 and 1878 was $328 792 12. The actual sum transferred in 1879 was $328 255 18, and doubling it, as the Auditor evidently has done in his communication, gives $656 510 36—a difference in favor of revenue for 1879 and 1880 of $72 281 56, which would almost swallow up the excessive appropriations $78 123 25, as estimated in the Auditor's comparative table. And to cover the difference it may be stated as an absolute fact that for pay of the General Assembly the amount in the general appropriation bill will not be exhausted, therefore the $10 000 in the supplemental bill of $87,-557 50 for that purpose will not be touched, and the debit side of the comparative table should have to balance it, $4 158 48 from the credit side, instead of being in excess.

The auditor does well to avoid the transfers in making his figures. But the people want no evasions of that character. Plain, stubborn facts are demanded and the comparative table when properly made, including everything, shows that the expenditures authorized for 1879 and 1880 are not in excess of the actual expenditures of 1877 and 1878.

Again, on the 11th day of April, 1879, in his quarterly report to the Governor, the Auditor states that in consequence of the decreased valuation of property there will be a reduction of the income of the State in two years of $447,789 72, or $223 894 86 per annum. He repeats that statement in the present communication, and intends to convey the idea that the State will need that sum to make her income in the next two years what it was in the two just past; ergo, there will be a great deficiency, the expenditures being the same. The tax levy for revenue purposes is 20 cents on the $100. No part of the State's current expenses is paid out of any other fund. The interest fund, which arises out of a further tax of 20 cents on the $100, is devoted entirely to the interest on the State debt, and is equal to the demands made upon it.

The decreased valuation, the Auditor says, is $55,973 317, and at 20 cents on the $100 the income would be $111 945 63 per annum less than heretofore, but the balance in the Treasury on January 1, 1879, to start the two years, was $120 224 95; so the deficiency dreaded is already overcome for 1879.

It seems to be the design in thus confounding the two funds—revenue and interest—to make the figures as large as possible. Again, a rule of the Treasury Department is, and it is perfectly safe, having been tested repeatedly, that the receipts from back taxes and delinquent lists of former years will more than equal the delinquency on the current tax-books. The Auditor's estimate for 1879, which includes the actual receipts to May 1st, of the revenue fund, is $1,232,492 69. The actual receipts of the same fund for 1878, not including the balance from 1877, were $1 452,564 05. The difference in favor of the receipts over the estimates is $220 071 36. Taking from this the actual falling off on account of decreased valuation, found to be $111 945 61, the estimate is then below the actual receipts of 1878 some $98 124 75, and adding to this the balance from 1877, with which 1878 started in, we have $176 195 23, which the Auditor seems to ignore entirely. But 1879 is $42,154 48 better off than 1878 was, since that sum is the difference of balance between the two years, inherited from those preceding. This would swell the sum which is ignored by the Auditor to $218 349 71, on the proposition that the receipts will only be short the amount estimated from the decreased valuation. The Auditor gives no other reason for shortage.

Again, the tax books of 1879 on the reduced valuation will produce $1,110 000 in round numbers, and to this must be added the licenses which the Auditor, on page 20 of his biennial report shows, was $268,-277.11. This will give as the probable receipts of 1879 the sum of $1,378 277 11, as against $1 452 564 05 in 1878. But on May 16th the Auditor tells the General Assembly that $499 180 48 has already been expended for 1879, and that the other eight months will cost $516 000, making a total for 1879 of $1,015,180 43, adding to this the transfer to school moneys, which was $328,255 18, we have $1 343 4 5.61 as the expenses as against $1,378,277 11, receipts.

Place the balance from 1878 with the difference between these sums, and we have about the same for a balance on Jan. 1, 1880, as demonstrated before the Senate caucus by Mr. Noland.

Again, Mr. Holliday does not give the revenue the benefit of the decreased valuation of property, in this, that he estimates that in 1880 the transfer to school moneys will be the same as in 1879, the sum of $328,-255 19, whereas if the revenue falls short $111 945 63, the school moneys will fall short one-fourth of that sum, and there will be the sum of $27,983.66, which the schools will not get from revenue in 1880, and this amount must come out of his estimated deficiency of January, 1881.

Again, the Auditor in his quarterly report to the Governor April 11th, 1879 informs His Excellency that the decreased valuation will make a reduction of revenues in two years of $447 789 72 and now, notwithstanding this tremendous reduction, he informs the General Assembly that the probable deficiency in January, 1881, will be only $140,-789 42.

THIRTEENTHLY.

Again, Mr. Holladay states the footing of the general appropriation bill at $1 885,-880 35 and yet that amount includes the $60 000 for support and $40 000 for new buildings at the penitentiary, which will not be needed, since the convicts remain at the coal mines. It also includes $75 000 for pay of guards, of which amount the warden thinks he will need but one-half. Two of these items he virtually admits will not be needed, since he did not include them in his table, and yet counts them in his comparative table, because if he did not, he would not be able to show that the present General Assembly had appropriated more than was expended in the two years past. He places the expenditures in 1877 and 1878 at $2 086,-625 49. Taking the penitentiary appropriations above cited from the total appropriations for 1879 and 1880, and there remains $1 029 748 77 or $56 876 72 less than was expended in 1877 and 1878. Since the Auditor can draw no warrant when there is no appropriation, it is safe to assume that the expenditures will be $56 876 72 less than in 1877 and 1878, and if the revenues were sufficient, (the Auditor admits they were, and $120 224 95 over,) to pay the expenditures of 1877 and 1878, it is clear that they will have $56 876 72 less to pay in 1879 and 1880, which is more than one half of the anticipated deficiency from decreased valuation.

SENATE.

The first thing called up in the Senate this morning was the non-forfeiture insurance bill, passed with amendments by the House.

Senator Ballingal moved that the House amendment be non-concurred in, which motion was agreed to.

Outside of the above, the Senate proceedings would be a repetition of the proceedings of the House, as they consisted entirely of the adoption of reports and passage of bills passed by the House yesterday afternoon and this morning.

THE ANVIL CHORUS.

A Sort of Telephonic Resume of the General Situation.

General Carpenter Promulgates Orders for the Concentration of Immigrants.

Chetopa is Crowded With Men, Women, Children and Dogs.

All of Whom Are Rushing "On to Oklahoma."

[Special Dispatch to the Kansas City Times.]

HEADQUARTERS IN THE SADDLE, OKLAHOMA FRONTIER, May 17, '79.

Please announce that all parties who have been holding back to hear from me, should now move without delay. The time has come. Parties from Platte, Saline, and Lafayette should start on Monday. I will meet them at Coffeyville the last of the week.

C. C. CARPENTER.

Chetopa Ram Jam Full of Immigrants.

[Special Dispatch to the Kansas City Times.]

CHETOPA, KAS., May 17, 1879.—Still they crowd on toward the happy land of Oklahoma. Chetopa is now crowded full of wagons, men, women, children and dogs, all marching to the "new land." It is almost impossible to find sleeping apartments, for the crowds that stop here for guides to pilot them across the prairies. Hay-mows, wood-sheds, and loose boards are sought after for resting places. Provisions have advanced, and farmers are jubilant. Knowing that the great rush cannot last till the new crops come in, many have abandoned their fields of fine corn and put their teams on the road at ten to fifteen dollars a day. We want mechanics, especially blacksmiths and wagonmakers, as the number here (twenty-three) cannot begin to do the work. We have now nine hundred soldiers here, but the crowds take them into the various saloons and treat them, when all is friendship. A deputation from five or six tribes of Indians is in town to give a friendly invitation to all who want to come into any part of the Indian Territory.

R. T. MALONE.

BUSINESS BRIEFS.

D. & R. G. SUBSCRIPTIONS.

NEW YORK, May 17.—The Denver & Rio Grand Railroad Company's subscription closed to-day at noon. There were over $10,400 000 bonds subscribed for at 90 cents; only $5,000,000 were asked and the subscriptions will be scaled to that amount.

Gen. Palmer, the President of the road, states that this sum will be used to complete at once the lines from Canon City to Leadville and Ten Mile, 150 miles from Alamosa westward to the San Juan mines, 110 miles, and from Alamosa southward to Albuquerque, in New Mexico, 105 miles.

The recent decision of the Supreme Court gives them the prior right of location in the Grand Canon of the Arkansas river, and on all the other routes named in the charter. The Grand Canon of the Arkansas which is the only practicable route for a railroad to Leadville except across the mountain ranges, will enable them to complete the road to that point by September 1st, by using the roadbed already graded by the Atchison, Topeka & Santa Fe Railroad Co. prior to the decision of the Supreme Court. Whether they will pay for the grading or not will be adjudicated in the United States Courts. They expect to complete the other lines within a year.

POLITICAL.

DEMOCRATIC NOMINATIONS.

CHICAGO, May 17.—The Cook County Democratic Convention to-day renominated Circuit Judges W. K. McAllister and Jno. G. Rogers, and nominated also Thomas Moran, Murray F. Tuley and W. H. Barnum.

Indications.

WASHINGTON, D. C., May 18, 1 a. m.—For the Upper Mississippi and Lower Missouri valleys, rising or stationary followed by falling barometer; cooler followed by warmer; northeast to southeast winds; clearer, partly cloudy weather, and possibly followed by local rains.

CARPENTER AND POPE.

Behold them both—each pursuing the other, and both slightly in advance. Such are the hazards of war. It is always either a fight or a foot-race. O'LEARY and ROWELL may well envy these champion pedestrians. "On, on to Oklahoma!" shouts Black Hills CARPENTER. "I am first at last, though I was behind before, responds Bull Run POPE. May the best legs win!

THE PEN IS MIGHTIER THAN THE SWORD.

PRESIDENT'S PROCLAMATION.—You are instructed to direct the agents and officers of the Indian service to use their utmost vigilance in the removal of such unauthorized persons as may attempt to appropriate by settlement, any lands of the Indian Territory, and make prompt report of any and all such cases of attempted trespass for the information of the Interior Department.

COLUMBIA.—The ceded lands of the Indian Territory belong to the people of the United States, and are as legally open to settlement under the Homestead and Preemption acts as the public lands in any State or Territory of the Union. You might as well attempt to dam Niagara with a bulrush as check the tidal rush to the Indian Territory. On to Oklahoma!

CARPENTER AS MOSES.

"But why MOSES?" asks the curious reader.

Answer—Because MOSES was a great popular leader, and so is CARPENTER. MOSES hid in the bulrushes—so did CARPENTER. MOSES slew the Egyptian, and CARPENTER "slewed" himself. MOSES exodized from Egypt, and CARPENTER to the Black Hills. MOSES numbered the people—ditto CARPENTER, and gave MOSES big odds. MOSES propounded the Decalogue, and CARPENTER'S martial conundrums affright the soul of the War Department. MOSES broke his two tables—CARPENTER has mashed many a faro-table. MOSES himself was no warrior—he fought by proxy—so does CARPENTER. MOSES sent out spies—so did CARPENTER. MOSES set up a brazen serpent—CARPENTER has "seen snakes" in abundance. MOSES did not enter the Promised Land—neither will CARPENTER. MOSES died with his boots on—so will CARPENTER. The Lord took MOSES—the Devil take CARPENTER!

CRIMES.

SHOOTING AT SEDALIA.

SEDALIA, May 17.—This morning about 8 o'clock, a fatal shooting affray occurred about seven miles north of this city. The parties were a young man named Caleb Lowry, son of Judge Wm. Lowry, aged 20 years, and Bard Smith aged 21 son of Col. J. D Smith. The parties are both of eminently respectable families and have always stood well in the county. There has been an old grudge existing between the parties for over a year and yesterday morning they met on the road. Young Smith being in a wagon with his brother, and young Lowry on horseback. As soon as the parties met Smith jumped out of his wagon and pulled his pistol, and Lowry also pulled his. Smith fired five shots and Lowry but one, which missed. One of Smith's shots took effect on Lowry's right groin, passing through his body and coming out near his backbone; another passed through his leg, through the saddle and into the horse. Lowry fell from his horse, and Smith jumped into his wagon and drove off. Lowry will not live till morning.

THE EASTON MURDER.

TOPEKA, May 17.—A man giving his name as Anderson, was arrested last night in Carbondale and brought here this morning. He is supposed to be the murderer of Mrs Costello at Easton, and answers the description very well gave, that his beard is short and shows no gray. When arrested, he wore several suits of clothes of good quality, and had a dirk knife which he attempted to use when arrested. He claims to be a druggist from Western Virginia, and appears very much afraid of being lynched if he is taken to Leavenworth county. A constable from Easton is expected to-night to identify him.

A BLOODY MURDER.

CINCINNATI, O., May 17.—The body of an unknown man was found in Spring Grove Cemetery this morning, with the head crushed. By the side of the body was found a club and a large stone covered with blood and brains. No clue to the murderer has yet been gained. No one recognized the dead man. When the body was stripped the letters "G. W." were found written on the right arm.

WIFE MURDER.

INDIANAPOLIS, May 17.—Patrick Welsh, a laborer at Amboy, a small town near Terre Haute, Ind., murdered his wife last night. Welsh come home drunk and commenced demolishing his furniture; Mrs. Welsh attempting to leave the house was overtaken by her husband, who, after violently kicking her, shot her twice with a revolver.

THE RUSSIAN TERROR.

The Rendezvous That Cost Serge Lawrowski His Nose and Ears—The Fate of President Novikoff and of the Informer Koprowski.

[London Telegraph.]

A few weeks ago Serge Lawrowski, one of the ablest detectives attached to the Third Department, was sent from St. Petersburg to Poltava with instructions to get at the secrets of the Nihilistic organization there established. Arrived at Poltava, Lawrowski displayed great activity in guiding the researches of the local police, made many acquaintances in different characters, being an expert in changing his appearance and manner, and was hopeful of success in his mission, when his evil fortune prompted him to fall in love with the pretty daughter of a priest, named Achristoff. This girl, only 17 years of age, was affiliated to the associations, and had been planted upon Lawrowski by order of the Poltava Committee, with the object of betraying him into their hands. After a fortnight's ardent courtship, Mlle. Achristoff allowed herself to be persuaded to give her admirer a rendezvous by night in a garden just outside the town.

When Lawrowski reached the trysting place he was surrounded and seized by five masked men, armed with revolvers and knives, who bound him to a tree and then cut off his nose and ears. Bleeding and unable to shout for assistance, as he had been gagged by his mutilators, he remained where they left him in an agony of pain until early morning, when he was found senseless and all but dead from loss of blood. An open letter in his pocket contained the following ferocious announcement: "We cut off his nose because he is a sleuthhound, and his ears because he has proved himself an ass, in that he paid court to one of Us!" Mlle. Achristoff has vanished from Poltava, and all the efforts of the police to track her to her hiding-place have proved utterly ineffectual. Meanwhile Lawrowski lies in a hopeless condition; and even should he rally from the utter exhaustion induced by the hemorrhage suffered during that terrible night, he will bear hideous witness on his disfigured countenance as long as he may live, to the pitiless anger of the Poltava Committee.

The *St Petersburger-Zeitung* reports four attempts at assassination committed at Kasan, the victims of which have one and all been State officials of high rank. Three of the four persons attacked have died of their wounds. One of these latter, Novikoff, the President of the district, walked into the principal restaurant of Kasan a few minutes before he was shot, and said to one of the waiters: "Friend, give me a dram; perhaps it will be the last I shall ever drink." A glass of vodki was brought to him, and the waiter noticed that Novikoff's hand shook as he lifted the liquor to his lips. Immediately afterward he left the restaurant; but, as he opened the door, a bullet struck him full in the breast, inflicting an injury which has since proved fatal. The agents of the Committee actually engaged in these outrages have been arrested. Two are workingmen, one is Boyar, and another is a handsome and highly educated girl of seventeen.

The latest news from Kieff indicates that the revolutionary propaganda is assuming extraordinary dimensions in that province. Eight peasants were brought into the provincial capital in chains from a village named Chramowko, about sixteen wersts from, Kiew, accused of distributing Socialist pamphlets and insurrectionary proclamations at the fairs and markets of the district. These men confessed under pressure that they had succeeded in circulating some 40 000 of these proclamations among the country folk. In another village, Toporewko, a secret printing press was discovered by the police in the school house of the Commune. Their search was instituted upon the strength of information supplied by the scribe of the Mir, a man named Koprowski. Next morning he was found dead in his bed with a knife plunged to the hilt in his breast.

PERSONAL.

JAY GOULD'S MOVEMENTS.

ST. LOUIS, May 17.—Jay Gould and party, consisting of Russell Sage, Solon Humphrey, A. L Hopkins and S T. Smith, arrived here this evening by special train, having made the run from Toledo, 413 miles, in eleven hours. The party will leave for Kansas City in the morning, and will probably go thence to Denver over the Kansas Pacific.

IN MEMORIAM.

MEMPHIS, May 17.—The graves of the Confederate dead in Elmwood Cemetery were decorated to-day. The ceremonies were of a most imposing nature. Colonel Luke W. Findlay delivered the address.

OVER THE RIVER.

PHILADELPHIA, May 17.—Judge Asa Packer died to-night, in the 73d year of his age. His funeral will take place at Mauch Chunk, Tuesday.

WASHINGTON WAIFS.

America's Ambitious Statesmen Wrangle Over the Silver Issue.

A Superfluity of Words and a Modicum of Good Horse-Sense.

WASHINGTON, May 17.—The Senate's executive session to-day was wholly devoted to an animated discussion of the report of the Judiciary Committee on the question of the right of the Senate to confirm nominations for army appointments and promotions above the rank of Captain, in view of the act of April 18, 1878, which prohibited such appointments and promotions until after the report of the joint committee commonly known as the Burnside Commission shall be made and acted on by Congress.

The conclusion of the Judiciary committee that this prohibitory clause is still in force, was to-day supported in an argument by Messrs. Garland, Maxey and Thurman, and was combatted by Messrs. Randolph, Hoar, Butler, Logan and Burnside. A number of other Senators participated briefly in the debate, but the foregoing were the principal speakers. The advocates of the Judiciary Committee's views argued that, although the various proceedings were taken in each house of the Forty-fifth Congress upon the report submitted by the Burnside Commission, no act either in affirmance or disaffirmance thereof, ever received the concurrence of both Houses, and therefore that no action of "Congress" has yet been taken upon that report. It was also argued that it would be unwise for the Senate to confirm the pending nominations because in the event of a different construction being placed upon the law by the House of Representatives court there would be great trouble and confusion in readjusting the ranks of the officers whose promotions might then prove to have been illegal. The result is considered doubtful, although recommendations of the Judiciary Committee are usually sustained.

ARREARS OF PENSIONS.

WASHINGTON, May 17.—In response to a letter addressed by Secretary Schurz, inquiring what amount of funds can be made available for the payment of arrears due upon the pensions allowed prior to January 25th, 1879, the Secretary of the Treasury states that including the amount already paid, $1 500 000 will be available prior to July 1st, and $4 000 000 monthly thereafter.

At this rate nearly the whole of the next fiscal year will be required to complete the payment of these arrears. The Commissioner of Pensions, in view of this, has issued a circular letter to all applicants for arrears, saying that a comparatively small number of cases only can be adjusted monthly, and therefore some delay may occur in the settlement of the claims, but settlements will be made in such order as to distribute the payments equally among the several pension agencies, as near as may be.

CONGRESSIONAL.

SENATE.

During the debate on the amendment on the subject of clerks in the Postoffice department a colloquy occurred between Messrs. SAULSBURY and WINDOM, in which the latter said he would not join the former in his wish to economize expenses by reducing the army, which is required for the protection of the frontier against the attacks of Indians. A discussion followed with Messrs. Saulsbury, Conkling and Edwards, using the name of Gen. Schenck on the use of troops in Maryland and Delaware.

Mr. LOGAN said there was no more honorable man than Gen. Schenck when treason stalked about the land and the nation was rolling and rocking to and fro like a distressed vessel on a stormy sea. Gen. Schenck reached forth his hand in his country's defence. He was one of a band of patriots who defied treason and risked his life and all other things precious for the preservation of the Union.

He did not claim that Gen. Schenck was entitled to credit for being a great patriot, but because he was a patriot was no reason why he should be maligned here or elsewhere. Gen. Schenck was a crippled man, a pensioner for wounds received in his country's defense, and he was a patriot and honest man, notwithstanding the sneers of the Senator from Delaware.

After a short executive session, the Senate adjourned.

HOUSE.

Mr. SPRINGER spoke in favor of his amendment, to which Belford's amendment was offered. It would make a difference between the value of bullion and the value of coin, and inure to the Government instead of bullion owners. It would give the bullionholder 84 cents for his bullion, which it was worth, and not 100 cents, which it was not worth. It would put into the Treasury the difference between the bullion and coin value of silver and keep it there as a trust fund for the people of the United States. (Applause on the Republican side).

MR BUCKNER opposed Mr. Springer's amendment as a proposition utterly destructive of the whole theory on which the bill was founded. It was a worse blow at silver than the proposition of the Secretary of the Treasury to stop its coinage at $50,000 000. This amendment cut the throat of the silver dollar, and if it was put upon the bill he would vote against the bill, because it would then put into the hands of the Secretary of the Treasury the very power he desired, and would virtually stop the coinage of another silver dollar.

Mr. NEWBERRY opposed the bill. It was not based upon facts but upon theories, opinions and guesses of the wildest kind. He criticized the provision in the eighth section that certificates issued "shall not exceed 20 per cent beyond the amount of coin and bullion in the Treasury."

What was that 20 per cent. It was simply fiat. It was a tail to the greenback kite. It was legislation for the rich man, for the banker and broker. Why were the streets of Washington to-day filled with men who had bullion piled up in New York, if not for the purpose of seeing that this bill was passed and of lobbying it through. He was thinking of offering an amendment to the bill providing that an owner of paper pulp might deposit the same at the Treasury and receive therefor legal tender notes of the same dimensions as those now in use.

Mr. BRIGHT (Tenn.) said that the question was whether the government should have a seigniorage on coin or whether the country should have a free coinage and argued that when a seigniorage was put upon the coin it would be driven out of the mints. He opposed Mr. Springer's amendment as amounting to little less than a tax of sixteen per cent on the coinage of silver bullion.

Soon afterwards a vote was taken on Belford's amendment, and it was defeated—yeas 87, nays 130.

Mr. EWING offered an amendment to Mr. Springer's amendment. It provides that the Secretary of the Treasury shall issue and deliver to the depositor of silver bullion certificates to an amount equal to the value of such bullion, and that silver dollars coined from such bullion to the extent of forty per cent. of such certificates, shall be held for the redemption thereof, and the remainder applied to the payment of the interest of the public debt.

Mr. GARFIELD said that Congress had never legislated on any question that reached further both territorially and in time and touched more vital interests than those touched by this and similar bills within recent years and notably within recent months. The leading thinkers in the civilized world have become alarmed at the attitude of the two precious metals in relation to each other and they were clearly of the opinion that by some wise, broad and judicious arrangement both metals might be kept in service for the currency of the world.

Even England which for more than half a century had believed in a single gold standard, was now seriously meditating how she might harness both of those forces to the monetary power of the world. Yet outside of this chamber and capital there was not a single bi-metallic authority in the world who considered it safe to plunge out into the wider coinage of silver at the present time anywhere. France and the Latin Union, which had believed in bi-metallism and maintained it against all comers, and had advocated it throughout the world, were not coining silver and had not done so since 1874. The most strenuous advocates of bimetallism now said it would be ruinous to bimetallism for France or the Latin Union to coin any more silver; and yet the United States Government, which had coined in less than two years, more of silver dollars than had previously been coined, from the foundation of the Government, and ten times more than had been coined in the seventy years of its existence, was to-day facing the world and denying the universal opinion about bimetallism, by saying that America, single handed, could enter the contest and settle this mighty question alone. This was madness. He had once seen a dog on a great stack of hay which had been floated out into the wide overflowed bed of a river; for a little while the dog appeared perfectly happy. The hay stack was there; the stack-pin was there, and he thought that the world was all right; but bye and bye he began to discover that the barn and the house and the surroundings were not all there, as they had been before he went to sleep, and he began to understand that he could not quite command the prospect as he had done. So in the United States, we were all afloat on this mighty question, and we "bay the moon" as we float down the whirling tide and say, "We are wise; we have been launched on a wide current which sweeps over the whole world, and we bark from our hay stacks as if we commanded the whole. For heaven's sake let us take some account of the flood; let us understand that the deluge means something and try, if we can, to get our bearings before we undertake to fix it all up in a House of Representatives.

To-day we are coining one-third of the silver that is being coined in the world. China is doing another third, and the nations of the globe are using the other for subsidiary coin. If we want to join China and part company with all the civilized nations of the Western Word, let us put it in this bill. What this country needs most of all is that this Congress go home (laughter and applause on the Republican side), and let these forces of business and peace and order and brotherhood work in their natural way and bring us into light, stability and peace. Even now our administration is opening negotiations with all the Eastern nations to see if there cannot be an international arrangement whereby this question of bi-metallism may be wisely settled.

Mr. WARNER said he was glad the present administration had been induced by the action of this House to open correspondence on this question with foreign countries, and he hoped that action would be backed up by the vote of the House. He has well declared himself to be an enthusiastic bimetallist, but was opposed to the bill and to Mr. Springer's amendment thereto, because, if the bill passed, the gold would leave the country and the currency would be contracted to the extent of two hundred millions.

A vote was then taken on Mr. Ewing's amendment, and it was adopted—yeas 106, nays 103.

The Speaker casting the deciding vote, amid applause on the Democratic side.

Mr. Springer's amendment as amended by Mr. Ewing was then rejected—yeas 38, nays 171.

The House then, on motion of Mr. CLYMER, adjourned until Tuesday.

The Forbidden Land

But the boastful Carpenter was soon to be put to the test. The Secretary of War, George W. McCrary, presently advised Schurz that he had enough troops at strategic points to take care of the intruders. At Forts Sill, Reno, Supply, and Gibson, in the Indian Territory, there were 535 men of the Fourth and Tenth regiments of cavalry, and 229 of the Sixteenth and Nineteenth regiments of Infantry. At Fort Elliott, in the Texas Panhandle, there were 55 men of the Fourth Cavalry and 91 of the Nineteenth Infantry. And at Forts Riley, Wallace, and Hays, in Kansas, there were others. Patrols were employed along the border and within the area threatened by intruders, and numerous arrests were made and parties expelled. Other troops appeared on the streets of border towns, and their officers read to attentive listeners the President's proclamation and warned that their orders were to use force if the proclamation was not heeded.

At this juncture Inspector John McNeal of the Indian Service met Carpenter on the streets of Independence and warned him against his proposed venture. He reminded the would-be invader that "the jig was up," that he must leave the country or else he might be forced to wear handcuffs to complete his clownish attire. Carpenter blustered and sought to evade McNeal's accusations. But his spirit was weak and soon he was making tracks for Kansas City. A disappointed disciple at Independence wrote on May 7 that his home town was no longer booming. "The 'whoop-her-up' feeling of a week ago has subsided." All wondered what had become of Carpenter. More than once riders and movers coming to Independence, Coffeyville, or other towns reported having seen a man answering to his description here or there. But his whereabouts for several days was unknown. It was finally learned that he was hiding in Kansas City. So the "children of Israel" now looked for another Moses to lead them to the Land of Promise.

49

5 : A "New Philadelphia"

*W*HILE Assistant Doorkeeper Dave Payne was maintaining a watch over the House of Representatives gallery in Washington he met and had several conferences with E. C. Boudinot, probable employee of the Missouri, Kansas and Texas Railraod and proponent of opening Indian Territory to settlement. Already Payne had manifested great interest in such a venture. He had explored the country while with the Nineteenth Kansas Volunteers, and before he went to Washington he had sought to interest others in a colonization society. Moreover, he had carefully studied the treaties bearing on the Oklahoma problem and had consulted "eminent" lawyers with reference to homestead rights. There is good reason to believe that he and Boudinot had agreed upon some common plan of action, perhaps including the backing of one or more railroad corporations. O. E. Jefferson wrote in 1889 that it was logical to suppose that Frisco officials had employed Payne, since he was a prominent Kansas frontiersman and politician, and that he probably received "a salary from them during the first years of the boomer excitement." There is substantial proof, to be presented later in this narrative, that at least there was some railroad support.

Payne was an ideal leader of the Boomers, as the Oklahoma-bound emigrants were now called. His was a far more commanding personality than Carpenter's. In 1880 a contemporary

50

described him as a "stalwart young man, 35 or 40 years of age, pleasant and sociable in manner," who wore a broad-brimmed hat, blue flannel shirt, and heavy boots. Some of those who knew him during these early days have also made mention of his hypnotic eyes. C. P. Wickmiller of Kingfisher, Oklahoma, a surviving member of the invasion of 1883, says that Payne's eyes had peculiar yellow-gray flecks, unlike anything he had ever seen in the eyes of others.

When he lost his Assistant Doorkeeper job, Payne left Washington and visited his old home in Indiana. Here he borrowed two hundred dollars from his sister and then turned his steps toward Kansas. He arrived in Wichita in August, 1879, and he, Anna, and George (their son) boarded in a second-story apartment. Payne now began to work industriously but quietly among those interested in Oklahoma. He took enough time out, however, to revisit his old haunts in the Wichita Mountains and to travel from there eastward to the Canadian River, where he tentatively selected a site for his future "Oklahoma City."

The Wichita *Beacon* of February 11, 1905, mentions a preliminary organization of Payne's Oklahoma Colony as early as late December, 1879, when Payne, Frank B. Smith, proprietor of the *Beacon*, Frank Fisher, W. C. Glenn, and Oscar Smith met in the latter's office on the second floor of a building in the Allen block on Douglas Avenue to discuss ways and means of launching the colony. Yet little more was accomplished than the levying of a nominal fee of one dollar on those present, to provide for running expenses and to plan means for interesting substantial citizens.

William W. Bloss wrote five years later that during the winter of 1879–80 two organizations were created. The first was Payne's Oklahoma Colony, with D. L. Payne as president; Dr. R. B. Greenlee, vice-president; John Faulkenstein, treasurer; W. B. Hutchison, secretary; W. A. Shuman, corresponding secretary; and T. D. Craddock, general manager. The other organization was the Oklahoma Town Company (later changed to the Southwestern Colonization Society), largely composed of Wichita businessmen who took no part in the invasions. Its officers were John M. Steele, president; Payne, vice-president; and George M. Jackson, secretary. Both organizations, however, changed officers from time to time. Membership dues in Payne's Oklahoma Colony were at first fixed at two dollars, and in the Town Company at twenty-five dollars. In the Colony, members were entitled to all the rights and privileges the organization could afford, as well as a claim to 160 acres of land apiece. In the Society, a member was entitled to a town lot in the proposed capital. The Colony surveyor was also required to make a charge of two dollars for each homestead location, and the secretary fifty cents for the imprint of the Colony seal on each claim certificate, which he was allowed to keep. Then, finally, special collections were taken to pay Payne's attorneys, to defray railroad expenses of officials, and for other unexpected calls. It is not known how much money was raised to back all these colonization purposes, although Colonel Edward Hatch, in charge of Oklahoma troops, later said that he personally knew of $100,000 having been collected by Payne. Receipts for membership dues in the Colony numbered well above fourteen thousand by the time of Payne's death in 1884. The number of shares sold by the Society is not known, although in May, 1880, there was reported to be a rush for corner lots.

By January 1, 1880, Payne's Oklahoma Colony had received many recruits, and its president had issued his first proclamation. In it he again called attention to Boudinot's assertion that there were fourteen million acres of unoccupied land in the Indian Territory subject to homestead entry, and added that his association planned to occupy the same with a colony of five or ten thousand people. The date of the start of the first invasion was announced as March 25. Then followed detailed instructions: Each family or person joining the Colony must be supplied with ample means to support himself for a year; each family should have at least one team, a wagon, agricultural implements, and seed to plant, to the value of five hundred dollars. Single men who did not have this amount must go as employees of members of the Colony and must contract for work for a period of at least six months. Brickmakers, carpenters, artisans, and mechanics would be needed, and these classes were urged to join.

Payne suggested that wherever groups of Boomers came together in border towns they should perfect organizations by electing presidents, boards of directors, and such other officers as they would need. He warned that no intoxicating liquor would be allowed, and that the Boomers would not tolerate "hangers on and idlers." He promised, however, that if everything went well the Colony would presently assume much the same character as other thriving communities. He had made arrangements for a daily paper and schoolteachers, and would promise that within "three days after reaching the place of destination" the Colony would have schools in full operation.

Meanwhile the Colony had grown rapidly, claiming a membership of fifteen hundred by February 1. As in the previous year, covered wagons were on the move for Wichita and other border towns, and Boomers had high hopes of success. Payne continued his work of organization, going from town to town with his membership book and addressing groups wherever possible. He spoke to a large and interested audience at Wichita, another at Caldwell, and another at Coffeyville. A. H. Norwood, Postmaster of Claremore, Indian Territory, while visiting in Coffeyville, attended the Payne rally, and later reported to a Cherokee delegate in Washington, W. P. Adair, what he regarded as alarming news. He said that Payne called for a thousand recruits, a force sufficient to resist United States soldiers, Indians, or others who offered opposition. To maintain a semblance of compliance with the requirements of the Creek and Seminole treaties of 1866, another speaker on the same program proposed to take fifty Indians and fifty Negroes to Oklahoma, who in turn would employ the one thousand Boomers! If there were legal problems, he assured his listeners that the Boomers were backed by five firms of lawyers, as well as the Kansas City *Times*.

There were two reasons for Payne's proposing to launch his invasion during the spring of 1880. The first was that in his December, 1879, message to Congress, President Hayes had expressed a doubt that the federal government could keep Boomers out of Oklahoma. Then, second, the border press was giving front-page notice to Senator Vest's bill. The measure proposed the establishment of a United States court and a land office for the survey and allotment of land in the Indian Territory. Each Indian was to receive 160 acres, after which the balance was to be sold and the proceeds held in trust for the Indians. Payne argued that even the President could not deny the Boomers homestead rights and that the Vest bill, when enacted, would represent a surrender by Congress on the question.

The Kansas City *Times* was the most active of the western newspapers backing the opening of Oklahoma. On January 28, 1880, "writing Editor" Bloss informed Payne that the *Times* was still the "advocate of its original proposition." He spoke of a petition being circulated endorsing the Vest bill and concluded: "If the petition is seconded by a raid upon the Territory in the manner you propose Congress will be placed between two fires, the law abiding people who desire a peaceful investigation on the one hand and those who are determined to enter the public land. . . ." He promised to advertise the movement well and to join the first invasion party if possible.

Bloss evidently did his advertising well, for presently a giant mass meeting was held in the Kansas City board of trade hall. An

Oklahoma society was set up with J. M. Nave as president and W. H. Miller as secretary, and with more than thirteen hundred members. The meeting was addressed by Boudinot, B. J. Franklin, and others, each speaker stressing the fact that Oklahoma was in the public domain and therefore subject to homestead entry.

But the government had prepared a counter measure. On February 14, J. R. Hallowell, the United States District Attorney for Kansas, had written Attorney General Charles Devens that he had been unable to find any law under which he could order the arrest of Boomer agitators, unless, he said, it was Section 5440 of the *Revised Statutes,* relating to the use of United States mails to defraud. Since by circular Payne had falsely represented the Oklahoma lands as "public lands" and had used the federal mail service to disseminate these false claims, did this not constitute a violation of the law referred to? Unless some such step were taken at once, he advised, the government would court trouble, for already colonies at Chetopa, Coffeyville, Arkansas City, and Caldwell were preparing to join Payne's Wichita invaders.

Devens would not support Hallowell's proposal. In his reply to his ambitious district attorney he said that such a procedure was "risky," that violation of the law referred to would be hard to prove, and that unless the government secured a conviction it would be greatly embarrassed. Devens then initiated his own plan at the Kansas City meeting. United States Marshal C. C. Allen claimed the floor to read a message from the President to the audience. Some of the Boomers present sought to have him ruled out of order, but the chair was more lenient and allowed him to speak, whereupon he read a new proclamation, dated February 12, in which the President reaffirmed his policy of the preceding year to the effect that Oklahoma was yet a part of the Indian Territory and not subject to homestead entry.

The President's proclamation was also read elsewhere and,

although Boomer organizations were still effected, land-hungry members were not inclined to brave federal troops and the President's "stay out" warning. Consequently, when the March invasion date came, Payne could not muster enough hardy souls to go with him. The presence of two companies of troops at Caldwell and two at Coffeyville, with occasional patrols showing up all along the border, undoubtedly was convincing proof that the President meant to enforce his proclamation. The troops had been given orders to prevent invasion wherever possible, to warn those about to enter that such a venture was illegal, and to explain the folly of such a move.

Similar federal opposition had sent Carpenter in wild flight; but not Payne. The doughty captain argued plausibly that the government must make a show of opposition to save its face, and that if the Boomers went ahead with their plans there was no law or authority that could stop them. Nevertheless, his Colony melted away. Many a disappointed Boomer left Wichita and started for home, until only ten or twelve wagons remained. On April 2, Payne left Wichita and joined his camp on Cowskin River. The border press was more optimistic concerning the strength of those remaining than subsequent events would justify, estimating them variously at thirty, forty, and sixty-five men with teams.

There is little doubt that Payne was anxious to test the Oklahoma homestead issue before a federal court. He wrote District Attorney Hallowell on March 29 that he proposed to start for the Oklahoma lands with a colony on April 10, and requested that the government take some action against him before that time. He asked whether his declaration of purpose would not be equivalent to an actual invasion. Since most of his followers were poor farmers and could not afford to lose a year's crop, would it not be better to stop the movement now? Hallowell referred Payne's request to Devens, but nothing came of it. It was used by Payne, however, as a basis for a protest against his first arrest, as will be noticed shortly.

If General Pope had expected to prevent an Oklahoma invasion by a show of troops, he was soon disappointed. On May 2 the commanding officer at Caldwell reported that a party of Boomers headed by Payne had eluded his patrol and had crossed the Indian Territory line between Arkansas City and South Haven, and that he proposed to leave at daylight the following day with twenty men to head them off. He assured his superior that it was quite impossible for any Boomer party to reach the Canadian, for troops along the Kansas line and at Fort Reno were constantly scouting the country.

But Payne and his party of twenty-one adventurous men had done what the officer had declared could not be done. On the evening of April 26, 1880, they broke camp on Bitter Creek between South Haven and Arkansas City, about six miles east of South Haven, and quietly crossed the line. Payne threw out flankers along the line of march, and H. H. Stafford and Harry L. Hill, two seasoned plains scouts, were sent on in advance to mark the way and watch for patrols.

Toward midnight the wagon train neared the Chikaskia River, when the scouts returned to announce that a company of soldiers was at the ford. Payne had intended to move directly south and had ordered his engineer, George F. Goodrich, to mark the way, but now he was compelled to reroute his course. Immediately the wagons were turned to the left and a few hours later had crossed the river several miles below. Then the invaders followed the course of the river until near daylight, when they pulled down under the river bank into a copse of timber and went into camp. Here they remained until about noon the next day. Meanwhile the scouts were out watching the movements of federal troops. Near noon, Hill rode into camp reporting that he had sighted another squad of soldiers twelve miles in advance.

Payne again changed his plans. He had intended to travel down the Ponca Trail from the Chikaskia, but now he resolved to make a new road between the route first followed and the Ponca Trail, and instructed Goodrich accordingly. He crossed the Salt Fork of the Arkansas at the southwest section of the Nez Percé reservation. Nez Percé warriors here intercepted the invaders and grunted their displeasure, hinting that "they rather wanted the boys' scalps," but the Boomers turned the tide in their favor by presenting Chief Meridin with six pounds of tobacco and lesser chiefs with trifling gifts. Next the Boomers made a day's march directly to the southwest and encamped. The following day the course was directly southward over the Arkansas City cut-off of the Chisholm Trail. Red Rock Creek was approached from a ridge that led to its bluffs, and now with grubbing-hoe and spade the Boomers prepared a crossing. Then, by a coupling of teams "and a vigorous pull-all-together," the small caravan was landed on the south side. They camped here but were given little rest. A violent storm raged from late in the afternoon until almost midnight, the lightning flashing, the thunder rolling, and the rain falling in torrents.

The next morning the spirits of the Boomers were high. On to Oklahoma! No Indians or troops in sight! All about was a sward of luxuriant spring grass and flowers, fine trees, and rich meadows; and every wagon was well supplied with venison, turkey, and fish. What more could any man ask! On the last day of the month the wagon train had crossed Black Bear Creek and the Cimarron and had emerged into the beautiful Canadian Valley, crossing the river on May 2 and going into camp at Walton's ranch, within two miles of the spot afterwards selected as the townsite, or approximately one mile west of the Santa Fe Railroad in Oklahoma City, on a gently rising hill.

The Boomers had reason to be proud of their exploit. The trip had been made in six days, and they were within the very heart of the Oklahoma district. Payne now sent Hill to Wichita with the news of success. His announcement, as carried in the Kansas City *Times* and reprinted in the Topeka *Commonwealth* (May 13, 1880), ran:

North Canadian River, I.T.
May 3, 1880

To the Kansas City Times:

Please say to any that may wish to know that the public lands in the Indian Territory are not only open to settlement, but settled. We are here to stay; are building houses and making homes. Brought with me 153 men, all of them with good teams. Will have one thousand people here in thirty days.

Yours truly
D. L. PAYNE

There is a curious difference between Bloss' quotation of this announcement and that carried by the *Times.* For "153 men" Bloss had substituted "a gallant band of men," and he had qualified the last sentence to read: "*If unmolested* [present author's italics], will have one thousand people here in thirty days."

Presently the Boomer camp was a beehive of industry. Construction work on a strong pole stockade was commenced, a well was dug, and a liberal supply of firewood was hauled. It was feared that hostile Indians might attack and it was well thus to be prepared. Goodrich was also sent out with his surveying instruments, and presently all the colonists had located claims and laid the foundations for their future habitations.

After three days Lieutenant J. H. Pardee with a squad of troops rode into camp and informed Payne that he had orders to expel all intruders from Indian lands. However, Payne seemingly convinced Pardee that he and his party were not on Indian lands but in the "ceded district." Hill reported that Payne and Pardee had "much talk," the lieutenant inquiring fully as to what the Boomers intended to do and Payne insisting that he and his men were homesteaders. Pardee finally drew from his pocket his instructions, and after thoughtfully reading them over again he marked carefully the words that told him to eject any and all settlers "if found upon Indian lands or Indian reservations." Then he told Payne that his instructions evidently did not cover the ceded lands, and presently soldiers and Boomers had shaken "hands across the bloody chasm."

But Pardee and his men were not the last soldiers to visit Payne's camp. On Saturday afternoon, May 15, at four o'clock, Lieutenant G. H. G. Gale arrived with a squad of sixteen troopers of the Fourth Cavalry. Gale had left Fort Reno two days previously with instructions to run down a party of Boomers who had eluded the Kansas patrols, and had found the Boomer camp at a point about forty miles east of the post and about one and one-half miles south of the North Fork of the Canadian, or about one mile east of the present Santa Fe Railroad tracks. A disappointed Boomer later said that it was by mere chance that the camp was discovered. One of the wagons was exposed to view from the north side of the camp, which was situated in a fine cluster of oaks, and Gale, four miles distant, had chanced to see it. Between the troopers and the camp was a creek over which the Boomers had recently made a crossing, three hundred yards below the stockade. Once the camp was seen, Gale's men approached at a fast gallop, but as they advanced they were compelled to wheel to the right to make the crossing, thus exposing themselves to rifle fire had the Boomers sought to take advantage of it. But Payne and his men watched them advance without any show of hostility. So when Gale brought his squad to a plunging halt before the camp, he found the colonists in front of their stockade with Payne puffing his pipe composedly as though the soldiers were expected.

Bloss, who was present, later reported the following dialogue between the two leaders.

"Who are you, and what are you doing here?" Gale asked.

"Well sir," replied Capt. Payne, "we belong to the Oklahoma Colony and are attending strictly to our own business. We have been hard at work since our arrival staking our claims, laying foundations and so forth, and are now enjoying a short rest."

"I am a Lieutenant in the United States Army," said the officer, "and command you to surrender."

"All right," replied Payne, "I supposed you were hunting for us, and it affords me pleasure to surrender to so gallant and gentlemanly an officer."

The Lieutenant looked incredulous. He had formed the conclusion from hearsay that Payne was a desperado and would not surrender without a fight.

The officer still sat upon his horse, and his men were at a "ready," expecting the order to aim.

"I do not wish to make any mistake," said the Lieutenant, eying Payne very closely. "Do I understand that you all surrender?"

"Certainly," replied Capt. Payne; "every man of us. We understand the situation perfectly," he continued, "and you can rely upon our good faith."

At this juncture Tom Donnell, the federal scout, who had dismounted, approached him, remarking, "I believe you are Capt. Payne, are you not?"

"Yes," answered Payne, "and this is Tom Donnell, the Scout?"

"Correct," said Donnell, "I used to know you on the plains, and remember you well."

Lieutenant Gale then dismounted and was introduced by Donnell to Payne, and cordially shook hands.

It is probable that the substance of this conversation occurred between the two men, for it is quite in line with Payne's sense of the dramatic. Payne is reported to have told Gale that he was aware the troops had been searching for his Colony for several days, and added: "Our preliminary work is done. We are located, and we cheerfully surrender. But Lieutenant, if you will take a look over the ground you have come, you will see that if we had been disposed to fight we could have emptied all your saddles before you could have got near enough to demand surrender.

Dismount your men, rest your horses, and let the soldiers get themselves something to eat." After which speech, Bloss reports, Payne tossed out a side of bacon, a bag of flour, and a can of coffee, and pointed to a cooking outfit.

Since it was already five o'clock in the afternoon and the troops had been riding for hours without food, the invitation was accepted. Payne also persuaded Gale to remain in camp until the following morning, since seven of his men were out surveying. They all had taken claims, he said, and under the squatter laws their rights would attach, even if the Territory were not opened for ten years; and, although they were willing to leave the Territory, they would return later and claim their homesteads. If possible, it was their intention to test the case before a United States court.

The soldiers partook of a hearty supper and fraternized with the Boomers, and on the following morning prepared to break camp and start for Fort Reno. But before going, Gale curiously inspected the site which the Boomers had selected. And later, on June 3, 1880, the *Sumner County Press* (Wellington, Kansas) carried his impressions under the title, "A New Philadelphia." Gale said that the plan of the site was made somewhat after that of Philadelphia. On the knoll in the center a square park was laid out. From this radiated eight principal avenues, each being one mile in length and having at the end a small park. The trees had been trimmed along these avenues in such a way that, standing in the middle of Central Park, one could look down eight long avenues, free from brush and undergrowth, the trees presenting the appearance of having been set out and arranged in regular order like those of an old, settled town. He described the farming land bordering the site as rich, black loam, capable of raising anything that would grow in the climate, and that all vegetation gave every evidence that the country was unexcelled as an agricultural region. Goodrich reported that each square was 300 by

600 feet with streets 80 feet wide, and that the entire townsite comprised 720 squares.

At 6:30 A.M., May 16, the combined party of troopers and colonists started for Fort Reno, reaching their destination on the following day at 2:30 P.M. On the trunk of a tree growing on the site of the abandoned camp, Payne left the following notice:

Indian Territory, May 15, 1880

We have accepted the invitation of Lieutenant G. H. G. Gale, 4th United States Cavalry, to accompany him to Fort Reno, but will return as soon as convenient for us to do so. Make yourself at home, but leave things just as you found them.

D. L. PAYNE, *President*

It is probable that the wily Payne intended this as a warning to other Boomers as well as a pre-emption notice.

As previously stated, Payne's intentions were to have the Oklahoma land problem settled by a United States court as soon as possible. He had anticipated arrest, and perhaps had already worked out with legal counsel a line of procedure for such an event. As soon as he reached Fort Reno, therefore, he presented to Gale the following protest.

I, D. L. Payne, with thirteen others whose names are herewith attached, do most earnestly and solemnly protest against being removed from these lands belonging to the United States Government and thereby to the people of said government.

We protest because the lands from which we are about to be removed are free from Indian title and belong solely and exclusively to the government of the United States and in our opinion subject to settlement by the people of the United States and that they have legitimate and legal right to occupy the same. And we further protest because we made known to the officials of the United States our desire and wish and stated to them that we would at a certain time and on a certain day proceed to and move upon the said public lands; that they could at the time have made arrest, if necessary, and granted our request for a test case in which the title to the lands in question could be tested in the Federal Courts. . . . And lastly we protest against being removed . . . because we are doing what our fathers have done before us—to settle upon and occupy the Public Domain.

[*Here signed by Payne and his thirteen followers*]

Payne's protest was finally sent through regular military channels to Washington, but nothing came of it. Upon reaching Fort Reno, Gale turned over his prisoners to Captain G. W. Randall, commandant of the post, who upon the following day placed them in charge of Lieutenant J. H. Pardee and twenty-one men, to be escorted back across the Kansas boundary. But when the party reached Pole Cat Creek, Pardee received an order to hold them until further notice; so here Payne and his Boomers were detained until June 6, and finally released. Bloss explained the detention by the fact that a writ had been issued by Judge Campbell of the Thirteenth Judicial District of Kansas, commanding General Pope or any of his inferiors forthwith to bring Payne and his men before him and show cause why they should be detained. The halt, therefore, was to avoid service of the writ. While detained here, Payne also addressed a protest to General Pope, explaining that he and his men were homesteaders occupying a part of the public domain at the time of their arrest, and declaring that they were being illegally detained.

It was while in camp on Pole Cat Creek that Payne first suffered from sickness. On subsequent invasions it was his common fate. He exposed himself to all kinds of weather, sleeping for hours in wet clothes and often going for days with a cold. His rugged health was to break, finally, under such hardships and exposure.

When Payne and his small party came back to Wichita they were welcomed as returning heroes. Anna, George, and the families of Payne's followers were promised that soon homes would be provided for them in the "New Philadelphia."

6 : The Second Raid

WITHIN the short time between Payne's return from the first Oklahoma invasion and the start of the second, he did not have an idle moment. Although General Phil Sheridan had called him a "pestiferous fellow" and the editor of the *Cherokee Advocate* (Tahlequah, Indian Territory) had classed him as a "dime novel reader," the Boomer leader's popularity was undimmed. Eager throngs at Wellington, Arkansas City, Caldwell, and Wichita wanted to hear him; and he did not disappoint them. On the streets he was a conspicuous figure, generally towering well above the heads of those who would gather about to learn of his Oklahoma experiences. Payne held them spellbound by his glib, racy stories. He was the embodiment of enthusiasm and confidence. He assured his listeners that both the soldiers and the Indians recognized Boomer rights within the ceded lands. Had not Pardee refused to arrest him when convinced that the Boomers were not on Indian lands? Had not the Fort Reno commandant given him and his men the freedom of the post? Even General Pope, he boasted, had feared what the decision of Judge Campbell might be and had ordered that he be held on Pole Cat Creek for fifteen days. Moreover, he was prepared to say that his expedition had not failed. Each Boomer who accompanied him had staked out a claim that would attach, once the government permitted occupation, and the future capital of Oklahoma had been surveyed.

Payne's followers, too, were popular storytellers. Each gave enthusiastic endorsement to his leader's claims. In addition, they had been on a grand and glorious lark and could promise the same to all who would join the next expedition. At no time, they said, had they been without fish and wild game. Some confessed that in the beginning they had fears as to what the attitudes of the soldiers and Indians might be, but these were proven groundless.

In view of these exciting tales, many homeseekers now bought membership certificates in Payne's Oklahoma Colony. Most of them were willing to await the results of a second invasion, although the border press estimated those who were to follow Payne as being in the hundreds. Twenty-one Boomers in four wagons drawn by thirteen horses and mules left Arkansas City on July 6 in stormy weather. Heavy rains had caused all streams along Payne's line of march to be swollen with floodwaters, which probably caused many Boomers to hold back. When the small caravan reached the Chikaskia, the invaders found it full from bank to bank. After a brief consultation they decided to push on, and improvised a ferry by selecting a watertight wagon box to transport their baggage. The men swam along beside the wagon, clothed only by the turgid water, while the horses and mules floundered and struggled forward, drawing the cumbrous wagons, generally with the water well up around their necks and sometimes deep enough to force them to swim. Several trips with the wagon box were required before all the baggage was on the south bank.

From here Payne directed his course toward Yellow Bear's tepee on the Salt Fork, in the southwest corner of the Nez Percé reservation. But the Salt Fork, too, was a raging torrent, and now the disappointed leader ordered a halt. While they were encamped here, Chief Joseph visited the Boomers. He told them that he would allow them to camp on his reservation six days, and that on the following morning he would "furnish all necessary aid" (for fifteen dollars) to get them across the river. The Boomers were quite willing to pay this amount, but they did not like the delay. Captain Thomas B. Robinson's cavalry was at Caldwell, only twenty miles to the north, and might show up at any time, and other patrols would soon be out looking for them. Therefore speed was imperative, even though the river's channel was half a mile wide and an intervening island would lengthen the distance to be covered by another quarter of a mile.

A desperate situation and a need for quick action led the Boomers to decide upon an immediate crossing. They at once began the construction of a raft by lashing saplings crosswise over four small logs by means of lariats. Then a framework was superimposed for raising the baggage above the water, and when this was heavily loaded their flimsy craft was pushed from shore into the seething water.

But the improvised ferry could accommodate only a part of the baggage contained in the wagons, and another trip would be necessary before all could be successfully transported. "The men were stripped, swimming at the sides," wrote a Boomer. "The stream was swift and the channel deep and shallow at intervals. The raft was overloaded and in deep water the swimmers were compelled at times to wade and support it underneath to avoid swamping. Others swam at the front, pulling at the ropes. Payne, Sutter, Soper and Stafford supported the four corners, to guide and prevent capsizing, when the crossing was finally made in safety."

The work of transportation was accomplished on a second trip and with less difficulty, for the men had profited by their previous experience. Fortunately the water was not cold, although all the men were chilled by the long exposure. Payne, who had only recently recovered from malarial fever contracted while a prisoner on Pole Cat Creek, was so exhausted that he was unable to speak for some time.

That night the colonists went into camp on Red Rock Creek, for here another task awaited them to which their exhausted condition was unequal. But on the following morning they were up early, refreshed for their day's work. They cut down the steep bank of the creek to make a sharp incline to the water, and they let the wagons down this by means of ropes fastened to the rear axles, a tree serving as a snubbing post. Then on reaching the opposite side all hands were required at the ropes to help the mules haul the wagons up the steep and slippery incline.

This sort of routine was repeated at nearly every crossing until the weary Boomers arrived at the Cimarron. This stream was known to be reasonably shallow, but it was full of washouts and the quicksands were treacherous. The river was about six hundred feet wide and the water was swift and filled with debris. Here again the men stripped their clothes from their bodies and prepared for their tasks. Payne and Stafford waded into the water and sought out the hidden holes that might swamp the wagons, swimming when they stepped into deeper water until they could stand again. Then the men were stationed at intervals to guide the wagons away from the deep holes, thus marking an irregular crossing. After much pulling and straining at the ropes and putting their shoulders to the wheels when these were endangered by quicksand, the Boomers were at last pleased to see all of their wagons across the river.

Both on the march and while encamped, the men were often wet and uncomfortable. Payne contracted inflammatory rheumatism, and his legs were soon swollen. Although suffering intense pain, he continued to direct the work of his men, hobbling about on improvised crutches.

Not long after crossing the Cimarron, the Boomers learned

that a cavalry patrol was near. Donnell and his Indian scouts had been seen at the former Boomer camp site. Indeed, a few days previously they had arrested near this spot other intruders who gave their names as W. F. Richardson, J. M. Stewart, Joe Stewart, and John Langfort. Payne reasoned that the cavalry officer would expect him and his party also to show up at their old camp, and decided to modify his plans. When he was within a day's journey of his former camp he changed his course so as to leave the road, and continued until he came to the Deep Fork, and thence journeyed up its valley on the north side. In this manner, wrote one of his men, he avoided "several bodies of troops who were in hot pursuit."

The camp of the second night after leaving the Cimarron was made in a dense grove of timber within a mile of the government road, and in an admirable hiding place. The valley was low, the hills stood back a distance of two hundred yards, and the trees furnished perfect concealment. Knowing that they would remain here for several days, and not caring to drink the muddy water from the creek, the Boomers dug a well. After making preliminary arrangements for their camp they located claims and surveyed the land for ten miles about them, under the direction of Stafford, since Goodrich had not come on this trip. While they were thus engaged, one of the optimistic home-steaders wrote back to the Wichita *Eagle:* "Arrived here on the 10th. Surveying and laying of foundations going on at a lively rate. Colony in excellent spirits. Oceans of timber, water, stones; forests full of deer, antelope, turkey; streams and rivers full of fish. . . . Indications of coal and iron, we take our choice. Six hundred claims taken and improvements made." Perhaps we should make allowance for such overflowing enthusiasm, for obviously six hundred claims had not been made.

But this was not the center of the "promised land." The Canadian Valley had been the Boomers' goal from the time they crossed the Kansas boundary. On July 14, therefore, they again moved forward with Payne and W. H. Smith going in advance to mark the way. Bloss states that the Boomers' wagons were discovered before they reached the Canadian, but the contemporary accounts of both the Boomers and the military authorities give every reason to believe that this was not true. They presently came to their old camp and found thriving the gardens which they had planted early in the spring. Here, too, they met Jack Beetle, "a scout from Texas," who told them that "a thousand men would be in the Territory in ten days." Already Payne had sent Hill back over the trail to Arkansas City, from which town he sent broadcast flattering reports on the new colony. He telegraphed to "numerous parties along the Atchison, Topeka and Santa Fe and Kansas Pacific railroads" to push on to Oklahoma at once.

Meanwhile, T. D. Craddock, at St. Louis, received other telegrams from prospective emigrants in Illinois that they were on the point of starting for the Indian Territory; and advices were received at the Wichita headquarters that the drought of western Kansas had driven thousands of settlers to make the same decision. Thus, had the second invasion been successful, there is no doubt that the Colony would shortly have been joined by many other Boomers.

But it was not successful. Hardly had Payne's party arrived on the site of the first Canadian camp when Donnell and twelve Indian scouts five miles away discovered the ruts made by the wagons. They followed these to the Canadian and found the Boomer camp.

Donnell seemed to be amused because of his success in this game of hide-and-seek, but Payne could hardly appreciate his levity. The scout in high spirits demanded the surrender of Payne's party. The Boomer leader ignored the demand and in turn asked, "How many men are in your force?" To this Donnell replied, "No one but the Indian scouts." Payne retorted that he did not propose to surrender to Indians. Donnell understood the Boomers' reluctance to surrender to the scouts and added that Pardee with a troop of cavalry was only a short distance away. "All right," the Boomer leader is reported as saying, "I will return, or send for him, or will remain here until he comes." This satisfied Donnell, and a scout was sent hurrying back over the trail after the troopers.

A short time later the lieutenant put in an appearance. But he had to wait here for instructions from his superior. He told Payne that in the meantime he and his men were at liberty to employ themselves as they saw fit, and could go hunting if Payne would be personally responsible. He called the Boomers "constructive prisoners" and would consider them as such only so long as they conducted themselves properly. Presently a courier brought Pardee orders to bring his prisoners to the former Pole Cat Creek camp, and soon he broke camp and started northward.

Payne and his twenty-two followers were turned over to Captain Robinson on Pole Cat Creek, where they were held from July 21 to August 7. Since all but four of the men arrested were first offenders, they were finally permitted to return to Kansas. But Payne and the old offenders were held. There is reason to believe that Payne now partook too freely of Robinson's "good cheer," as he was accused of doing, for the captain reported Payne as saying what he probably would not have said during his sober moments. First, he explained that he had gotten past the military patrols along the Kansas border by taking advantage of an excursion from Wichita to Arkansas City, his wagons crossing the line one at a time.

But his second admission was far more significant. He said that his invasion had been made on the advice of "eminent legal talent at Washington, Saint Louis and Kansas City," and had been strictly in accordance with instructions. Robinson was convinced that this was true. He wrote Pope that Payne's followers appeared to be more respectable than those of the former raid. "I think the majority of them are temporarily employed to go with Payne on this expedition and are unquestionably remunerated by some agent acting for the A. T. and S. F., M. K. and T., and the St. L. and S. F. railroads, and L. L. and G. railroad."

Payne was also reported to have told Robinson that all arrangements had been made to test the legal bearing of the case at Fort Smith, Arkansas, and that his backers expected to continue putting expeditions in the field until the government was forced to submit the matter to a federal court. "It appears that this move," wrote Robinson, "in aid of the extension of railroad lines across the Territory and the consequent settlement of lands contiguous to their lines is about the only one of any importance now threatening the Indian Territory."

Robinson's belief that Payne was backed by railroad corporations was shared by others. Chief D. W. Bushyhead of the Cherokees wrote Samuel Checote of the Creeks on September 10, 1880, that he had good reason to believe that a "strong combination" had been formed to force court action on the Oklahoma issue.

Since Payne was quite loquacious, Robinson sought to draw him out on the subject of how the Boomer Movement could be halted. "You certainly should have reasoned that out," Payne is reported to have replied. "Put a detachment south of Arkansas City on the Chikaskia to watch the trails and a detachment in 'Oklahoma.' That will end it so far as that place is concerned. These are the only lands we claim a right to settle."

Payne felt that Pope, in holding him and his friends for seventeen days on Pole Cat Creek, was again seeking to avoid court action. And there is every reason to believe that this was true. Indeed, Pope wrote to the Adjutant General that he did not consider it expedient "to undergo the expense and trouble of trying such people. It is precisely what they want and would certainly result in their being discharged from custody." But holding the prisoners for this period was illegal, and Payne was prompt in pointing it out to Pope. He cited Section 2151 of the *Revised Statutes,* which in part read: "No person apprehended by military force under the preceding section shall be retained longer than five days after his arrest...." The indignant general did not reply. Payne had likewise protested to Pardee, calling his attention to the fact that he and his men were homesteaders on the public domain, where they had commenced the erection of their dwellings. If they were to be taken anywhere, he said, it should be before Judge Isaac Parker at Fort Smith for trial.

Payne was to have his wish granted. When President Hayes heard that the Boomers had launched a second invasion across the Kansas line, he called his cabinet together for advice. Then he instructed Attorney General Devens to try the prisoners at Fort Smith on the charge of conspiracy to violate the Intercourse Act of 1834. So Payne and his four Boomer friends were first taken from Pole Cat Creek to Wichita and thence to Emporia, before they were sent on to Fort Smith. From here the prisoners were then sent by rail to Muskogee, Indian Territory, and from there by wagon to Fort Smith.

Correspondent Bloss affirmed that when Lieutenant Hewett and the five enlisted men arrived at Muskogee with their prisoners, Indians made an attempt to mob them. The quarters which they occupied upon their arrival, he said, were vacated early in the night, because it was uncomfortably warm, and the lieutenant and his party had camped in the open air. "In the morning it was found that an attack had been made by a party of Indians on the deserted house and several volleys fired through the windows and doors." For the remainder of the journey Hewett allowed Payne and his men to carry "a brace of 'navies' and an ample supply of cartridges."

When they finally arrived at Fort Smith, Payne was again afflicted with rheumatism and was suffering so much that he could hardly walk. In fact, his illness detained him at Fort Smith one week.

Judge Parker took no immediate action. He bound Payne over to appear before the November term of court and then allowed him to go his way. Payne had no money to pay his own and his party's fares back to Wichita, but a Fort Smith friend came to his rescue.

Upon his return journey, Payne traveled via Little Rock and St. Louis. At the latter place, the *Republican* announced the coming of Payne on the morning of September 1, stating that he was on his way to Wichita to "rally a new organization to number this time ten thousand." It had been the intention of local Boomers to have Payne address a huge mass meeting at St. Louis, but an urgent call from his headquarters at Wichita necessitated the abandonment of this plan.

Never did a returning hero from the field of battle meet with a greater home-town reception than did Payne. Two bands, Captain Thompson's cavalry troop, and committees of both political parties, besides a large concourse of citizens, all united in the demonstration. At the railroad station vehicles were provided and the party was driven to Eagle Hall, at the corner of Douglas Avenue and Main Street, where a still larger crowd of men, women, and children had assembled.

Captain Jackson, of St. Louis, an active participant in the Oklahoma movement, had accompanied Payne from St. Louis to Wichita and now addressed the audience. "You may go on now with your Oklahoma boom as you call it," he exultantly exclaimed, "with every hope of success in the near future. You have been under the impression that President Hayes was against you in this movement, but gentlemen . . . he is now a convert to the theory upon which we propose to settle this immense and beautiful public domain by education and civilization." Captain J. B. Carey gave Payne a formal and cordial welcome on behalf of Wichita, and Payne responded by saying that he greatly appreciated the honor bestowed upon him but believed that the "principle involved" and not Payne, the man, had elicited such enthusiasm.

The *Cherokee Advocate* of September 8 was much impressed with Payne's reception at Wichita and philosophically remarked, "Those men are able to enthusiastically receive any one for they have money and a railroad or two to back them. . . ."

7 : *Winter Booming*

*F*OR A TIME the Boomers enjoyed great good fortune, but it was not long before they were faced with one of their severest tests. Not only was there friction between the leaders at a moment of crisis, but one and all went through a heartbreaking siege of snow and ice, far from either home or Oklahoma and with no supplies of their own. But let's begin at the beginning.

Kansas border settlements were assailed by wild reports during the fall of 1880. The returning invaders had sown broadcast their stories of Oklahoma, the wonderland. South of Kansas was a virgin land, inexhaustible in its wide variety of resources; with mines, forests, and prairies; with mountains, cataracts, and canyons; and with valleys and streams. Here were the brightest skies, the grandest sunsets, the softest twilights; and the most brilliant moon and glittering stars, smiling their welcome to visitors. The landscapes were unsurpassed, covered with fragrant flowers; and gentle breezes caressed the green prairies, stretching in soft undulations far away, as if the ocean in its gentlest swell stood arrested with its rounded billows. This was the home of the wild horse, deer, elk, bear, turkey, grouse, and birds of song; and God had reserved it as man's paradise on earth.

Hard-bitten pioneers hardly accepted these reports, except with a grain of salt; but many a newcomer, ever ready to see what was over the next hill, was eager to prove them with his own eyes. During the day and far into the night, Payne's Oklahoma Colony headquarters at Wichita was thronged with inquirers. Would the government oppose the next invasion? What homestead claims were available? Were town lots in the capital yet to be had? When did Captain Payne propose to start for Oklahoma? Attending officials sought to satisfy their questioners; they distributed maps, circulars, and Surveyor Goodrich's engineering reports, and gave out promising assurances.

Payne was lionized, but he could hardly enjoy his unmeasured popularity because of his old rheumatic affliction. Yet he did not stop. Both from his headquarters and before town audiences he sent forth his good tidings. The government was helpless to deny homesteaders their rights! President Hayes's manifestoes were worth no more than the paper on which they were written! Typical of the propaganda distributed in Kansas, Texas, Arkansas, and Missouri towns is Payne's announcement found reprinted in the Wichita *Beacon* of November 3, 1880. It proclaimed that the time was fast approaching for a third Oklahoma invasion. All timid souls should take courage! The former expeditions were intended only to provoke court action (Payne did not mention here, as before, the tentative establishment of claims and the survey of the future capital). For these, large numbers were unnecessary. "But the situation is now changed," the announcement read. It was of the utmost importance that a large Colony move at once upon the ceded lands so that the President would not dare interfere without the sanction of Congress. All should hold themselves ready to move on five days' notice. "We shall carry heavy freights, and rally in such force as shall insure the success of the expedition. . . ." Every colonist should take assorted hardware and implements essential to pioneer settlement, and should also provide himself with subsistence for at least thirty days. Then it concluded: "We shall go to stay!"

The Boomer Movement was now at the height of its popularity. Over four thousand names were enrolled on the colony roster in Kansas alone, and mass meetings and subsidiary colonies were launched in other border states.

Commercial and business interests of St. Louis caught the enthusiasm, and at a municipal rally a committee of leading jurists was appointed to investigate the status of the ceded land and report back. Those attending the meeting were told that the bearing of the Oklahoma issue upon the commercial welfare of St. Louis could not be overrated. The survey of the Atlantic and Pacific Railroad (then owned by the St. Louis and San Francisco interests) crossed the Indian Territory from Vinita, extending westward to Albuquerque, New Mexico, where it intersected the Santa Fe. Since the former road was operated entirely in the interests of St. Louis, all good citizens were asked to support the city leaders in their new move to capitalize on the Indian Territory movement. By extending the Atlantic and Pacific, St. Louis was certain to reap a great trade harvest, for the road would cross the Texas cattle trails and the enormous herds would be diverted to St. Louis instead of crossing the Kansas line (as many had done) and being shipped thence to Chicago. Payne was in St. Louis at this time and attended one of these mass meetings. From here he sent back to the Kansas towns another appeal for members. Again he declared, "We go this time to stay," and promised that the Colony would have a school started three days after the grounds had been reached. (Prospective Boomers were anxious about their children's schooling.) In addition, he promised that his Colony would set up two sawmills "and thus be able to furnish all the native lumber required to build houses; and will also have a printing office and publish a daily newspaper."

Captain Thomas B. Robinson, at Caldwell, became alarmed at the wide approval given Payne's advertising and the active support extended by the border press. On November 13 he sent Lieutenant C. C. Hewett hurrying down to Arkansas City to investigate a purported imminent invasion. Hewett arrived on the next day and made a quiet inquiry, but he was able to report to his superior that there was little evidence of invasion preparations, although he found a few Boomers in town. United States Marshal E. T. Heine, however, told him that evidently some Boomers were entering the Indian Territory as hunters, and that South Haven was a gathering point. Agent Whiting, of the Ponca Agency, also reported southbound hunters, but said that many of these had been turned back by the Indian police.

There was more truth in these reports than Hewett was willing to believe. A Fort Reno observer stated on November 20 that a cavalry patrol had recently brought into the post from "Saint's Rest" (as the former Boomer camp was called) twenty-two Boomers, who were kept under guard during the visitation of a violent blizzard and then were sent home "to their wives and mothers."

From Arkansas City Hewett went on to Wichita. Here he sought to conceal his identity as he went about the streets talking to the people. In this he was partly successful. From a Boomer who did not know him and who did not suspect his purpose, he learned that November 25 had been fixed as the tentative date for starting for Oklahoma. But later others recognized him. Then boldly he entered Boomer headquarters on Douglas Avenue and talked with Editor Hutchison of the Caldwell *Commercial*, Bloss of the Kansas City *Times* and Chicago *Times,* and four others. The Boomers did not mince words. They told Hewett that they proposed to enter Oklahoma in spite of all that the troops might do, although they would not tell the exact time of starting. They claimed a membership of five thousand.

Before the November starting time had arrived, Payne became seriously ill, and the date was reset for December 6, the irrepressible leader announcing: "We will positively cross the line for Oklahoma at that time." This date was chosen because Congress would be in session and it was hoped that it would modify Hayes "stay out" proclamation. In an enthusiastic Wichita meeting Payne was again named commander-in-chief, with Hill Maidt, of Dallas, and Stafford as lieutenants. The chief of scouts was Hill, and the quartermaster was David Aspland. Payne had designated "Major" Maidt as military commander of the expedition, since he had seen four years of service in the Regular Army and had served as an Indian fighter under General W. S. Harney on the Pacific Coast.

Although General Pope had not replied to Payne's protest on Pole Cat Creek, he now sent General C. H. Smith, second in command of the Department of Missouri, and Captain C. B. Hall, Nineteenth Infantry, to visit Boomer headquarters. These officers called upon Payne, explaining that they merely came on a courtesy visit and not as spies or to gratify an impertinent curiosity. Then they seated themselves and amiably discussed the Boomer issue. Smith assured Payne that he had the kindest feelings toward him and some sympathy for the Oklahoma enterprise, but that this was as far as he could go. He was a soldier and in this instance had but one duty to perform—to expel, by force if necessary, all Oklahoma invaders.

The week preceding the announced start of the Boomers was a busy one for border towns. Although each shared in the harvest of Boomer buying, Wichita, the Colony's headquarters, was most favored. During daylight hours the streets were crowded with wagons, hacks, and buggies. Merchants were so confident of Boomer success that for purchases made they accepted Oklahoma Town Company stock, "of which there were many thousands of dollars in circulation." Yet they discounted it from 50 to 80 per cent. Correspondent Bloss estimated the amount of business in Wichita at twenty thousand dollars! This also encouraged the sale of shares, as seen in an early December special dispatch to the *Sumner County Press*, which stated that twelve hundred dollars in shares had been sold during two days at Hunnewell.

Winter Booming

On December 7 about two hundred Boomers with sixty-eight wagons were encamped on the Arkansas River, about one mile south of Arkansas City. Here a mass meeting was called to encourage faint-hearted members. Payne and Editor McIntyre of the *Democrat* addressed them. Then a memorial was adopted calling upon the President to withdraw his proclamation. But there was an ever-present reminder of government displeasure near at hand. Lieutenant Mason, with Company H of the Tenth Cavalry (Negroes), was encamped within a few hundred yards on the opposite bank of the river.

The Boomers were not intimidated. On December 9 they broke camp and moved out in good order, closely followed by Mason and his troopers. They had not advanced far, however, before the soldiers were thrown directly between their wagon train and the Indian Territory boundary. But Payne had no intention of crossing the boundary here. When within a short distance of the cavalry, he turned sharply to the east and paralleled the section line. Then Mason quickly redisposed his force and followed the wagons to Chilocco Creek, where colonists and troopers again went into camp.

Many a merry gibe was directed at the soldiers by the high-spirited Boomers. An Indian summer day, warm sunshine, and the excitement of launching a new venture were all enlivening.

Citizens of near-by towns were curious to know how the Boomers fared and drove out to their camp. A large delegation, including Ma Haines and several other women "as a social escort," was entertained at dinner. And when the campfires were lighted they joined the pilgrims in singing and in lively banter. Lieutenant Mason also came (by invitation), and expressed a wish to read his orders. The colonists, curious to know what to expect, listened with respectful attention. Then Mason read President Hayes's proclamation and said, as General Smith had said before him, that he had no other choice but to enforce it insofar as he was able. At this announcement the colonists cheered loudly, evidently feeling that it was the usual federal "stay out" gesture.

Early the next morning, while the smoke rose lazily from smouldering campfires, the Boomers stood for military inspection, with the Stars and Stripes prominently displayed. Then promptly at ten o'clock they broke camp and resumed their line of march, the flag mounted on the front wagon. The troops were in a parallel column and between the wagons and the Indian Territory boundary. That evening the prospective invaders pitched camp on Bitter Creek, and the next evening on Shoo-fly, a small, wooded tributary of the Chikaskia, near Hunnewell; and Lieutenant Mason and his cavalry encamped on the same stream, a few hundred yards away, on the south side of the Indian Territory line.

Colonel J. J. Coppinger had arrived in the meantime and had superseded Mason to the command of the troopers. Both officers now visited Payne's Shoo-fly camp and urged the Boomers not to attempt invasion at this time. Payne would not promise this but he did pledge himself not to cross the Territory line without giving notice to the federal officers. Maidt, Bloss, and other Boomer leaders present angrily protested this pledge. Then Payne informed Coppinger that since there was divided opinion, thereby challenging his leadership, he would formally resign his command in favor of Maidt.

Coppinger then asked the new leader what his policy would be. Maidt replied that the settlers were thoroughly organized and ready for any eventuality, but that he would leave the decision to the captains of his men, and he summoned them to appear. When all these had assembled, Maidt asked their advice; and they voted unanimously to cross the line at all hazards. Before leaving, Coppinger warned that his men had "shoot" orders.

On the following morning (Sunday), religious services were held in camp. An invitation had been extended to a pastor of a South Haven Church, two miles distant, to conduct the services, but he was ill and could not come. Also invitations had been sent to Hunnewell, Arkansas City, Caldwell, and Winfield, and delegations from these towns, including women and children, now arrived. The ladies assisted in singing "Hold the Fort" (adapted to the tune of "America"), "Oklahoma Still," and "The Star-Spangled Banner." The federal officers and soldiers also attended and some joined in the rousing songs. In the evening a second service was held, attended by a large gathering of people who had come from many miles around. The services were conducted by an ordained Methodist minister, the Reverend W. Broadhurst.

There was much criticism of the morning service. Chaplain Cory preached from a passage in Exodus, speaking of President Hayes as Pharaoh, Oklahoma as Canaan, the colonists as the Lord's people, Major Maidt as Moses, and he, the chaplain, as Aaron. And strangely enough his sermon was concluded with three cheers for the President and a "tiger" for the troops! Then J. T. Weaver, a not-too-saintly Boomer, helped to conclude the services. The Wichita *Eagle* of December 23 thus ridiculed the affair: "The Boomers have a chaplain, Weaver, everybody in Wichita knows Weaver, the jolly J. T., who never fails of a chance to stand up with the crowd and take 'suthin' for his stomach's sake. Well, he has been playing chaplain for the boys on the border. Wouldn't the old frequenters of the corner enjoy hearing Weaver pray just once! He preaches, too, the dispatches inform us, or did before the Boomers ran so short on grub. Weaver, a year since, was going to build a distillery in Wichita, but whisky has come to be about as uncertain as the Oklahoma enterprise. Imagine Dave Payne with his hat off and head bowed to a reverential angle while Weaver offers up his morning supplications, and Hutch [Hutchison] and Maidt and the rest of the boys impatiently rubbing the frozen ground with their knees, waiting for the amen! . . . Lord, if that crowd has the cheek to face heaven for an endorsement, we don't blame the poet who writ,

" 'As long as the lamp holds out, etc.' "

But Payne, when he heard of them, was not greatly perturbed by these verbal thrusts. In comparing his influence with that of his critics, he said that he could call four thousand men together at a moment's notice when he chose to do so.

The cavalry was not entirely successful in thwarting the designs of the Boomers. While encamped here Payne sent Hill and Craddock into the Indian Territory to report on conditions. They successfully eluded the watchful soldiers and scouted through Oklahoma for fourteen days, visiting their old Canadian camp and other points. When they returned to the Kansas Boomer camp they reported that they had met fifty wagons at an appointed rendezvous in Oklahoma, concealed from the Indian scouts. But the members of this party finally broke camp and returned to their several homes when they learned that the Kansas Boomers could not join them. Most of them, Hill and Craddock reported, were from Arkansas, the Chickasaw Nation, and Texas. Smaller parties were also encountered, and there were many claims staked out.

There was an Arkansas emigrant and his family, however, that Hill and Craddock had not seen. On December 8 they had come to Fort Reno to tell a pitiful story. The man had read Payne's Boomer literature describing Oklahoma as the wonderful land, and had promptly set out with his family of five (a girl fifteen years of age, and four boys) to claim it. He had loaded all his worldly goods into his wagon, bringing also sixty head of cattle. The party was caught in the December snowstorm, however, and marooned twenty-six days without seeing any persons but themselves. Thus they were thrown on the mercies of the Fort Reno soldiers, tired, footsore, and without provisions or money, their stock jaded and almost starved. Major Randall allowed them to remain until the storm had abated and then permitted them to depart for their former home, poorer but wiser.

Presently the Caldwell Boomers fell on evil days. A blizzard swept down from the north bringing snow and ice. "The ragged patriots hump over the flickering flames of an expiring buffalo chip, eying askance at the well fed blue coats, wondering whether they are natural born fools or only dupes and adventurers," wrote a scoffer. There is no doubt that their experiences were trying in the extreme, and that many ardent Boomers feared the approach of winter and went home.

But hope crushed to the earth will rise again! At the Shoo-fly meeting, Dr. Robert Wilson was unanimously chosen to go to Washington and present the Boomer cause to the President, and those left in camp doggedly held on until he could report.

The border press continued its ridicule. "Oh, why shouldn't the spirit of 'small fry' be proud?" asked the *Cheyenne Transporter* (Darlington, Indian Territory). "Payne, Boudinot, Carpenter, and the whole outfit are a set of plotting hirelings of the railroad companies," joined in the *Sumner County Press*, which in another issue scoffed: "Behold these lilies of the field; they toil not, neither do they spin; and yet they are gorgeously arrayed, have pockets plethoric with railroad passes, while their aldermaniac proportions suggest good living and frequent infractions of the constitutional amendment."

On the morning of December 14 the Colony broke camp and moved toward Caldwell. When the long train pulled through Hunnewell hundreds of citizens thronged the streets, cheering and waving hats and handkerchiefs. The same kind of demonstration was also accorded the Boomers at Caldwell.

Within two miles of town the wagon train was met by a cavalcade of men and women on horses and in carriages, headed by a brass band. And when they reached town, they marched and counter-marched, the band playing, the drums beating, the flags waving.

The colonists made a detour outside the city limits and went into camp on Bluff Creek, and the troops pitched camp near by. Two days later Payne addressed a mass meeting of Boomers and Caldwell citizens. His speech was somewhat inflammatory, and Boomer feeling ran so high that some proposed to burn in effigy the Senators and Representatives in Congress who were known to oppose the opening of Oklahoma.

It is interesting to notice here that although Maidt was the nominal leader of the Boomers, Payne continued to dominate their every action. Some charged that in the face of a crisis he had shown the white feather, and that he had taken comfortable quarters in Wichita while they were freezing; others thought his designation of Maidt as leader was to divert the attention of Colonel Coppinger. But the average Boomer was yet loyal to his old leader and was ready to listen to him. The *Sumner County Press* reporter was not too much impressed with the Boomer leaders in the Shoo-fly camp, whom he named as "Major H. M. Maidt of Dallas, Texas; Major W. W. Bloss, Adjutant and correspondent of the Chicago *Times;* Major George M. Jackson of St. Louis, agent of the Associated Press; Dr. Wilson, Colony surgeon; and Colonel Payne of Oklahoma." He found that at dinner each greedily helped himself to meat, bread, and coffee without waiting for the others.

Meanwhile, cold weather continued to chill both the bodies and the spirits of the Boomers. Snow had fallen and the mercury continued to drop from day to day. The troopers swore at the determined campers because they, too, were forced to undergo great hardship. Boomer camp supplies were running low, and soon the horses were without forage. The disheartened Boomers were now at the end of their rope, and the approaching Christmas caused them to think of warm fires, Christmas trees, and families. Just at this critical juncture, however, Caldwell citizens gave them two dressed hogs. And on the next day, December 24, they also sent large quantities of hay, corn, flour, and bacon; in fact, several wagonloads of supplies for both man and beast. Even then there were a few Boomers who left camp, declaring that if they could not have the milk and honey of Oklahoma, they did not propose to substitute "donated hog meat!"

Christmas morning dawned cold and clear. The Boomers celebrated with a discharge of musketry and side arms, followed by a dress parade and the usual colony meeting. Then Payne invited his poorly clothed, shivering fellow sufferers to come to his tent for his compliments from a Christmas canteen. But Steward Brophy, the "Mickey Free" of the camp, turned the favors on Payne by handing him a well-stuffed stocking containing two handsome revolvers and a generous roll of greenbacks, the compliments of Caldwell admirers. Generously, too, the same donors had presented the camp with a fat beef, dressed with gay ribbons and rosettes. And they supplemented it with game brought in by their own hunters—turkey, raccoon, opossum, quail, rabbit, and venison. They "fabulated" a wild boar's head in the shape of a Kansas porker's head, decorated with "appropriate emblems of Oklahoma." All in camp were now merry. In the afternoon both soldiers and Boomers hilariously stormed the streets of Caldwell, setting off firecrackers and skyrockets and firing muskets and pistols.

On the following day a psychological letdown came, one which was to grow. The weather remained cold and the Boomer camp was soon without supplies again, although its inhabitants had dug themselves in. Editor W. B. Hutchison of the Caldwell *Commercial*, a Boomer agitator, visited the camp presently and found his friends snug enough. He reported that despite the severity of the weather they were as happy as any set of men he had ever seen. They had dug into the second bank of Fall Creek bottom and had provided quarters, had cut out fireplaces, and had otherwise made themselves comfortable, so that in many respects they were better fortified against winter's assault than many settlers of the Kansas prairies.

This report was too optimistic, for the Boomer camp quickly melted away. One disheartened camper told Payne that New Year's Day was approaching and he wanted to be with his family; another excused himself to attend pressing business matters. Thus in ones and twos they drove away. But there were a faithful few who held on, who would not go until Dr. Wilson had reported from Washington. The hostile press said that the President had rebuffed the Boomer emissary; but the irrepressible George M. Jackson brought to camp another story. He had a letter from Wilson, who reported that Hayes had received him graciously, had given the Oklahoma issue favorable consideration, and had promised to be guided by the opinion of the Attorney General. It is probable that actually Hayes was unfriendly, for a delegation of Philadelphia women had come to Washington bringing a petition which they claimed was signed by a hundred thousand people, asking that Indian Territory be preserved for the Indians. Thus the Boomers were put back where they were in the beginning, and many were now willing to go home.

For several weeks Payne had been convinced of the failure of his winter enterprise but had held on to meet the wishes of Maidt, Bloss, and others. Now, however, on December 28, he advised his followers to return to their homes and await a more propitious time. "These lands are ours," he said, "and we want to take possession of them before planting time." He promised that he would send them secret instructions as to a spring invasion date and that in ones and twos they could then cross the boundary and thus avoid the soldiers.

8 : Before Judge Isaac C. Parker

*T*HE *HARD WINTER* of 1880–81 was trying on the nerves and patience of Boomers and soldiers. The colonist had little regard for the trooper who would deny him a homestead in Oklahoma, and the trooper returned this dislike with full measure running over. This ill-concealed hostility was also occasionally revealed in the relations between federal officers and Boomer leaders. Early in January Lieutenant Wood roundly denounced William W. Bloss in a Caldwell hotel, and added that if he had his way he would go down to the Boomer camp and kill every one of those "blankety-blanks." Although passing through the lobby at the time, Bloss did not hear these slighting remarks, but a talebearer afterwards informed him of them. Immediately he sent Wood a challenge to a duel, but Major George M. Randall, Wood's superior, salved Bloss's wounded feelings and further trouble was averted.

Some of the Boomers were enterprising, despite the reports of their foes to the contrary. They reoccupied the Fall Creek camp and secured employment in freighting for the government. The editor of the *Cherokee Advocate*, on January 26, 1881, grudgingly admitted that the "colonists have gone to work" hauling supplies from Wichita to Camp Wood, near Payne's old camp site on the Canadian. "The soldiers were getting tired of watching the boomers," he said, "and are giving them work. . . . The colonists think that while they are getting pay from

89

Uncle Sam, they are at the same time helping along their scheme of locating on the coveted soil. It is said that many of the freighters before they return, embrace the opportunity of locating claims."

On February 23 two federal scouts rode into Wichita and reported finding the remains of a lost Boomer. While on patrol of the ceded land a few days before, they had crossed a heavily wooded creek emptying into the Canadian. There on its bank, in a copse of ice-coated timber and leaning against a tree as though for protection, were the frozen remains of a Boomer. His body was thinly clad in a suit of brown with buckskin leggings, and on his head was a coonskin cap. Nearby were his gun and his faithful dog. The scene overawed the hardened soldiers and "they did not have the heart to disturb his frigid repose."

But soon came spring, with its perennial hope as well as its birds and flowers. All eyes now turned to Fort Smith, for the Oklahoma issue hung on Payne's case before Judge Parker. If the government were not successful in convicting Payne, then the ceded lands would be quickly occupied by ambitious home-seekers.

Leaders of the Five Civilized Tribes also saw the importance of this case. As early as September 10, 1880, Principal Chief D. W. Bushyhead, of the Cherokees, had written to Samuel Checote, of the Creeks, to warn of their common peril in the trial of the "notorious Captain Payne" and to suggest an "international" council to determine a proper course of action. As a result, delegates from the Five Tribes assembled at Eufaula on October 20 for a two-day meeting. Here the forthcoming trial was discussed at great length. Bushyhead pointed out that Payne was a mere puppet in the affair; railroad interests, backed by greedy St. Louis and Kansas City businessmen, constituted a "powerful combination" to force the issue. Each tribe was asked to contribute to a defense fund prorated as follows: Cherokees, $1,450; Choctaws, $1,450; Creeks, $1,040; Chickasaws, $540; and Seminoles, $340. Growing out of this proposal, a defense commission was named, consisting of G. W. Grayson (chairman, Creek), James Thompson (Choctaw), Thomas Cloud (Seminole), and D. W. C. Duncan (Cherokee), who should have the power to employ outside counsel if they saw fit.

Tribal councils subsequently ratified the resolution and on December 15 the committee met at Eufaula and discussed the advisability of employing outside counsel, but deferred a final decision until a later meeting. Then they voted to visit the Boomer camp near Caldwell, since it would be difficult to plan a course of action until they had firsthand knowledge of the Boomers.

The Indian committeemen arrived in Caldwell on December 17 and were immediately driven out to the Fall Creek camp. News of their coming had preceded them and they were given a friendly welcome, since the Boomers did not care to offend the representatives of those tribes which they had sought to keep on good terms. But the visitors were in no mood for friendly intercourse; they had come to meet their foes and to give them sound advice. "We found their number to be about seventy-five," wrote Grayson, "instead of many hundreds as they and certain newspapers in their interests had so often falsely reported. They had thirty-two pretty good lumber wagons with shabby teams. They presented a most miserable appearance. They are evidently the dregs of the white population of Kansas and adjoining States. They bear the aspect of a desperate, uncultured band of frontier ruffians—just such fellows as are usually found in a muss with the Indians. They were destitute of everything that might indicate, on their part, either an ability or a disposition to enter into and develop the resources of any new country. While at the same time they carried themselves disencumbered of everything that might impede their movements as a band of organized desperadoes."

Nor was Grayson favorably impressed with the Boomer leaders present, who perhaps included Payne. "Payne and one Jackson are their recognized leaders," he continued. "Payne does not spend much of his time in the camp of his followers, but lounges about the saloons and other places of dissipation drumming up recruits for his crowd and strengthening the faith of those that grow weak. Jackson moves in the footsteps of Payne. He claims to be a Socialist on the land question—that is, he is a member of that class of cutthroats. . . ."

But Grayson did not tell how he had angrily lectured the Boomers. As he sought to dissuade the Boomers from further effort to invade the ceded lands, he was met by a firm refusal. Then, it seems, his anger flared up. "We are doing all we can to prevent the opening of the country," he stormed, "and you had as well go home, for we have bought and can buy your Congressmen like so many sheep and cattle!" Even then the colonists refrained from angry retort; and the visitors finally left with the parting shot that even if the government permitted the Boomers to enter Oklahoma, which it wouldn't, the Indians would ban together to raise an army of five thousand men and drive them out.

Payne may have been the saloon habitué, as charged by Grayson, but certainly he did not spend all his time there. He interested himself in the Ojo Caliente Mining Company as a paid-up stockholder, probably using money from his Colony fund to meet assessments. Then he sought to encourage a "Freedmen's Oklahoma Association" headed by a St. Louis Negro, Miller Turner, but Commissioner W. A. Williamson of the General Land Office denied all but Indian Territory Negroes rights under the treaties of 1866.

It was in connection with his Oklahoma Colony that he showed most interest. To this end he had sought congressional support. On January 15 "Major" Bloss was in Topeka urging the legislature to instruct the Kansas delegation in Washington to support a resolution introduced by Representative Dunn, of Arkansas, declaring the ceded land of the Indian Territory open to settlement. At the same time Payne was working with Surveyor Craddock in platting still another "Oklahoma City." Since his "New Philadelphia" of 1880 had gained wide publicity, he hoped to dazzle the eyes of his followers with his new plan.

In St. Louis Payne was able to find backers of his proposed city. His plan embraced a four-story hotel to cost not less than fifty thousand dollars, the stock of which was to be raised among cattle shippers who were intrigued with the idea that the new "Oklahoma City" would become the great shipping point of the Southwest. James D. Potter, of Crosswhite, Potter and Company, St. Louis, was to be president of the hotel company. A fountain was to furnish the hostelry with water, which would be forced up to the fourth floor. The building was to be located at the intersection of two broad avenues, running east and west and north and south. The railroad depot and manufacturing plants were to be in the northern part of the city so that the citizens would be free from smoke. At the south end of town would be the courthouse, and at the west end, the state capitol and governor's mansion.

Payne promised that within three days after a favorable decision by Judge Parker on the Oklahoma issue he would have settlers on the ground ready to make his "dream city" a reality. Indeed, the optimistic captain was so obsessed with his plan that he would not take time out to accept Buffalo Bill's invitation to attend a roundup on his ranch, although the famous scout flattered Payne by saying that the "world is preparing to throw great coffers of wealth and happiness at your feet."

As early as September 8, 1880, the *Cherokee Advocate*, the leading sponsor of Indian rights, had sought to anticipate Payne's defense. It believed that the Boomer leader would claim that the

Creek and Seminole cessions constituted "reacquired" public domain and as such were subject to homestead entry under the homestead and pre-emption laws. The *Advocate* ruefully admitted that Payne had a good arguing point. The Nonintercourse Law of 1834 had described a certain tract as the Indian country, but since this early date the boundaries of the Indian country had been modified again and again by numerous laws in order to meet white men's needs for homes. Thus the cessions of 1866 by the Creeks and Seminoles were precisely of this sort, and the Oklahoma cessions were now a part of the public domain.

This was clever deduction. These claims were presented before Judge Isaac C. Parker at Fort Smith on March 7, the November hearing having been deferred until this time. The scene was tense, for on the judge's decision rested the future of the Oklahoma movement as well as the welfare of the Five Civilized Tribes. The Indian defense commission had decided not to employ outside counsel and was itself present, with D. W. C. Duncan as spokesman, to lend support to the able United States District Attorney, William H. H. Clayton. And Payne was well represented by James M. Baker, of St. Louis, and Thomas H. Barnes and William Walker, with the first-named attorney as his principal spokesman.

The government's main thesis was that under the Nonintercourse Law of June 30, 1834, and a later enactment of August 18, 1856, unauthorized white men were not permitted within the Indian Territory. The first intrusion called only for expulsion with a warning not to return, but the second carried a fine of a thousand dollars. Now the ceded lands of the Creeks and Seminoles were yet a part of the Indian Territory. Payne and his associates had been expelled from them on or about May 3 by the military with a warning that a subsequent violation of the law would incur a penalty. And, notwithstanding this warning, Payne and some of those previously expelled had again been arrested within the same area and were now subject to the penalty provided.

But Baker sought to prove that Payne and his associates had not been arrested within the Indian Territory, either on May 3 or August 10; that the region in which they were apprehended by the military was a part of the public domain, ceded by the Seminoles by the treaty of March 21, 1866; and that the government had previously recognized it as such by granting to the Atlantic and Pacific Railroad the odd sections of land therein reaching back forty miles on either side of the roadbed, within which zone, on the even sections, the Boomers had staked their claims. Thus the soldiers had unlawfully seized Payne and his fellow homesteaders while they were peacefully occupying their legal claims under the pre-emption and homestead laws.

Judge Parker listened quietly to the arguments presented by the two sides and then announced that he would defer his decision until the next term of court, starting on May 2. And at this later date, he declared against Payne. He first pointed out that the defense had claimed Payne's homestead rights, under the laws of 1841 and 1862, to Section 14, Township 11, Range 3 North, west of the Indian meridian. This could not be, said Parker, for under the homestead and pre-emption laws a citizen could not claim more than 160 acres of land, even though it was on the public domain. Then he sought to answer the question, "Did Payne have a right to pre-empt or homestead a claim on the land ceded by the Seminoles?" In Section 2258 of the *Revised Statutes* he read that "lands included in any reservation by any treaty, or proclamation of the President for any purpose shall not be subject to the right of pre-emption, unless otherwise specially provided by law." The only question to be decided then was the expressed purpose of the government in 1866 in the disposal of the cession, since no subsequent law had changed it. This, he pointed out, was made plain by the wording, "In compliance with a desire of the United States to locate other Indians and freedmen thereon." This being true, the cession was yet a part of the Indian Territory, and Payne was liable to the penalty of a thousand dollars as provided under the Nonintercourse Law.

Payne was not present when the decision was announced. On April 12 he had made an announcement of a Colony meeting in Wichita for May 3, stating that the Boomers would be on the eve of another start for their new homes, that the decision of Judge Parker would be ready, and that he would announce it at that time. The meeting was held as scheduled, with eighty-seven members of the Colony present, many from other states. Payne's solemn countenance revealed that he had disappointing news. All listened intently as he read a telegram announcing the adverse decision, and their faces, too, "visibly lengthened." But Payne insisted that they stand by their organization until victory should crown their endeavors. On their part, the Boomers endorsed a resolution urging Payne to renew his efforts to effect a lodgment in the Territory, criticizing the place of the trial and asking a change of venue.

The government's case was a civil suit in the nature of an action of debt to recover from Payne a penalty of one thousand dollars. But he had no property or wealth against which an assessment could be levied, and no other penalty was provided! The government's victory, then, was a hollow one, since Payne was now free to resume his Boomer activity. Commissioner Hiram Price of the Indian Office complained at this lamentable weakness of the law, and recommended to the Secretary of the Interior, S. J. Kirkwood, a measure that would provide for the first offense a penalty of not more than five hundred dollars and a prison term of not more than one year at hard labor; for subsequent offenses, a fine of not less than five hundred dollars and not more than a thousand, and imprisonment of not less than one year and not more than two; and that wagons and teams and other property be held for a recovery suit. But nothing was done about his proposal.

For several weeks after the Fort Smith decision, Payne's spirits were at a low ebb. Boudinot wrote him on June 7 that he had seen a "bush sign" at Vinita making fun of him, and significantly added: "When that road [St. Louis and San Francisco] is built west from Vinita they will laugh out of the other side of their mouths." But in the same letter he chided his friend "that you should not have lost your fool temper and sailed away at me."

By mid-July Payne had recovered his equipoise and had traveled southward to visit relations at Gainesville, Texas. Not only a plausible talker, but also supplied with maps, he lectured at Gainesville, Denison, and other north Texas towns, trying to recruit another colony of "dupes." He seemed plentifully supplied with money and promised to pay the editor of the Denison *Tribune* for his influence in sponsoring a new boom, but his offer was declined. He told the Texans that Judge Parker had only decided "a demurer" and not the question of the right to settle Oklahoma. The *Indian Journal* (Muskogee, Indian Territory) took notice of Payne's Texas visit and stated that since he had "plenty of money furnished by railroads or other parties, he would undoubtedly secure some 'gudgeons' to join him."

From Gainesville, in company with friends, Payne went into the Indian Territory, crossing the Red River near Red River Crossing and traveling up Cache Creek to the Wichita Mountains, skirting Oklahoma on the west. He inspected the spurs of these mountains for ore and then traveled eastward to his old camp site, where a small party of Texas Boomers were camped. Here Lieutenant Pardee with some troops and Indian scouts found a part of them. Pardee told the Boomers that he would furnish them an escort back across the Kansas line. But they replied that they were capable of finding their way out. Then Pardee arrested them and took them to Fort Reno, where they were held two days and nights without provisions. Finally they were conducted back toward Kansas and freed within eight miles of the boundary. Payne and a fellow Boomer, H. B. Jones, were not with the main party at the time of Pardee's appearance and succeeded in getting back to Kansas first. Payne thereby secured a writ of habeas corpus from Judge Torrance, of Winfield, to serve on Pardee. But he was quite chagrined when Pardee did not cross the boundary. Nor were the soldiers and scouts in a very good humor. An Arapaho scout is reported to have said: "You take he out he comes backee; kill the son of a bitch and he no comes backee."

Payne presently showed up again in Wichita with the startling announcement that he had brought "a large lot of specimens of galena and some very fine silver ore," which, thought the *Beacon* of August 3, "remove all doubts of the presence of rich minerals" in Oklahoma. Since Payne had received considerable accessions to his Colony in 1880 by a similar report, it is probable that he thought of the same expedient to arouse again the waning hopes of the faithful few.

Meanwhile the border press discussed Payne's movements pro and con. The "dupes" of which the editor of the *Sumner County Press* wrote soon swelled the Colony ranks. The *Cherokee Advocate* on December 2, 1881, returned to its chronic grievance by saying that "The regular raid of Oklahoma colonists has commenced," and the Kansas City *Times* certainly gave it little comfort by stating that "Captain Payne will open up Oklahoma to settlement without the interference from the Government." But it seems that such optimism was premature, for on December 10 the *Cheyenne Transporter* mentioned "a body of soldiers in Oklahoma in anticipation of Payne's threatened raid from Gainesville." Whatever the designs of the Boomer leader may have been, no other aggressive move was made at this time.

9 : *Resourceful Payne*

*N*OTWITHSTANDING the discouragement resulting
from the Fort Smith decision of the previous year, 1882
opened auspiciously for the Boomers. On January 5, O. B. Gunn,
of Kansas City, and B. F. Hobart, a banker of Oswego, Kansas,
were awarded a contract for the grading and masonry on a sixty-
two-mile extension of the St. Louis and San Francisco Railroad,
west of Vinita, Indian Territory. The editor of the Caldwell
Commercial saw a Boomer advantage in this, and wrote: "It is
safe to predict that by next fall Oklahoma settlers can ride into
and out of their claims with impunity. This is the opening wedge
that will open up Indian Territory to white settlement."

But more than one western editor was still hostile to the intruders. On January 25, 1882, the editor of the *Cheyenne Transporter* tauntingly inquired, "What has become of our valiant
Oklahoma knight, Captain Payne? . . . Come Captain, it is about
time for you to rise up and explain." But there was little need for
explanation, for soon Payne's activities were given wide publicity.
Indeed, three days later his attorney, H. G. Ruggles, filed suit in
the First Judicial Court of Kansas against Major General Pope
on two causes for action. The first claimed damages of fifteen
thousand dollars for Dave's arrest, detention, and ejectment from
Oklahoma, purportedly a part of the public domain, in May,
1880; the second, damages for ten thousand dollars for the same
causes in July following.

And even while the *Transporter* editor was penning these lines about him, Payne and a party of surveyors were prisoners of Captain George M. Randall. Fourteen days later, A. P. Lewis, of Falls City, Nebraska, and four other members of Payne's recent fiasco showed up at Wichita to report the failure of their venture. Already Wichitans knew that Payne had postponed an earlier attempt because of the "illness of his chaplain," and had smiled at the Kansas City *Journal's* remark that "Just what use Payne has for a chaplain while violating the laws of his country is a conundrum." But few had heard that at last Payne with a band of surveyors had crossed the line. The return of Lewis's party, therefore, caused much excitement. Lewis said that the surveyors had crossed the Indian Territory line about January 1 and had traveled without interference to Deep Fork, where they had camped for four days. Then they had moved on southward to the North Canadian and had spent several days in hunting deer, antelope, and wild turkey.

On the afternoon of January 24, reported Lewis, they were arrested by a cavalry patrol under Randall and taken to Fort Reno and placed in the guardhouse. When they inquired of Captain Bennett, post commandant, as to why they were arrested, he told them that he had orders to expel all intruders from Oklahoma. They then asked him for food but he replied that he had no authority to issue rations. If they had money they could make all necessary purchases from the commissary. Nor would he feed their horses, complained Lewis. At midnight, January 25, the Boomers were awakened from sleep and told that they must present themselves for inspection, which Boomer Lewis seemed to regard as sheer nonsense. Then on the following day they were released, after giving their promises that they would return to Kansas without delay. So they had come to Wichita.

In February, Payne and his friend Tom Craddock were again back in Oklahoma. They built a dugout on "Cedar Creek," near their old camp but where it would be hard for the soldiers to find, and made preparations for a permanent stay. Then Craddock journeyed back to Wichita to recruit colonists and to procure supplies, promising to return shortly. Payne evidently found another Boomer also going to Kansas and by him forwarded a letter which was published in the Kansas City *Times* on February 25:

Oklahoma, I.T., February 16, 1882

Dear—— ———:

Have my house up and living in it. Am making a garden. The weather warm. Grass up green. The spring has fully come here, bees flying round the house, and we are feasting on honey. Tell the folks there to come on with plows, seeds, etc. I will be planting corn in two weeks from now. Please send me all the news you can send me by Mr. T. B. Fager, who will give you this.

Cheerfully yours,
D. L. PAYNE

At the same time Payne was making a diary record of his stay, which is somewhat in contrast to his published letter. On February 17, 1882, he begins thus "Today went with Tom to our old trail, 10 miles northwest. He went on to Wichita. This leaves me alone and I will be until his return 12 or 14 days from now. Will be lonesome but will hope for the best, trusting in Him who guards and watches over all."

What Payne had referred to in his published letters as a "house" was in his penciled diary a dugout, made in an embankment near the creek and near two springs; so near, indeed, that the dampness brought back his old rheumatic trouble. Yet he managed to keep busy. On February 18 he spent the day making clay pots in which to put ferns, digging up some Green River roots to make pipes, gathering some ferns, and going to his traps. Then he closed his day's record: "Now half past three. Oh for something to read until night!"

The next day was cold and wet. "If I have counted right it is

Sunday," he estimated. "Rained and sleeted most all day. Bad storm, stayed in dugout all day; only out long enough to get wood and go to my trap." But in rummaging through his trunk he found three old newspapers which afforded him some interest. Then he read his Bible, which "Sister Jennie" had given him for a Christmas present. He was grateful to her for such a gift, now that he was lonely and had time for introspection.

It was still gloomy the following day, snowing and sleeting. His spirits were low. "Killed nothing; seen nothing," was the discouraging diary entry. "Mended my clothes. Am feeding the birds that swarm around my door. They chatter and sing and seem to relish the crum[b]s thrown to them." Then there were clear days. On February 22 he was visited by an old Shawnee Indian who, although unable to speak much English, took dinner with him. Payne added, "I could make out about all he said. Said he would come again in two days." Then Dave again turned his attention to the Bible. He also hunted through the woods with his two dogs, Nellie and Jim, but complained that the Indians had chased away all the game and that he had no success.

On February 26 he was again visited by the Shawnee and two other Indians who stayed three or four hours. One of his guests was an Oto whom he did not like. "They asked me many questions about government land, the soldiers, railroads, etc.," wrote Payne. "The Oto said soldiers past to the north five miles west of me day before yesterday, that they would go to the Cimmeron River and come back in two days. . . . He would not tell them I was here but better leave for white settlement."

Now began Payne's trials—sickness, hunger, loneliness. After a period of ten days he began to complain that his dugout was so damp that he had to keep a fire going all the time. Two Indian boys visited his dugout on February 27 and traded him meat for coffee. But the Oto showed up again, and in an ugly mood. Payne was suspicious of him. "Said he was going to some of his tribe that was camped on the Cimmeron," wrote Payne. "Started up north, crossed the creek to the west side and hid. Watched for some time but did not go and found that he went westward to Fort Reno. Think that he went there to inform the soldiers that I was here." Then on the next day still another Indian came; he told Dave that he was a Cheyenne, but he rode the same horse ridden by the Oto on the previous day. He also wanted to frighten Payne, and did to some extent, for thus runs the diary: "I would like to get out of here if I could. But I cannot do so without losing all that I have got. So will take my chances." The Cheyenne had been "an impudent cuss" and was mad because Dave gave him only cold food and would not cook him warm bread.

Dave was also visited by Indians on other days, and on one occasion while he was absent. On the night of Friday, March 3, he was ill and not able to make a fire. The next morning he reflected, "Bad enough to be alone so long when one is well but worse when sick. Not a soul came today." He earnestly looked and prayed for the return of his friend Tom, but one day passed miserably much like the other, while he suffered from rheumatism and lack of food. Since Tom did not show up, he thought of the expediency of getting the old Shawnee to go with him to a cow ranch north of the Cimarron. On March 5 he arose early and started for the Indian's home. When he arrived his host told him that his work horses were out in the woods but that he would send his son after them, and that if the boy came back in time he would come to Payne's dugout the next morning, load his things in his wagon, and carry him across Deep Fork. Payne then started homeward. But he "took a stitch or kech" in his right hip and was drenched with rain until he arrived at his dugout. On the next day he was greatly discouraged, for the Indian did not show up. Dave again expressed an earnest wish that Tom would come.

On March 7 and 8 it snowed and stormed heavily, but it cleared again on the third day. Then Payne became ill again.

At 4:20 P.M. on March 10 he wrote: "Have headache badly. Am getting out of patience and out of heart. Some one ought to have reached here by this time. Will if well enough go again in the morning and see if I can not get the 'old Indian' to take me to the Cimmeron River." But he was not well enough the next day, and wrote: "Last night I suffered terrible the forepart of the night with headache. I cannot describe it but it was in the back of my head mainly and seemed to throb and go with the pulsations of the heart and sometime the heart seemed to stop or transfer as it were its beatings to the back and lower part of the head." But determinedly he started out for the "old Indian's" camp, and was again stricken with his "kech" and compelled to return home, "to do, I know not what." He complained that he was "awful billious" but had no medicine, "not even a pill." On March 12, however, Tom at last came, accompanied by a "Mr. Miller"; and soon they had put Dave's trunk and bedding in their wagon and were on their way back to Kansas.

Ordinarily such hard experiences would have discouraged an aspiring leader, but Dave was no ordinary man. On April 26 the Wichita *Beacon* mentioned a proposed invasion, stating that "Captain Payne, Mr. E. H. Nugent, ex-city councilman, and others, left Wichita for Hunnewell, Monday evening." At the latter point the Boomer caravan of thirty wagons was joined by an additional fifty from Parsons. "The Parsons outfit had farming implements, building material and a printing office," and was composed of "respectable men," according to an army scout.

From Hunnewell the Boomers moved south, crossed the Indian Territory line, and traveled to a creek "some distance from the old camp" without having seen soldiers or Indians. This was Deep Fork, about six or seven miles northeast of present-day Oklahoma City. They immediately set to work to establish their colony. One of their number, George McNeal, wrote back to his brother Jacoby that Nugent's house was finished. They had also built a hotel, the Erastus House; had started one for "Captain" Lewis, as well as twenty others; and had planted gardens. On May 24 the *Beacon* reported that a courier had arrived in Wichita bringing letters from Nugent and announcing that he (the courier) would return shortly at the head of another caravan.

But this attempt met the same fate that the others had. On May 28 even Payne and Nugent were back in Wichita, having been brought to Hunnewell by Fort Reno soldiers. Only the main leaders of the Colony had been arrested, Randall believing that others would presently leave. And in this he was right. The *Transporter* of June 10 reported that a few days previously "a disconsolate outfit consisting of 8 wagons" had passed Fort Reno on its way to Texas and that others had been sent northward toward the Kansas border.

Evidently one enterprising Boomer, "Captain" J. H. Leroy, felt that the Boomer cause now needed stimulation, for on May 22, 1882, the Kansas City *Star* carried his exciting though fantastic report. He said that he had just arrived from Oklahoma and that he wished to correct a false rumor to the effect that Captain Payne and Captain Warner had been arrested and were now held as prisoners at Fort Sill. He asserted that this was not so, and that "the few troops, 400 to 500, that were sent to arrest Payne and Warner have been captured by Payne's and Warner's men and disarmed. . . . The Payne and Warner men number 4,000, with daily additions." It is probable that this started the wagons of adventurers rolling toward the Kansas border, for before long they were collecting in considerable numbers at Hunnewell, Wichita, and elsewhere.

Then came alarming news! It was rumored that Payne had abandoned the cause altogether until Congress should act on the matter. Payne took little notice of the rumor until many Boomers had started for their old homes. Then he acted. On June 28 he asked the editor of the *Beacon* to announce that the story was false and that soon he would re-enter the forbidden land. He was to say further that "the oft repeated statement that any one of us was ever held to bail or fined, is false. . . . We have been always pleading for a trial, but have failed, they [the officers] refusing to go into court with us, and for the reason that they knew they would be defeated—that we were able to and would show that the lands from which we have been removed, were a part of the public domain—and that when shown in court, would open up to settlement the lands in question." Just how Dave could reconcile this assertion with the results of his trial at Fort Smith the previous year is not known. Nor did he explain why he had not appealed to the Supreme Court from Judge Parker's decision.

In the same article Dave challenged any federal officer, Indian agent, or lawyer to prove that he had violated any law in going into Oklahoma. Then he announced that a new start for the Oklahoma lands would be made on July 20, and concluded with the warning: "There are not corporations, Indian (stealing) agents, hells or devils enough to keep us from them. We will have them, and when we go again, we will stay on them. No more squaw fights or foolishness with federal officers, Indian agents or corporations. They have played the squaw man and squaw fight with us for four years. Everybody sees that it is a farce. No more of it for us. They might as well stand from under. We go at the time stated and to stay and will stay." Perhaps the reader will remember that this was not the Boomer leader's first "go to stay" announcement.

In addition, Payne had prepared a pamphlet for general distribution. It reviewed at great length the land problem in the Indian Territory, pointed out that the Atlantic and Pacific Railroad had a large land grant in Oklahoma, that an act of Congress (1878) had provided that wherever there was a railroad grant the provisions of the pre-emption and homestead laws would likewise apply, and that Attorney General Charles Devens had ruled that the Atlantic and Pacific yet held valid rights. The pamphlet also identified another type of intruder. "It may be stated that cattlemen are fencing in what they call ranches from 20 to 30 miles square. These ranches are over the Oklahoma country, and yet we are not allowed to stay on or improve a small farm of 160 acres. These cattlemen are protected by the same United States soldiers that have always taken us out. These cattlemen are, in one form and another, connected with other corporations and monopolies, therefore have little trouble in getting the ear of the powers that be in Washington." The pamphlet ended by warning that here was the last chance to get "a choice, valuable and beautiful home for nothing. . . . Come and go with us to this beautiful land and secure for yourself and children homes in the richest, most beautiful and best country that the great Creator, in His goodness, has made for man. By being one of the first on the ground, you can secure a claim (160 acres of land) that will be worth $20 to $50 per acre in one year."

There is little doubt that this and similar appeals had made converts of men in responsible position. Payne's notebook of 1882 shows that he made considerable progress in the sale of Colony shares. He disposed of 40 shares to Buffalo Bill; 40 to Judge Slone (probably "Sloan"); 80 to the Kansas City *Times*, through Dr. Mumford, September 6; 200 to G. D. Baker of the Topeka *Commonwealth*; 80 to J. W. McMillan; 40 to Editor Sol Miller of the *War Chief*; 420 again to Dr. Mumford, October 14; 40 to D. L. Payne on November 12 and the same number on December 20; 5,000 to the Chicago *Times*, on October 20; 5,000 to surveyors of the Atlantic and Pacific Railroad, on October 20; 40 to "Colonel" John Martin, as attorney fees; 40 to Thomas Fenlon; and 40 to Judge Price.

At the same time Dave was advancing the Boomer cause among the rank and file. On April 24, B. W. Lower wrote Payne that "Dock and I have 40 calls a day to know about Oklahoma," and that if he were given a few lots in the prospective capital, he would move a printing press there. Still another enthusiastic Boomer wrote that he would soon sell his property and would donate the proceeds therefrom to the Oklahoma movement if the money were needed.

Such enthusiastic endorsement of an outlawed movement drove ranking military officers to bitter retort. Major General Pope wrote Lieutenant General Sheridan on May 23 that Payne was a convicted criminal before the United States court and ought to be dealt with more severely than other intruders. And as to the anomaly of the situation, he added: "It seems absurd to keep military forces constantly scouting that region to keep this one man out, when for him there is absolutely no penalty for a repetition of his offense." General W. T. Sherman suggested to Secretary Lincoln that Payne and his fellow invaders could be held in prison at Fort Sill and made to work like other prisoners. But Lincoln thought that this would be stretching his authority too far. Then William A. Phillips, special agent and counsel of the Cherokees, had still another suggestion. He wrote Commissioner Hiram Price that Payne could be prosecuted as a common swindler, since he had sold certificates for town lots in Oklahoma, to which he had no more right than he had to sell rooms in the Capitol at Washington!

But the opinions of the legalists were somewhat divided. For example, on March 25, 1882, Judge George W. McCrary of the United States Circuit Court, Eighth Judicial District, wrote to Senator George F. Hoar that in a recent case before him in Minneapolis he had occasion to find that Section 1 of the Indian Intercourse Act, defining the Indian country and its boundaries, had been nullified by the *Revised Statutes*. So he warned that there was now no area that could be legally defined as Indian country! Unless Congress immediately came to the relief of the hard-pressed Indian Bureau, he thought, the present legal status favored the Boomers. Agent D. B. Dyer, of the Quapaw reservation, was quite alarmed at McCrary's opinion and wrote Commissioner Price on August 19 that unless Congress enacted a new corrective measure the Indians could not be protected much longer against the "worst class of outlaws that can be found on the borders of a Western state."

Just how this opinion was made public is not known, but Payne and his backers were soon making the most of it. The border press gave it wide circulation. Payne was quite pleased, and seemed to think that the chances of his suit against Pope were visibly brightened. Pope evidently thought so, too, for anxiously he conferred with District Attorney Hallowell. But there was little cause for alarm. The case had been set for February 25; it was then postponed and finally dropped.

In July, Payne went to Washington to forward the Boomer cause. While there he called on government officials, including Secretary of the Interior Henry M. Teller. According to a report which Payne gave on his return journey to Wichita, Teller talked with him quite frankly and amiably. He admitted, said Payne, that the Boomers had an advantage over the government, but warned that they had better not press it. In any event, why wouldn't it be advisable to await the action of Congress so that the Boomers would find, when once they did get in, the framework of organized courts and government? To this Payne replied, "If the government will let us alone we'll ask no favors." He said that the Boomers would go in such force as to discourage any opposition by Indians or cattlemen, and that there were then ten thousand members of the Oklahoma Colony distributed along the border.

Payne also sought the favors of other officials, even including President Chester A. Arthur. He demanded of him the "protection of the flag" in his settlement of the public domain of Oklahoma. To all he said that his next invasion was scheduled for July

20. Yet he tarried in Washington long past this date; so long that a border editor scoffed that he must be enjoying "the sweets of Washington!"

At long last he was back on the border, offering plausible excuse for not fulfilling his July 20 appointment. The troops were watchful, but once more Payne proved a master of strategy, and again he crossed the boundary.

But his actions at this time are hard to explain. On October 5 William H. Osburn, an ardent Boomer, in telling a reporter of the Topeka *Commonwealth* the story of this ill-starred invasion, said that Payne's party made a start for Oklahoma from Hunnewell on August 3. If so, Payne evidently sought his own arrest and trial, for on August 2 he addressed a letter to the "Commanding Officer" at Fort Reno, giving his location at the time as "Camp on N. W. ¼ Section, 26 T., NW. R. 2 W." (two miles east of the present town of Wicher, Oklahoma). Thus the letter was evidently mailed from Hunnewell before the start was made. In it, Payne employed clumsy legalistic phraseology:

We as settlers on the Public lands situated in the Indian Territory (Oklahoma) do very respectfully but most earnestly ask that you will state to the Hon. Secretary of War by telegraph (or otherwise) that we as citizens refuse to submit to arrest and further if you are authorised to use violence in making such arrests, or in using the United States Army as a Possee Comatatus (or Police force) in making such arrest and removal; and believing that you will be generous enough to ask him, the Hon. Secretary of War, these questions. Please state to him that we refuse to submit to the arrest on the advice of men who are eminent as councilors at law and high officials in authority, and at the same time please telegraph him full text of Hon. George W. McCrary's letter to Hon. G. F. Hoar, United States Senator, and at the same time asking if United States Senate Bill No. 2100 has become a law. Common fairness is all that we ask and as an Army officer, we not only hope, but ask that you will be fair enough to comply with our very humble though earnest request.

Not until four days later did Payne and his party of twenty-six men, women, and children (including Anna and George) reach Deep Fork, a few miles north of present Oklahoma City, after an uneventful journey. They immediately turned to the task of staking claims, although some of the invaders moved on southward to the North Canadian. By August 12 all the Deep Fork settlers had become located, and they had begun to dig wells and build houses. While thus engaged, on August 26, Second Lieutenant C. W. Taylor and a detachment of the Ninth Cavalry (Negroes), or "Yellow Legs," as the Boomers contemptuously called them, appeared. Taylor harshly ordered the Boomers to reload their wagons and move out. They refused. Then he turned to his reluctant troopers and commanded them to hitch the intruders' teams to their wagons and load therein both the recalcitrant Boomers and their household effects. But this was not done without resistance. According to Osburn, a few days later, Payne did not resist arrest, but he himself fought the troopers until they tied him to his wagon. Then the others also engaged the soldiers and "a rough and tumble fight" followed. Finally, however, those resisting were bound and dumped into their wagons as though they were sacks of shelled corn. The first offenders were permitted to return to Kansas; others, including Mrs. Osburn and her child, were taken to Fort Reno.

When they arrived at the post—again according to Osburn—the Boomers were subjected to cruelty. They were denied food for twenty hours, although Mrs. Osburn and her child were ill. "After holding us there without accommodations, in rain and sun for eight days," continued Osburn, "they sent a tent and stove, after 36 hours of rain and still raining, and after eleven days they sent a Jesse James gang and stole our property."

But the reader must make due allowance for Osburn's anger. Obviously some disposition must be made of the Boomers' property. In fact, Captain F. T. Bennett at the post immediately wired the Adjutant General, stating that he had taken over the intruders' "horses, wagons and other property" and asking what should be done with them. Official records are silent concerning final action. They do reveal, however, that every consideration was shown the Boomers. Yet one hardly knows what to believe, for Payne, too, complained bitterly. He told Bennett that he had served on the border for twenty-five years and had seen the workings of "vigilant committees," but that he had never known one to drag sick women and children around over the country for revenge or to separate old and feeble men from their property.

The Secretary of War now ordered Captain Bennett to turn Payne's party over to United States Marshal Thomas Boles at Fort Smith, for trial. There is good reason to believe that Payne was elated at this turn in his fortunes. When Bennett informed him that he and his party were to be sent under guard to Fort Smith, he replied that he was "willing and anxious" to go. Still, seven of the prisoners had "chills and fever," and he feared that a wagon trip across the rough country between Fort Reno and Fort Smith would tax the strength of all, especially Mrs. Osburn and her child, who were critically ill. If they should journey via Fort Sill and Henrietta, Texas, he urged, the trip could be made in one-fourth the time of a more direct wagon journey, for from Henrietta they could travel to Fort Smith on a railroad train.

Then, too, Payne informed Bennett that he was prepared to prove that Indians living between the two posts and along the wagon road had offered rewards for Boomer lives. He warned that a force of a hundred soldiers would hardly be sufficient to protect the prisoners against these "vicious mobs."

Bennett decided to accede to Payne's request, although later he admitted that in doing so he was tricked and that the purported troubles were trumped up. On September 11 the prisoners were turned over to Taylor and two companies of the Twentieth In-

Payne in camp on Deep Fork, 1882

Office of

Payne's Oklahoma Colony,

A. B. Calvert, Sec'y.

Wichita, Kans., May 21st 1883.

Friend Garrison
Belton Tex.

Dear sir your favor recd
this mail containing P.O. Order all right— And will
forward you 57 blanks more Do the best you can for
the cause for we are needing all we can get financially
As we are out at least five dollars a day for rent postage
and advertising. I sent you paper last week. Will send you
one this week. Our time is set to leave the Kans. line at
Arkansas City Kans. June 20th from there we will have 110
miles to travel by waggons. which will take us 5 days
to reach our destination. (North Canadian River) I have
nothing new to tell you only our cause is brightening all the
while Men of money and sense are falling in to line.
We are receiving daily from forty to fifty letters The people
are waking up they say the country is bound to open
that it can not lay Idle. And when the people says open
it opens (the people are the Government) I will write you
more about meeting you in my next Resp. Yours
hop Success is ours &c I await your early ans A. B. Calvert—
Sect.

A typical specimen of Boomer enthusiasm

fantry and a Negro trooper of the Ninth Cavalry. From Fort
Reno they traveled southward via Fort Sill.

After a tedious journey of seven days, they arrived at Henrietta on Sunday, September 17, and pitched camp near the Denver and Rio Grande Railroad depot until the next day. Here
Osburn was allowed to procure the services of a physician for his
wife and child. And on Monday Payne was also allowed to go
into town with some of his men to make certain purchases. On
the journey southward he had assured Taylor that he would
make no trouble. But when Payne reached town he engaged a
lawyer, who presently sent a deputy sheriff back to the depot
armed with a writ of habeas corpus to serve on Taylor, demanding the surrender of Payne and party to local authorities. The
angry Taylor refused, telling the Henrietta officer that his
charges were federal prisoners guilty of violating the Nonintercourse Law. Either the deputy was ignorant of the implications
of Taylor's statement or he felt that his writ was mandatory, for
he went away with a threat that he would return with a posse
to force compliance.

By this time Payne and his men had returned to the depot.
While in town Dave had become quite drunk, but he was sober
enough to be disappointed because of Taylor's refusal. Taylor
was nervous and anxiously awaited the eastbound train. And
much to his delight it arrived before long. This was indeed fortunate, for hardly had he loaded his prisoners and soldiers aboard
one of the cars when the county sheriff came hastening up with
a considerable posse. Gruffly he demanded Taylor's arrest for
refusing to recognize the writ previously served on him and
also asked the other Boomers to surrender. But again, in crisp,
angry words, Taylor refused. The posse then moved forward
and boarded the train, but found itself confronted by the drawn
bayonets of the soldiers. As the train moved slowly out of the
station, the sheriff and his men hastily leaped to the ground.

"Payne seemed chagrinned and surprised at this failure of his plan," Taylor reported a short time later, "and became quite abusive and boisterous; so much so that I was on the point of gagging him." But again the resourceful Boomer showed enough presence of mind to become quiet. Yet he warned Taylor that other efforts would be made to rescue him, either at Decatur or Dallas, and this caused the officer great uneasiness. No further hostile demonstration was made, however, and the trip to Fort Smith via Dallas and Texarkana was completed in peace.

At Fort Smith, on September 20, Taylor turned his prisoners over to Marshal Boles. Still there was no federal law under which Payne could be tried, since already, without success, the maximum penalty of a thousand dollars had been assessed. So Payne was released to appear at the next term of court, and his associates—Addison P. Lewis, Emmett Lewis, Addison Lewis, Jr., Dicy Dixon, William H. Miller, Edward Hatfield, Albert C. McCord, William H. Osburn, and the latter's wife and child —were freed on the same terms. At a later hearing, all charges against them were dropped.

In his later report, Taylor expressed great satisfaction at having accomplished his difficult task. At times his position had been most trying. For example, Osburn had protested very bitterly against the removal of his wife and child from Henrietta while they were yet critically ill; and the local physician, Dr. McGee, had also warned against such a move. But at the time he surrendered his prisoners into the hands of the capable United States Marshal at Fort Smith, the condition of the sick was much improved.

Yet Taylor was not free from all responsibility. While he was at Fort Smith, Payne's attorney entered suit against him in the Sebastian Circuit Court on the grounds of assault and false imprisonment; and not caring to stand the cost of the impending case, Taylor appealed for War Department support. The Attorney General named District Attorney W. H. H. Clayton, of Fort Smith, to appear for the officer, who then was permitted to return to his post of duty. Later the case was dismissed.

Hardly was Payne back in Wichita before he had laid the foundations for a new venture. He could now play the role of a martyr—and did, to good effect. To all listeners he told of his cruel treatment, as well as that of the unfortunate sick.

10 : *Trial by Blizzard*

PATRICK HENRY had his George III, but David Lewis Payne was not quite sure who his principal adversary was. At one time it was Hiram Price, Commissioner of Indian Affairs; at another, it was Major General John Pope, commander of the Department of Missouri, within which was the Indian Territory; at still another, it was the officer in charge of the troopers who expelled him from Oklahoma; and again, it was the cowman who fenced in a large part of Oklahoma.

Still, as a frontier leader, Payne was superb—impetuous and rough enough to please adventurers and sufficiently a dreamer to attract homeseekers. He shared uncomplainingly with his fellows in hardship, toil, and danger; and he measured up well to every test—in conferences with federal officials, in stump-speaking, and in determination and resourcefulness. Always his course was unswerving. Oklahoma was a part of the public domain and subject to settlement under the pre-emption and homestead laws. On this point he was firm, even though he was lampooned by hostile editors, rebuffed by the military, and scolded by Washington officials. He was almost as well versed in Indian laws, treaties, and in court decisions bearing on Indian affairs as were the best lawyers, and could quote glibly from them. Much buffeting about had left him embittered, grim, determined; neither argument, threat, nor cajolery had changed him. His ringing challenge was "On to Oklahoma!"; it was an obses-

116

sion, a tantalizing mirage which ever danced before him. And so through trial, hardship, suffering, and devotion to his cause, he emerged, in the eyes of his followers, a martyr, a peerless hero.

By early January, 1883, Boomers were collecting at Wichita, Hunnewell, Arkansas City, and Caldwell. Judge McCrary's recent opinion, the refusal of federal officials again to bring Payne to trial, and the clumsy maneuvering of cattle interests to absorb the Cherokee Strip—all made hundreds of converts to the Boomer cause. Fully six hundred Colony certificates were sold in Arkansas City alone during January. Nowhere along the border did the idea of a permanent Indian Territory meet with public favor. A Caldwell editor complained of timber thieves who stripped the region between the Kansas line and the Cimarron of fine trees; one at Wichita thought that cattlemen were overreaching the Indians and robbing them of their valuable grazing lands; and another at Arkansas City pictured the Indian Territory as "the grandest nuisance on God's earth," in that it was filled with "robbers, cutthroats and highwaymen." This last editor wrote that "the devil and all his angels seem to have gathered there where they are protected from the hand of a just law." Texas and Arkansas editors heartily agreed with him. To them, it was either the man with a plow or the outlaw with a gun, between whom they would choose the former.

By the dawn of the new year, a perceptible change had come in the attitude of the Kansas border press. Cattlemen ranging their herds on the Cherokee Strip and in Oklahoma had recently become alarmed at the Boomer Movement, fearing that it would imperil their interests. Therefore they organized to oppose the invaders, and subsidized the newspapers by liberal amounts of advertising. Then attacks on the "Oklahomaites" were more frequent, the weight of which was reflected in the metropolitan press. Boomer leaders were aware of the source of this hostile criticism and decided to counteract it by setting up their own

organ, the *Oklahoma War Chief;* and under the editorship of
A. W. Harris, the first issue saw the light of day on January
12, 1883.

But there were also a few border-town editors who were not
influenced by the cattlemen. It seems that while in Fort Smith a
short time before, Payne had won the favor of the editor of the
Herald, for on December 28 the latter wrote encouragingly of
the Boomer Movement, stating that Payne's Wichita office was
thronged daily by prospective colonists and that the movement
was in a healthy condition. "Treaties," he added, "are ropes of
sand in all such cases." Then on January 12, Payne and Harris
visited Arkansas City to select a rendezvous camp from which to
invade Oklahoma. And while there they called on the editor of
the *Democrat,* who heretofore had not been too friendly toward
them. But Payne satisfied him "beyond a doubt" that Oklahoma
was government land and subject to settlement.

While Payne was occupied thus, W. W. Bloss wrote him that
an Oklahoma and Kansas City Colony had sprung up, headed
by B. S. Waldren. Payne was quite alarmed at this news and called
a meeting of his own colony in Wichita to consider it. After going
into the matter at some length, the Boomers adopted a motion
to contact the Kansas City organization through a committee, of
which Payne was chairman. Dave forthwith composed a letter
appealing to the Kansas Cityans to subordinate their colony to
that already set up. He pointed out that Payne's Oklahoma Colony had pioneered in this field, had spent large sums of money
in buying maps, certificates, and posters, and in surveying the
country to be settled. When Payne's letter was received by the
Kansas City Colony it seemed to meet with little favor. Payne's
personal representative for the occasion, "Oklahoma Ben"
Lower, wrote back discouraging news. "I think they aim to
monopolize the whole business, town and all," he said.

By January 12 all differences between the two organizations

were evidently ironed out, for the Oklahoma and Kansas City Colony set up a committee consisting of President Waldren, P. H. Frybarger, P. H. Heydon, L. E. Chessman, and George C. Banta to extend Payne's Oklahoma Colony a cordial invitation to rendezvous with them at Coffeyville preparatory to an Oklahoma invasion. But the Wichitans did not accept. Payne, Osburn, and E. A. Reiman, acting as a committee for the latter, wrote in reply that the date set by the Kansas Cityans to come to Coffeyville was that fixed by Payne's Colony to start from Arkansas City for Oklahoma. They hastened to add, however, that they would be pleased if the Kansas City Boomers would join them in Oklahoma.

The Boomers in camp at Arkansas City, about five hundred in number, waited in eager expectancy for Payne's "Forward!" Around a huge campfire here on the cold night of January 19 they held a lively meeting at which "Oklahoma Still" and other Boomer songs were sung. Then Payne addressed them. Also, Harris announced that while he had been in Kansas City, recently, Waldren had asked him to say to the Payne colonists that he and his colonists would follow into Oklahoma from Coffeyville. Harris said that wherever he had gone in recent weeks he had found "most people wide awake." C. C. Pratt, of Towanda and Eldorado, had told him that there was great interest at these places and estimated that fifty Boomers would soon join their Arkansas City camp. A "Mr. Eidenbaugh," of Belle Plaine, counted twenty or twenty-five teams. Payne added that he had found the situation the same wherever he had gone; that at Douglass he had been received most enthusiastically, and W. L. Couch, a prominent citizen, had promised to bring several others with him before a southward start was made.

No doubt Payne's and Harris's reports were based on fact. The Caldwell *Commercial* of February 1, 1883, stated that large numbers of Boomers were concentrating at "Arkansas City,

Coffeyville, and various other points along the Kansas border."
But it also mentioned that federal troopers were engaged in active patrol to frustrate any movement. Colonel J. D. Bingham, of Caldwell, was not content to assume the defensive. On January 30 he sent a special agent, C. F. Somner, to investigate the extent of Boomer activity. Somner arrived at Arkansas City and inquired the way to the Boomer camp, and was told that already the invaders were on the move for Oklahoma.

But the Boomers were not far away. Couch, of Douglass, had arrived on January 31 with twenty men in five wagons, and they had been named by Payne to head the caravan. At eleven o'clock the next morning the wagon train moved southward in a long column, estimated by Payne at more than a hundred wagons. A blizzard had blown up, bringing fitful gusts of snow and sleet, causing the wagoners to walk beside their teams to keep warm or to hide their faces behind their turned-up coat collars. "Scrouching down over his horse," Payne rode in advance of the flag-bearing wagon. Women and children within the wagons sought the protection of blankets or quilts.

After traveling southward for about four miles, the caravan then turned sharply to the west and followed the state line, finally encamping on Bitter Creek, about sixteen miles from Arkansas City. Hardly had it halted before Boomers were scurrying here and there looking for firewood, which was found in abundance along the creek. Soon campfires were leaping merrily, and before them the half-frozen travelers were thankfully extending their hands and feet.

It was here that Somner found them. He had procured a horse at Arkansas City and had followed their trail into camp. He, too, was cold and sought the nearest campfire. When he was warm, he began his inspection. Payne and other Boomer leaders were suspicious of him, although he was dressed as a civilian. He asked annoying questions. Where were they headed? By what route did they expect to travel? Were other parties to join them en route? Somner received evasive answers. Then he turned his attention to the campers. He counted eighty-seven wagons in camp, of which five or six were drawn by oxen and the others by horses. He also saw four carriages and four cows. At Arkansas City he had been told that there were 157 wagons in the train; if so, the others had gone farther down the creek to have the advantage of windbreaks. Each wagon was filled with provisions and forage and had a bale of hay tied outside. Some were loaded with furniture and agricultural implements.

The Boomers impressed Somner favorably. They seemed to be, he said, "a well-to-do, quiet set of farmers." In fact, some were leading businessmen of Arkansas City and other Kansas towns. Among the "better class," he mentioned "Mr. and Mrs. Haynes of Wichita; Mr. and Mrs. A. McDonald of McPherson; J. B. Cooper, a newspaper man of Moline; Doctor and Mrs. McIlvaine of McPherson; Mr. and Mrs. R. A. Cameron of El Dorado; and a lawyer, J. K. Rogers of Carrolton, Missouri." He did not name Ma Haines and her son, George, who were also present.

While Somner was visiting the Bitter Creek camp, the Boomers cleverly sought to trick him into court action. He was told that one of the Boomers from Wichita, E. N. Achley, carried in his wagon a full load of whiskey and cigars, as he intended to open a saloon in Oklahoma. Of course Somner's informants knew that a heavy prison sentence awaited anyone who was convicted of selling liquor in the Indian Territory. Still they hoped to prove that Oklahoma was not in the restricted area.

Somner attended the evening meeting of the Boomers. While the wind was howling about the wagons, driving squalls of sleet and snow before it, the undaunted campers had assembled. The meeting was opened by prayer, and then Payne in angry tones denounced the government for its inconsistent Oklahoma policy and for the favoritism shown the cattlemen. "The cattle rings are allowed to fence in huge tracts of Oklahoma land," he shouted, "while we are denied the right to homestead 160-acres." But border people were becoming aroused, he assured his listeners. To prove this he read aloud a telegram from Texas Boomers assembled at the Red River Crossing of the Chisholm Trail on their way to join him on the North Canadian.

Somner was unfavorably impressed with Payne himself. Arkansas City citizens had prejudiced him. He reported to Colonel Bingham that they regarded Payne "as a professional dead beat, a worthless drunken loafer, who for the last three years has not earned a single dollar by honest means or labor and whose sole objects in starting these booms are merely gain." He found it "astonishing that so many apparently good, honest and intelligent people could be led astray by such a miserable wretch." He was told at Arkansas City that every member of Payne's Oklahoma Colony paid two and a half dollars for a certificate, of which fifty cents was retained by the secretary and the other two dollars by Payne, and that Payne issued "Land Certificates" to those who did not care to go with an invading party. These persons were guaranteed 160 acres of land for which they paid only the certificate fee of twenty-five dollars.

When Somner left the Bitter Creek camp, he next visited Boomers at Coffeyville. He found here about thirty-five adults, most of whom had taken refuge in livery stables because of the extreme cold. The thermometer read from twelve to fifteen degrees below zero. "These people," he reported, "have mostly all come from Missouri, are a rough looking lot, but seem to have plenty of provisions." Their horses and mules were poor. They grumbled to him because others who had promised to meet them here had not shown up. Nevertheless, they intended to move along the Kansas boundary until they came to the old Fort Cobb road, and then to travel over it to the Cimarron.

Trial by Blizzard

The Arkansas City Boomers left their Bitter Creek camp at half-past eight o'clock on the morning of February 2 and journeyed southward to Deer Creek. The weather was too cold to go farther, so they remained here for the next day. In a penciled notebook diary which Payne kept while on the trip, he wrote that here his feet, fingers, and nose were frozen. "But Mrs. Haines and Little George," he said, "stand the cold like heroes." His last entry for the day was, "I am not well."

On February 4 the Boomers resumed their course southward until they came to Red Rock Creek, where they went into camp, protected from the cold wind by a grove of trees. While they were here a Boomer scout brought news that troops were in front of them, but none appeared. When on the following day they reached the Salt Fork of the Arkansas, the ice on the river was so thick as to permit the entire wagon train to cross to the other side. From here the trail continued southward over ridges and divides. The face of the country was broken and scarce of timber, but well watered. The wagons now became scattered and it was not until nine o'clock at night that all were reunited at Beaver Creek. Its banks were precipitous and it was necessary for the Boomers to use ropes to let the wagons down into its channel and to draw them out on the opposite side.

In the afternoon of February 6 the pilgrims crossed the Cimarron. Since the river water was salty, they pitched camp at a fine spring a mile beyond, within the edge of the Cross Timbers. At this point, before journeying on to the Canadian, Payne made his last speech to his shivering comrades. He appeared in fine fettle and held his listeners enthralled for more than an hour, speaking with great eloquence. He and his comrades were pioneers in a great cause, he said, and would be so counted by historians of the future. Their material reward would be fine homes and opportunities to rear a great commonwealth in the wilderness. The Boomers probably needed this verbal stimulant, for when the meeting had broken up they spread their blankets on frozen ground.

The following morning, when the sun's rays came stealing over the eastern hills to light up the ice-coated trees in dazzling brilliance like hundreds of inverted, giant chandeliers, the Boomers were up and about their tasks. Around the campfires the aroma of coffee and frying bacon whetted hearty appetites, but breakfast was eaten hastily and the journey continued.

In the scrub-oak forest on either side of the trail, hunting now began in earnest, and deer and turkey in large numbers were killed, so that every wagon was well supplied. Council Creek, a small spring-fed stream, was reached and crossed about noon; and near three o'clock in the afternoon the Boomers had their first sight of the "Yellow Legs"—twelve Negro troopers of the Ninth Cavalry under the command of Lieutenant Stevens. The soldiers approached at an easy canter, Stevens saluting the hindmost teamster as he passed. But when he neared the head of the train he reined in beside Payne and told him that he was under arrest.

Payne did not halt. He replied to the nervous officer that he and his men were in a hurry to get to the North Canadian and could not afford to stop now, but that if the troopers would journey with them, they would soon pitch camp. Since there was little else that Stevens could do with so small a force, he reluctantly consented. Then a short time later the two forces camped on Coffee Creek.

The wagons moved out again on the following morning, toward the south, escorted by the troopers. During the night Stevens had sent a courier to Captain Carroll's camp, not far distant, asking for aid.

While the caravan was moving southward, Harry Stafford, scout and guide, rode in advance to direct the course of soldiers and Boomers. The settlers were delighted with the country and said that it was all that Payne had reported—rich bottoms, good water, and large timber. Deep Fork was reached just above its confluence with Coffee Creek, and now all hands set to work to bridge it with brush, logs, big weeds, and dirt.

While the others were thus engaged, a young photographer, C. P. Wickmiller, who had joined the expedition at Payne's invitation, crossed the yet incompleted bridge to an elevated tableland on the south side so that he could have a good view of the train of covered wagons as they stood in a long curved line bending around the brow of the hill between Coffee Creek and Deep Fork. But the eager Boomers stopped their work and rushed forward for the picture so that little of the train appeared in the photograph later finished.*

Finally the creek was behind them and the journey was resumed toward the North Canadian. The Boomers crossed the divide between Deep Fork and the North Canadian on the afternoon of February 8, and at last came in sight of their goal. "The scene was magnificent," wrote a pleased pilgrim, "and was greeted by the Colonists with a spontaneous cheer that ought to have been heard at Washington. Stretching away as far almost as the eye could reach lay the level land, the river and foothills skirted with large, beautiful timber of walnut, white oak, ash, beech, hackberry, and hickory, while between was the rich bottom land nude of timber or brush and ready for the plow."

Descending from the crest of a hill, the Boomers moved down into the valley and camped on the north side of the river at the foot of a protecting bluff. Payne recorded in his diary that the camp was located on Section 16, Township 13, Range 1 West.† It was called Camp Alice in honor of Alice McPherson, a Boomer's small daughter.

*The present site of the crossing is south of Highway 66, a short distance west of Arcadia, Oklahoma, near a country road crossing of the near-by railroad.

†Today the site is about three miles north and slightly west of Jones, Oklahoma.

Here the Boomers had some protection against the cold wind and zestfully set to work to make their camp comfortable. But about five o'clock in the afternoon Captain Carroll and two troops (about ninety men) of the Ninth Cavalry arrived. Carroll was not intimidated as Stevens had seemingly been, although the Boomers were numerous and armed with Winchesters and shotguns. He was kind but firm. He handed the chairman of the Boomer committee his orders, saying that he had come to "order out" or "help out" the intruders.

Naturally the Boomers were excited. They had suffered greatly from cold and exposure on the road and were not ready to accept defeat. Some were for fighting. Indeed, Osburn said a short time later that during the trip Payne had made a very inflammatory speech declaring in part that "he would rather have his arms cut off, his throat cut and the streams run red with blood than to be arrested and prevented from settling in Oklahoma." If Payne made this statement, he was probably under the influence of liquor, for contemporary evidence seems to show that he was often drunk during this period. It should also be remembered that after the expedition Osburn was not on good terms with Payne.

Carroll undoubtedly was "the man for the place," for he sought to soothe the ruffled feelings of the Boomers. "I have nothing to do with the laws," he told them, "but I am here in obedience to orders and have a duty to perform." He would arrest old offenders and take them to Fort Reno, but he would allow all others to go back to Kansas or the states from which they came.

A rift now appeared in the Boomer camp. With the appearance of the soldiers, the invaders had agreed among themselves not to identify the leaders and old offenders for the military officers. Then when Carroll came to Camp Alice and demanded their surrender, Payne either forgot his pledge or else felt that conditions were such that it was no longer necessary to keep it. He explained in his diary that Carroll sent for him, and that they had "angry words." Then he, Stafford, Goodrich, and Osburn were put under arrest, along with seven others who refused to return to Kansas. Osburn offered some resistance and was treated with less consideration than the others. All that Payne wrote about Osburn's behavior was that "the soldiers went through camp to find Captain Osburn. This seemed to scare all our folks out of their better judgment and soon all said they would leave except probly fifty. No use to try to stay with these now and I advise all to accept the situation and go with the others." A disgruntled member of the party, however, charged that Payne cared little, that presently he was in Lieutenant Stevens' tent "smoking Havanas."

Osburn felt that Payne had shown little courage and was willing to forget the interests of all. Payne's friends, however, complained that Osburn had "hidden out while Carroll was present" and had run from trouble. But prior to this "he was active, with his pencil behind his ear and certificate book under his arm, looking after the little two dollars that prompts him to duty." Couch believed that Payne was in the right. He had not revealed his identity, he said, until the camp was breaking up and wagons were starting for Kansas, and then he had asked Carroll for a stay of five days to allow the Boomers to rest after their long journey. This period of time would enable the Kansas City and Texas colonists to reach the North Canadian, and perhaps, too, Washington would be heard from. "Osburn tried to be cute," thought Couch, and resisted arrest.

There is little doubt that the Boomers were jittery, as a camp incident proved. An impromptu meeting had been called to quiet the excited Boomers who were preparing to leave. A speaker, mounted on a large tree stump to which had been lashed the American flag, was appealing for sober action on the part of all.

Then a voice rang out, "There's a spy in camp!" This caused much excitement and milling about, and another angrily called, "Get a rope, let's hang him!" Then Couch leaped to the top of the stump and with outstretched hands shouted: "Men, we are American citizens and are here under the protection of the American flag. We are here to do no wrong but to try to build homes. Let's not do anything that would class us as criminals. If there is a spy among us, let him spy. We are doing nothing against our government and he can do us no harm." This quieted the men. Upon inquiry, they found the "spy" to be a harmless government teamster.

On February 11 Captain Carroll sent his prisoners to Fort Reno under military escort. Both while at Camp Alice and on the journey to Fort Reno, the Negro troopers took every occasion to express their displeasure toward the Boomers for having exposed them in such severe weather. They remarked that they were forbidden to shoot them, were too cold and weak to drive them out, and saw no reason why the Boomers did not defy them and stay! Osburn, too, raised the question of why Major General Pope would send out troops in such freezing weather. He found forty or more men in the Fort Reno hospital severely "frosted," some to lose hands, some feet.

Payne also had suffered from cold and was ill for most of the invasion. His diary record of February 15 reads: "Have been sick for two days with my old army complaint and have a fearful cough. Both together have hurt me terible." Fortunately, however, he and his associates were treated kindly. Payne said he was furnished with comfortable quarters; and while at Fort Reno Osburn wrote, "After the first day at 10 o'clock, we were under the charge of Captain R. M. Taylor, who gave us papers to read and treated us kindly."

On Sunday, February 18, a sergeant and six enlisted men escorted the captives back to Kansas, traveling northward via

A photograph made by C. P. Wickmiller in February, 1883, as the Boomers crossed Deep Fork. The child in the foreground is Alice McPherson, for whom Camp Alice on the North Canadian was named.

A photograph made by the author and Eugene Couch in 1942. The split rock on the hillside and the hill contour are the identifying features.

Camp Alice on the North Canadian, from a photograph by C. P. Wickmiller at the time of its establishment. The location, as given by Payne in his notebook diary of February, 1883, was "Section 16, Township 13, Range 1 West."

The site at present, about eighteen miles east of Oklahoma City and three and one-half miles northwest of Jones; from a photograph by the author and Eugene Couch in February, 1942.

Kingfisher Creek, Buffalo Springs, Sun Creek, and thence on to Caldwell.

Little more is known of the Waldren and Texas parties. If the Texans crossed the Red River, they were evidently intercepted and turned back by a patrol from Fort Sill. But on this the official records are silent. A railway mail clerk at Tulsa, Indian Territory, reported that on February 7 "twelve teams and 150 heavily armed men" had passed this town on their way to the North Canadian. These were probably the Missourians who had been camped at Coffeyville and who, no doubt, had effected a union with the Kansas City Boomers, for the *Cheyenne Transporter* on February 26 reported that the Kansas City Colony had followed Payne "a few days afterwards, and were the hardest looking lot of boomers we have seen." This tallies with Somner's appraisal of the Coffeyville camp. They came as far south as the Cimarron, but here Waldren was arrested and taken to Fort Reno; and, indeed, he was sent on to Kansas five days before Payne reached the post. Waldren was in Kansas City on March 8, and while there reported that he would head another expedition to Oklahoma shortly, but there is no record of his having done so. Those who went with him to the Cimarron were permitted to return to Kansas without escort.

11 : *Boomer Dissension*

*T*HERE is little doubt that the cattlemen were the Boomers' cleverest foes. Working behind the screen of "Indian rights," and with large sums of money, they stayed well within the bounds of legitimacy. Ever since the close of the Civil War they had driven their herds across the Indian Territory and had ranged them on its fine grasslands. In the beginning the Indians had opposed the trail drivers, but when they were given "mohaw" (beef) they were inclined to offer little opposition. From 1875 to 1882, Texans drove 2,093,132 cattle northward over Indian Territory trails, according to Joseph G. McCoy, a contemporary cattle buyer; and by 1883, cowmen's range leases almost checkerboarded the Comanche-Kiowa and Cheyenne-Arapaho reservations and the Cherokee Strip. Moreover, thousands of cattle were driven into the Territory from neighboring ranges. The Chisholm Trail entered the Indian Territory on the south at Red River Crossing, in the northwest corner of Cooke County, Texas, and extended northward to Abilene, Kansas, on the Kansas Pacific Railroad, via the present Comanche-Chickasha-Kingfisher approach. Farther west, the Western Trail crossed the South Fork of the Red River at Doan's Store, north of Vernon, Texas, and then took a northerly course via Camp Supply, Indian Territory, to Dodge City, Kansas, on the Santa Fe Railroad.

On either side of these two important cow trails was excellent pasture, and here trail drivers on their way to Kansas often allowed their herds to rest and graze for days or weeks. Commissioner Price, of the Indian Service, protested this trespass of Indian land to Secretary Kirkwood, who in turn asked Secretary of War Robert T. Lincoln for troops to expel the offending cowmen. The request was acceded to reluctantly, but as often as the soldiers drove the cattlemen out they returned again. Military officers, from General Pope to post commanders, protested against such constant police duty. It was difficult enough, they argued, to patrol the Kansas and Texas boundaries and to expel the Boomers; it was quite impossible to keep out the persistent cattlemen with their tens of thousands of wild cattle.

In the summer of 1881 Ikard and Harrold brought herds into Old Greer County, between the two forks of the Red River; and by the next year sixty thousand cattle ranged there. Occasionally these strayed across the North Fork onto the rich pasture lands of the Comanches and Kiowas, as did thousands of others from northern Texas. Officers sent out with troop patrols to expel them reported that it was impossible to know who were intruding cattlemen and who were trail drivers, and that they could not expel all of them.

In 1882 Agent P. B. Hunt, of the Comanche-Kiowa reservation, without the permission of Commissioner Price entered into a range agreement with the cattlemen and Indians whereby the ranchers were allowed the temporary privilege of ranging the reservation in consideration of a liberal supply of beef which they should donate to augment the government's slender allowance to the Indians. In later months and years this agreement was renewed from time to time, the cattlemen bribing important chiefs and headmen to keep down opposition.

The same thing happened on the Cheyenne-Arapaho reservation. Here, on January 8, 1883, Agent John D. Miles negotiated a range agreement between twenty-five chiefs and headmen of the Cheyennes and Arapahoes on the one hand and seven cattlemen on the other, whereby the latter were granted the right to range their cattle on 3,117,880 acres of reservation land for a rental of two cents an acre, payable semiannually in advance. Secretary of the Interior Kirkwood had been powerless to prevent these encroachments, since he had received only the nominal support of the War Department. Now his successor, Henry M. Teller, adopted a new policy. He would not lend official sanction to lease agreements but he would interpose no objection to them if the Indians did not, for he considered the cattlemen as only "temporary occupants." Nor did he see any reason why herds should not be allowed to graze the Oklahoma district so long as their owners did not make permanent improvements. Such arrangements, of course, were certain to cause trouble, for cattlemen and Indians not parties to these agreements would offer opposition.

There was still another Indian Territory area in which many cattlemen ranged their herds by 1883. During the 1870's Kansans had allowed their cattle to drift over the free range and into the Cherokee Strip. This region was a vast sea of grass, greater than the state of Massachusetts, and visited only occasionally by its owners, the Cherokees. So many ranchers were within the region by 1879 that a Cherokee agent rode out to collect "grazier" fees. He met with considerable success and presently established an office at Caldwell where he could keep a watchful eye on the cowmen.

The cowmen profited greatly from this arrangement and felt sufficiently secure in their rights to erect fences and construct ranchhouses and stock pens. In 1880 they effected a loose association at Caldwell to safeguard their rights and to make roundup regulations; three years later they entered a more formal organization, known as the Cherokee Strip Live Stock Association. In the summer of 1883 two members of the Association, Charles

Eldred and Major Andrew Drumm, went to Tahlequah, the Cherokee capital, and lobbied a lease bill through the council, probably bribing legislature members in doing so. Soon they were back in Caldwell with a five-year lease of the Strip for an annual rental of a hundred thousand dollars, to be paid semi-annually in advance. The Department of the Interior recognized such an agreement, for the Cherokees yet had control of the Strip under a provision of their treaty with the government in 1866. With this advantage, the cowmen now fenced their properties, built ranchhouses and stock pens, and settled down to permanent occupation. But they were closely watched by the envious Boomers, who looked upon all such agreements as rank discriminations against them. There is no doubt that this unjust favoritism shown the cattlemen created much sympathy among border settlers for the Boomer cause.

Thus by 1883 the lines of factions warring for the control of Oklahoma were sharply drawn. The railroads with charters from Congress backed the Boomers, for they could reap the full benefits of projecting lines across the Indian Territory only when the region was settled. But both the cowman and the Indian saw that this would mean the end of their mutually satisfactory contracts. Once the government permitted the Boomers to settle within the country, the large ranches would be broken up into 160-acre farms and the grasslands plowed under. Neither group of contestants observed the niceties of ethics in advancing its cause. Money was spent lavishly, powerful lobbies were established in Washington, and the best of legal talent was procured to take every advantage of the law.

In a sense, the Indians and cattlemen were supported by the federal government, for Indian Bureau officials insisted on observing the letter of the law in protecting Indian rights. Troops were thrown into the field against the Boomers, but, as has been noticed, the performance of their tasks was difficult. Cavalry patrols combed Oklahoma weekly and fortnightly, and camps were established well within the zone of occupation, but Boomer parties of ones and twos eluded the patrols and hid here and there. Often these remained long enough to stake choice claims; and, occasionally, when they had returned to Kansas, they engaged in heated controversies others who had already staked these claims. Finally, Payne was forced to take a hand. This was not a disagreeable task, for it afforded the resourceful captain an opportunity to give legitimacy to his organized movement. He announced through the *War Chief* shortly after his winter invasion that those going to Oklahoma to seek claims must be accompanied by the Colony surveyor so that no one would claim property already staked. Over and over he stressed the point that under the Pre-emption Law Boomer claims thus established would be valid once the country was opened to settlement.

There is little doubt that this repeated assertion gave force and drive to the Boomer Movement. How else could one explain the fact that poor Oklahoma claimants had repeatedly made donations to the Boomer cause even to the point of sacrificing family needs? They realized that their expenditure of time, labor, and money could only be fruitful if and when Oklahoma was opened to settlement. This, of course, was a desperate gamble, an economic cow which Payne milked dry from year to year. Always there was need for money—to pay a Washington agent's expenses, to employ attorneys, or to launch a newspaper.

During the stressful spring of 1883, the *Oklahoma War Chief* was a large factor in preventing Colony disintegration. But Payne's official organ was almost as migratory as the cause it represented. It was published at Wichita from January 12 to March 9, 1883; at Geuda Springs from March 23 to July 19, 1883 (and on August 30, 1884); at Rock Falls, within the Cherokee Strip, from April 26 to May 3, 1884. Then it was brought back to Arkansas City, where one issue was published on May 10, 1884, and others from February 3 to June 11 in the next year. It was at South Haven from October 23 to December 4, 1884; and finally at Caldwell from June 18, 1885, to August 12, 1886. Although Payne generally shaped editorial policies and was in a real sense managing editor, another generally bore the title. For example, A. W. Harris was listed as the first editor, at Wichita; then William Gordon's name was carried by the issue of April 26, 1884 (Vol. I, No. 27); and finally, Gordon and J. B. Cooper were coeditors at Rock Falls.

Had it not been for the cohesive influence of the *Oklahoma War Chief*, the Boomer Movement might have disintegrated because of dissension. In the summer of 1882, while Payne was in Topeka conferring with his lawyers concerning his suit against Lincoln and Pope, a rump assembly of twelve Boomers had elected Osburn as secretary of the Colony and Nugent as treasurer. Payne was surprised and somewhat suspicious of this coup when he returned to Wichita, but he tentatively agreed to accept the results of the election until a full meeting could pass on the matter. Then, at the Arkansas City winter camp, the same faction sought Nugent's confirmation as treasurer over Payne's opposition, but the move was defeated. By this time factionalism was in the open and there was even talk of supplanting Dave as leader, but he managed to weather the storm. After a start was made for Oklahoma, dissension continued to stalk the Boomer trail like a grim specter. It rent the Colony ranks at Camp Alice, as has already been noticed.

When Payne returned to Wichita, he was bitterly disappointed because of Colony disaffection and called a meeting of the Boomers on February 27. The minutes of the occasion are quite clear as to what followed. As usual, Payne addressed those present. He angrily complained of being mistreated by certain disgruntled members of the Colony while on the last trip, and said that he would no longer do business with them. Also, he hinted broadly that the Colony must make a choice as to whom it would have as leader. The secretary closed his record of the meeting by saying that it was whispered about town that those who opposed Payne planned to organize a new colony.

This was indeed true, as is seen in Osburn's letter published in the *Oklahoma War Chief* of March 9, 1883. The letter attempted to justify Osburn's actions at Camp Alice and to condemn Payne's surrender. All the way to the North Canadian, ran the accusation, the Boomers had repeatedly pledged each other not to submit to arrest so long as it was possible to hold out. Payne had violated this pledge at the first opportunity and had left to others the odium of military displeasure because of opposition. Osburn said that he had steadfastly refused to forsake his "loyal friends" and had resisted four attempts at his capture, turning a deaf ear to two Boomer committees who exhausted their persuasive powers on him. He had finally surrendered "only by the consent of the brave boys" who held out with him.

But the real purpose of Osburn's letter was now revealed. He said that there was much dissatisfaction with Payne's leadership, and many could no longer follow him. It was because of this that he had decided to set up the W. H. Osburn Oklahoma Colony with an office on the south side of Douglas Avenue, next door to Freeman's Restaurant, in Wichita. He would receive into his organization all members of the Payne's Oklahoma Colony without additional charge, and he would guarantee a safe, conservative course. He would assure all members that he would not attempt an invasion of Oklahoma unless there was a large chance of success. And to assure this, he proposed to petition Congress to remove all legal barriers to settlement.

If Payne's followers were jolted by this blow, they were sent reeling by Nugent's attack. On March 29, his "Inside of the Oklahoma Boom" appeared in the *Eagle*, running in part as follows:

I will state that last May, 1882, while at Hunnewell, Cap came to me and said: "Nugent, there are parties here who want to buy me out, and there are but two men I can trust, you and Berry Eastus, and as Berry is not here, I will fetch them to you and introduce them, and tell them to talk to you about it. And you tell them that Capt. Payne will not trouble them providing they will pay two hundred and sixty thousand, but no less. Now I want you to do this for me, for I won't dare to sell to them myself."

I said, "No, Cap; for if the Colony was to find it out, they would hang you sure."

"Well," said Cap, "you catch my meaning."

I then said, "Cap, what are you going to do with the parties that have suffered, worked, spent their time and money as much as you have?"

"Oh," said Payne, "I can easily satisfy them, but I shan't be seen for a few days."

Nugent said that he had reported Payne's action to a Colony assembly, at which time "Cap" had acknowledged it. So he had naturally supposed that Payne had sold out on the last invasion. He blamed himself for not having told of the plot before, but he had held off because he felt that Payne might prove true when he was responsible for the five hundred or more who went with him. This had not been true. Now, however, he felt compelled to speak. He said Payne had often attracted colonists by his "We are going to stay this time for sure," but that it was only to get their money. Then there were "other things" which the people of Wichita knew: "The money he gets for a certificate he most always spends in the saloons. He has lived with an unmarried woman here for years, who has a boy nine or ten years old. . . . It has been said to me . . . he certainly is the best educated dead beat in the State."

The verbal war between the rival factions had now reached its climax. The Augusta *Advance* championed Payne, claiming that Nugent was not worthy of belief and that he had "been kicked out of the Oklahoma organization." But the *Eagle* tartly replied that the *Advance* editor was either "excessively impressible or very cheeky," for if he stood as well in Augusta as Nugent did in Wichita he would not "be running a patent newspaper long." The Caldwell *Commercial* also came to Nugent's support by saying that he was "a plain, honest man, who had told in a plain honest way, the true inwardness of Payne's operations."

Payne, too, replied to Nugent. On April 13 he wrote (almost incoherently) to the editor of the *Eagle:* "I have never paid attention to say nothing geting down low enough to answer any of vile lying stuff that has been thrown at me since I comenced my work to open Oklahoma to settlement and would not now only for the fact that you Editorialy Endorse this scandal thrown at me or at any rate say that one of the men writing or flinging scandal the old Broken Down and Broken Up Bloated Up Drunkard E. H. Nugent is an honest and truthful man." If he were honest, Dave continued, why had he given countenance to the scheme? As to being in debt, Nugent was similarly obligated. Eight members of the Nugent family held certificates of membership in his Payne's Oklahoma Colony, he charged, and Nugent himself held five thousand dollars of Colony stock he had never paid for. "But I am wasting too much time on the old Broken Up Broken Down Bloated Up disapointed old Scandal Monger," he concluded. "I will not deal in Slander and Scandal to answer that part of his letter. But just very, very mildly hint to him that stones should not be thrown from very delicately Constructed Glass Houses."

Payne evidently expected the editor of the *Eagle* to publish his letter, but it was withheld. Then he wrote the editor a brief note, signed "Assassinated," in which he complained that he was denied the very means of defense his assassin had used in attacking him. The *Oklahoma War Chief*, of May 17, however, ran the first letter, but it was now toned down in spirit. In it Payne made the additional point that Nugent had been motivated in his attack by anger because of his defeat for the Oklahoma governorship. He said that petitions by colonists, proposing Nugent as governor, were to be sent to E. C. Boudinot in Washington, endorsed by Sedgwick County officers and the *Eagle*. Then certain members of Congress were to approve them, after which they were to be presented to "Hon. Thomas Ryan who would be sure to secure the appointment at once." This, of course, was to be in the event that Oklahoma was opened to settlement.

Never did Payne's versatility show to better advantage than during this turbulent period. Osburn's and Nugent's criticisms undoubtedly caused many Boomers to desert the Colony, but they did not daunt the Boomer leader. In March he announced the removal of his headquarters from Wichita to Geuda Springs, obviously because of growing Wichita opposition. The new "capital," he believed, was one of the natural wonders of America because of its springs, widely known for their mineral-bearing waters of great medicinal value.

On May 17 he made a lengthy announcement stating that a new start for the "land of promise" would be made on June 25 and expressing the hope that the Boomers might be able to celebrate the coming Fourth of July with a barbecue on the banks of the North Canadian. But for some unknown reason (perhaps the recurrence of Payne's "old army complaint") the start was postponed, and instead the Fourth was celebrated at Geuda Springs. Payne arose from a sickbed to address the celebrants. As of old, he assured them that Oklahoma was a part of the public domain, that the government would soon be defeated in its effort to keep settlers out, and that presently all those who joined the Boomers would be rewarded with as fine lands as could be found on the American continent.

A few days later he was in Kansas City to reorganize Waldren's defunct "Colony," and wrote back to Secretary A. B. Calvert: "Send me a few of them location certificates. . . . All looks well here. . . . If you can manage to do it, have one thousand or two thousand certificates of membership printed."

Then Payne went to Topeka to confer with his attorneys, Wood, Waters, and Ensminger, in regard to his proposed injunction against Secretary Lincoln and General Pope. So he asked J. B. Cooper and his new understudy, W. L. Couch, to look after the collecting of a five-hundred-dollar defense fund for his lawyers and to organize branch colonies and attend to other routine matters. In this work Couch proved more than an understudy; he was conspicuously successful. He was energetic, a convincing speaker, an earnest worker, and logical in argument. The *War Chief* enthusiastically backed him with Payne's and Harris's editorials and with supporting articles from others. The Geuda Springs headquarters also sent out numerous handbills and here and there put up large posters, keeping alive Boomer claims.

One can well believe that a resurrection of a purported silver discovery in the Wichita Mountains was a part of Payne's new strategy, for a similar boom had been successfully launched in 1882. In this instance, E. A. Reiman, an ardent Payne follower and a former Texas surveyor, had made the "lucky find." He reported that a short time before, while he and a party of surveyors had been working in the canyons and "breaks" north of the Pease River, near the Medicine Mounds, Texas, they had found large copper nuggets. They had then made more careful examination of the vicinity and had found an abandoned copper mine, above the entrance of which was fixed this legend, scrawled on a board: "Mercia Costello, San Antonio, A.D. 1847." They now concluded that the mineral-bearing structure extended to the Wichita Mountains farther north, and so had traveled to them. As they had calculated, wrote Reiman, in these mountains they found a rich vein of silver. Eagerly they prepared to sink a shaft to begin mining, when much to their disappointment Cheyenne warriors appeared and forced them to desist. This story was given wide circulation and undoubtedly had much to do with the rapid growth of the Oklahoma movement.

But one is less able to explain Payne's purpose in his proposal to the Absentee Shawnees. On July 3, 1883, Jacob V. Carter, agent of the Sac and Fox reservation, wrote Commissioner Price that Payne had interfered with the government's efforts to persuade these Indians to return to their former reservation. He said that Payne had proposed that the Absentee Shawnees allow the Boomers to settle among them there along the banks of the North Canadian. If they would do this the Boomers would protect them and would be good neighbors, and each Indian and white man could occupy 160 acres. But if the Indians returned to their old reservation, each would be allowed only half that amount of land. Carter felt that Payne's action was ground for a successful lawsuit against him if the government chose to press it. But his recommendation was ignored by the Attorney General.

Perhaps Attorney General Benjamin Harris Brewster was more interested in the pending suit against Secretary Lincoln and General Pope. Payne's attorneys were energetically pressing their case. And at the same time Payne was sending out repeated appeals to his followers to go the limit in raising the defense fund. He wanted the injunction to be based on the proposition that Oklahoma was a part of the public domain, for this would mean that if the decision of the court was in his favor the country would be open to settlement. In fact, Wood made such a proposal to Hallowell, stating that if he would agree, the Boomers would accept the court's decision as final. If it went against them, they would disband, pull stakes, and go home; if it were favorable, they would occupy Oklahoma. Official records do not reveal why Hallowell refused Wood's proposal, but it is probable that it did not meet with Brewster's approval. Finally the case was brought before Judge McCrary, of Keokuk, Iowa, and the injunction was denied, the judge refusing to allow agents of the federal government to be hauled before its own court for the faithful performance of their duties!

After McCrary's ruling, Hallowell turned the tables on Payne. On September 12, Payne, Cooper, Calvert, and A. W. Haynes, as officers of the Colony, were arrested on a charge of conspiracy to violate the laws of the United States by their efforts to settle Oklahoma. After a preliminary hearing at Leavenworth, the case was postponed until a later term of Judge Foster's court at Topeka. So once again Boomer agents sought to raise a defense fund; but they met with some opposition. On September 20, Emporia friends warned Payne that people were opposed to "any further unwarranted raids into Oklahoma." They complained that "there has been raised a vast sum of money, and it seems your Treasurer is bankrupt, and several officers to pay." They were willing to pay a "handsome assessment" if the proper course were pursued. Why not employ as defense attorney such a man as Robert Ingersoll, Benjamin Butler, or Roscoe Conkling, instead of some unknown firm of lawyers? Here again was evidence of Boomer dissension. In November, 1884, however, the indictments were quashed.

12 : *W. L. Couch Leads the Way*

PAYNE'S indomitable will and amazing resourcefulness enabled him to weather every storm. No sort of trial, disappointment, or criticism had caused him to abandon his Oklahoma enterprise. His enemies and critics had referred to him as a "deadbeat," "loafer," "vagabond," "convicted criminal," "drunkard," "libertine," "gambler," and "notorious Boomer." But he had ignored all criticisms. It was not until Nugent had written about the purported sell-out plot that he had lost his self-possession and had become almost incoherently abusive in his reply. The breach was soon closed, however, and by the fall of 1883 both Osburn and Nugent were reconciled to Payne's leadership. Once more along the Kansas–Indian Territory line was heard the challenging cry, "On to Oklahoma"; and again Boomer wagons began to collect at Caldwell, Arkansas City, and Wichita preparatory to a new Indian Territory invasion. But Payne could not lead the new movement, for he had to attend to legal matters in Topeka; so he urged W. L. Couch, the vice-president of the Colony, to head it. Payne could have designated no abler man. Couch was sincere, convinced of the justice of his cause, determined, and honest, and he had the confidence of his fellows.

From 1880 to 1883, the Boomers had been subjected to all kinds of weather—storm, snow, sleet, rain, and warm sunshine. Now, early in August, 1883, with the start of the new invasion, the fiery sun caused the horizon line to dance in heat; and sweat-streaked teams of horses and mules pulled indifferently the heavily laden wagons, the teamsters urging them on with raucous shouts and flailing whips. From the Boomer camp near Arkansas City, the course followed by Couch's wagon train was that taken by Payne on his previous February invasion, and it was traveled without interruption until Payne's crossing of the Cimarron, near the mouth of Skeleton Creek, was reached. While the Boomers were resting here, Lieutenant Day and a detachment of the Ninth Cavalry appeared. Old offenders—Couch, Goodrich, Maidt, Burns, and Brown—were arrested and, as on previous occasions, conducted to Fort Reno. The others, or first offenders, were allowed to travel back to Kansas, after they had been warned not to return.

Day tarried in camp for some time while the surrounding country was searched for others, and allowed the Boomers many privileges. John W. McGrew wrote back to Payne: "Boys are out today, some on Deep Fork. Couch is a good commander and does all he can for the men. Mr. Slomans and the Duchman are all right, playing cards right by my side at this time." On August 22 Couch, too, wrote to Payne that he and others were prisoners on their way to Fort Reno, where they expected to remain until they could hear from Payne's injunction suit. He urged Payne to invade Oklahoma and "scatter over the country so they can't gather you." But on second thought, he felt that this might cause confusion, in that Payne's men would stake claims already awarded those who had previously entered.

Day lodged his prisoners in the Fort Reno guardhouse for several days and then conducted them back to the Kansas line. Couch later filed a complaint before District Attorney Hallowell because of a lengthy imprisonment (sections 2150 and 2151, *Revised Statutes*) and because he had been treated in "an inhuman manner." But it was ignored.

Couch was not yet through, though. In quick succession he

led two other invasions. A few days after his return to Kansas he headed a second party of thirty men back to Deep Fork, his brother, T. A. Couch, also coming along. They camped near the site of the present town of Luther, Oklahoma, and addressed themselves as before to the routine tasks of homesteading. But again the troopers came before much could be accomplished, this time under the command of Lieutenant Taylor. Eight Boomers —the two Couches, H. H. Stafford, and five others—were taken to Fort Reno, and the others were sent back to Kansas. At Fort Reno, Couch and his men were closely confined in a tent for several days but were finally sent out of the country. On this occasion, however, they were conducted southward to the Red River. They seem to have established friendly relations with their captors and to have looked upon the journey as a pleasant diversion. When they came to Texas, they procured horses and rode back over the trail with the troopers, enjoying not only their fellowship but also their bacon, beans, and hardtack!

As the combined party approached the Canadian, the Boomers left the soldiers and turned again toward Deep Fork. It is presumed, however, that they had been given permission to stay a day or two longer to complete the staking of their claims, for a short time later they again rode back to Kansas.

Couch led his third expedition into Oklahoma early in April, 1884. Evidently Boomer fears had been somewhat allayed by the consideration shown other invaders by the troopers, for this was the largest wagon train yet brought in. After they had distributed themselves along Deep Fork and the North Canadian, A. C. McCord wrote back to "friend Maidt" that the invaders numbered more than a thousand. He said that there were four camps along the North Canadian alone, the settlement extending for fifteen miles down the river. The central camp was at a spring on Section 26, Township 12, North Range 3 West, or where the Webster Junior High School building in Oklahoma City now stands. Again the Boomers were soon occupied in plowing, planting, building, and making other improvements.

"Captain" Couch's father was with this expedition also, and had selected a 160-acre claim on the north quarter section, Township 11, North Range 3 West. Since it was spring and the grass and flowers carpeted the landscape, his thoughts now turned to plowing and planting. But shortly after noon on Friday, April 24, while he was in the field, Lieutenant Day and a detachment of seven troopers approached at a gallop. "Stop that plowing!" shouted the angry officer. "You are under arrest!"

Boomer Couch resented the peremptory salutation and called back, without stopping his team, "Get off my land!" This, of course, Day did not do. Instead he commanded two of his troopers to seize Couch's mules, but as they dismounted and ran forward to do so, the plower lashed out with his blacksnake whip, causing his team to leap forward. The soldiers jumped back out of their path. Day then sent a trooper to his camp to bring up a wagon; when it arrived, accompanied by sixteen additional men, Couch was seized, bound hand and foot, and dumped into it, although he struggled fiercely.

The soldiers then started for the main Boomer camp, and when they had gone a short distance they overtook a horseman rounding up cattle. They questioned him briefly and came to the conclusion that he was a cowboy employed by a neighboring ranchman. For this reason they did not require him to accompany them. The supposed cowboy, however, was William L. Couch, the Boomer leader.

When Day and his soldiers reached the Boomer camp, the officer arrested a "Mr. McGregor," A. C. McCord, J. D. Odell, John McGrew, D. J. Greathouse, James O. Loughlan, N. T. Nix, M. W. Sawyer, and E. S. Wilcox. But none of these gave themselves up without protest, for they were thoroughly angry because of Day's treatment of M. H. Couch. Odell refused to submit to arrest and Day ordered two Negro soldiers to seize him. He struggled with his assailants but was soon overpowered, the Negroes tying his hands behind him. The teamster of Couch's wagon had aided in Odell's capture, and when he had climbed back to his wagon seat he found Couch free of his fetters. "Lawzee!" he is reported to have exclaimed, "what a powerful man, done gone and chawed these ropes off already!" The truth was that Couch had slipped a knife from his pocket while the troopers were struggling with Odell and had cut the ropes that bound him.

The next morning, as he started for Fort Reno with his prisoners, Day ordered Odell to climb into a wagon, but the stubborn Boomer refused. The now thoroughly angry officer ordered that he be tied to the wagon. So for twelve or thirteen miles without a stop he was led or dragged behind the wagon, and when a halt was made for lunch, Day still refused to allow his hands to be unbound. The Boomers were first taken to Fort Reno, and then after several days to the Kansas line near Caldwell, where they were surrendered to United States Marshals Williams and Myers, who next took them to Wichita. Here they appeared before the United States District Judge, who released them under a bond of $250 to appear on May 14. But at the later hearing their cases were dismissed.

Meanwhile William Couch, on the night following the arrest of his comrades, slipped into their camp, filled his haversack with food, and then hastened back to Kansas. Here he found awaiting him about a hundred Boomers, whom a few days later he led back to the south side of the Cimarron, at a big bend in the river opposite the mouth of Skeleton Creek. On May 7, Lieutenant Day with a detachment of twenty Negro troopers and six Indian scouts found them. At this time, as had been true on other occasions, many of the Boomers were out staking claims and hunting, but about twenty-five were in camp, building a log school-house. The soldiers approached with drawn revolvers, and Day peremptorily ordered the workmen to consider themselves under arrest. "By what authority?" asked Couch. "We are citizens of the United States and are within reach of the civil law and officers." He said he could not understand why soldiers should accost them in such a threatening manner. Day gave no direct reply. Instead, he turned to his waiting troopers and asked a part of them to seize the Boomers, the others to stand by with drawn revolvers, ready to fire!

Day, it seems, had hardly counted on the fierce resistance which the Boomers now offered. A wild scene ensued. The effort of the Negroes and Indians to carry out the order resulted in as many desperate fistfights as there were pairs of soldiers and Boomers—and the two forces were about equal. For several minutes the loud cursing of the contestants, and angry grunts and shouts as they exchanged blow for blow, caused a peaceful camp to become a battleground. Finally the settlers drove their assailants back, much to Day's chagrin and discomfiture. He now ordered his men to stand in line immediately in front of the milling Boomers, with pistols presented. One of the Boomers started for his wagon and refused to stop when Day called upon him to halt. Then excitedly the lieutenant twice ordered his men to fire, but they evidently had enough presence of mind to refuse. At this juncture, wrote Couch a few hours later, one of the settlers sought to appease the excited officer. He does not say who the "one" was, but it was probably he, since he was the leader. "Myself and companions are citizens of the United States and law-abiding men," he called. "We would not resist a legal arrest; but this attempt of yours is not in accordance with the law, nor with the Constitution of the United States, which guarantees to every citizen the security of his life, liberty and property, and safety from arrest without due process of law! We are not here to raise arms against the troops, but would you dare shoot un-armed citizens?"

Evidently this impassioned address brought Day to his senses and prevented bloodshed, for the angry Boomers were all on the point of ignoring the drawn pistols of the cavalrymen. The Boomers, too, regained their poise, saw that further resistance was useless, and surrendered. Couch said that the whole affair was not only frightful but disgraceful. Why should "a mob of negro soldiers and blanketed Indians thus attack with arms a party of peaceable unarmed citizens, cursing, and swearing that they would blow their ———— brains out." Later, Day sent those arrested back to Caldwell, where their arms were restored and they were freed.

The Boomers' experiences and observations while on their recent invasions of Oklahoma had greatly embittered them. Both the officers and Negro troopers had rendered mortal affronts by subjecting them to such treatment. Editor A. W. Harris of the *War Chief* pretty well revealed this in a news item on August 30, 1883, in which he "guessed" that Lieutenant Charles W. Taylor was one of a litter of mud turtles born of a Negro woman. John Haufbauer, of Derby, Kansas, also wrote Payne on August 31 in very much the same spirit. He was not trying to dictate, he said, but he wished to suggest that when the Boomers entered Oklahoma again they should go to stay "and not submit to any arrests or escorts whatever." And "if the soldiers bulldoses," he reasoned, "then we must bulldose, and not go out under any cir-cumstances whatever, unless our hands and feet are bound and we are carried out."

The homesteaders also felt that the federal government was deliberately favoring the cattlemen. Secretary Teller had per-mitted cowmen to range their herds in Oklahoma, and this, they felt, was rank favoritism. In Couch's Fort Reno letter to Payne, previously mentioned, he said that Williams Brothers, the Wyeth Cattle Company, the McClellan Cattle Company, Berry Brothers, and others had fenced in more than six hundred thousand acres of Oklahoma land and had made permanent improvements. Captain G. B. Russell, of Fort Reno, on May 15, 1884, supported Couch's contention in his report to the Adjutant General. He said that the fencing of land and the building of other permanent improvements by the cattlemen was a source of complaint among Payne's followers. "The complaint seems to be just," he concluded, "and it is recommended that . . . all cattlemen be warned to remove wire fences, houses, cribs, etc."

Senator Preston B. Plumb's interest in the Oklahoma country had also greatly offended the colonists. They felt that certainly he was not representing them in Washington while he was ranging cattle in Oklahoma. But on April 22, 1884, according to the *Beacon* (April 30), Plumb wrote to E. A. Reiman, of Wichita, that he then had no cattle in Oklahoma. "I haven't a dollar's worth down there and have not had for nearly two years," he maintained. Immediately the Boomer press challenged this statement. The Augusta *Gazette* retorted that Plumb might not have cattle in Oklahoma then but that he certainly had when Payne was first expelled. And the *Beacon* was even more caustic in replying that "Many men are liars, or Senator Plumb has owned cattle 'down there' within much less than a year from this date [May 14]!"

In this connection Nugent once more claimed the limelight. In May, 1884, he had visited Oklahoma and "found a few things" which he asserted he was able to prove. The first was that the stockmen had a committee appointed to make assessments for what they called a "corruption or sugar fund." The previous summer, he said, they were assessed 2½ per cent, which netted them $50,000. This was to be distributed among Indian chiefs, agents, and Washington officials, whom Nugent named. The cattlemen had set $75,000 for their new goal to protect them during the summer of 1884. But he found that many small stockmen were getting tired of "sugaring" the assessors. Peter Stewart, who had a small ranch, had informed him that he had already paid $300 and that he would contribute no more. Theodore Horsley swore that he would not pay another cent. In addition, he said that $40,000 of the current fund was yet to be raised, which was to be divided between a prominent Indian chief and government officials!

Nugent had also talked to Timothy Sullivan, who had a herd on the Cimarron, and had been told that the pocketbooks of the cattlemen were too large for the Boomers ever to get into Oklahoma. But he was sure that if a party of men should go to Oklahoma prepared, and with a fixed determination to stand their ground, they would succeed. He said that a "Mr. Lockridge" of the Peoria Cattle Company told him that he was satisfied that the Boomers had the cattlemen on the run and that he felt uneasy about it. So "all we want is men of nerve," Nugent thought. "Tell them to come on. I will wait here [Hunnewell] for them."

13 : *Payne Again in the Saddle*

AT NO TIME was Payne content to remain idle. Early in January, 1884, John S. Koller arranged a speaking tour for him, to extend as far east as St. Louis and Springfield, Missouri. In every town the colorful Boomer was heard by large, enthusiastic crowds, and many homeseekers were enrolled as colonists. While in Washington, later, Payne sought General Land Office Commissioner McFarland's opinion on the status of the Cherokee Strip; he reported upon his return to Kansas that the commissioner had ruled that the Strip had originally been given to the Cherokees as an outlet to the buffalo and salt plains and that it was no trespass for white men to go into it.

Judge McCrary's refusal to recognize the injunction against Secretary Lincoln and General Pope caused Payne bitter disappointment, but he did not propose to give up. Shortly after his visit to St. Louis he issued a call for the Boomers to assemble in Wichita. A large number of colonists attended the meeting to learn of their leader's future plans. Payne explained to them that he must go to Washington. There he could counteract the hostile influence of the "cattle ring" and Indian lobbyists. And if this were done, Congress would expel the cowmen from Oklahoma and pave the way for Boomer occupation. He also explained his "financial embarrassment," and the Boomers quickly donated a considerable sum of money for his expenses on the journey.

Dave stopped at St. Louis to follow up the work of his previous trip. The *Republican* of January 17 mentioned his arrival and stated that local Boomers were aiding him in setting up a branch colony. As usual, too, Payne exuded optimism. He assured his new friends that the government was now on the defense and that both Judge Parker and Judge McCrary in their court rulings had cleverly dodged the real issue involved. He could prove to any unbiased judge that Oklahoma was a part of the public domain and therefore subject to settlement. He also informed them that he had learned of Secretary Teller's plan to settle "niggers" in Oklahoma and thus cheat the white homeseekers!

Payne had left Wichita hurriedly and had not taken time to bid Mrs. Haines and his son good-by. But from St. Louis, on February 2, 1884, he wrote, explaining to "Dear Annie" that it hurt him to leave for Washington without seeing her and telling how much he was concerned about "little George," whom he had heard was ill. Still, he reasoned, he felt sure that Anna would have telegraphed him if George were not getting along all right. In leaving hurriedly, he had forgotten a very important file of memoranda, which he wanted her to send him. (It was probably the affidavits of those who had firsthand information about the cruelty of military officers and the malpractices of the cattlemen.) In closing his letter, Payne added this postscript: "This far in 1884, I have not taken a single drink, and do not think that I will take one in the year." But he was to be sorely tempted in Washington!

Boomers throughout Kansas were jubilant over Payne's going to Washington. "Pull all of the wires," urged a Wichitan on February 4, "and do anything to get your committee to investigate the case." A few days later N. T. Nix of Emporia also wrote: "Cap, go at them and make those Cattle Lords look down their noses!"

Payne needed little encouragement, for he had every intention of "going at them." In fact, his St. Louis stopover was pri-

marily to "pull wires," and the *Republican* of March 9 revealed
satisfactory results. It commented on Payne's protracted stay in
Washington and reported that Representative O'Neill, of St.
Louis, had presented to the House of Representatives a Boomer
petition signed "numerously," asking for the appointment of a
congressional committee to investigate the several settler ex-
pulsions from Oklahoma and the attendant land problem.

Payne's presence in Washington caused quite a stir. Wash-
ingtonians, who in the past had seen him listed in newspaper
headlines as the "notorious Captain," the "Oklahoma outlaw,"
and the "border dead beat," were entirely unprepared to meet
a strikingly handsome, tall, well-groomed frontiersman who had
a pleasing smile and friendly word for everyone. Dave was as
natural a showman as his good friend Buffalo Bill, who offered
him a "handsome salary" if he would join his "Wild West"
show. But Dave was more interested in his own show.

Payne was not afraid of Washington officials. His huge
frame darkened the office doorway of more than one Congress-
man and secretary. President Chester A. Arthur gave him an
audience and assured him that he would study seriously Boomer
rights in Oklahoma. Secretary Henry M. Teller found that Dave
was not quite the "ruffian" that he had judged him to be. And
even Secretary Lincoln received him courteously and promised
that federal troops would oust Oklahoma cattlemen. But Payne
was not deceived. He well understood how a politician could
pass the buck. He did not propose to return to Kansas without
being able to show positive results from his Washington visit.
He had brought with him a formidable bundle of affidavits of
Westerners who allegedly knew of "slush funds," trooper cruel-
ties, cattle rings, and malpractices of Indian agents; and he
would not allow polite, smiling officials to sidetrack him.

Everywhere he went—on the streets, into crowded hotels,
outer offices of executive secretaries, the Capitol—he told of

Boomer grievances, in season and out of season. The Washington *Gazette* stated that an outstanding western Senator and an Indian lobbyist bolted the capital to avoid testifying before a Senate committee.

Payne was also a frequent caller on Kansas and Missouri Representatives in Congress, and was bold in pushing his claims. He challenged General W. S. Rosecrans of the House Committee on Military Affairs to allow him to come before the committee to prove three things. He would show, first, that cattlemen, together with Indian chiefs and officials, had contributed to a "corruption fund"; second, that cattlemen had fenced in extensive areas of Oklahoma and had erected thereon permanent dwellings and other improvements, while Boomers were denied the right of homesteading; and, third, that "men and parties" contributing to the corruption fund had said that ranking United States government officials in Washington were to be paid for their protection of the cattlemen! He similarly challenged four other House and Senate committees, as well as Attorney General Benjamin H. Brewster, "Bro." H. M. Teller, Commissioner Hiram Price, and Secretary Lincoln.

Rosecrans was considerably impressed by Payne's charges, and on April 5 wrote in reply: "Several members of the committee have read the letter, and one of them in my presence said that he had no doubt you could prove those facts. All I can say is that the matter may be ripened so that you can have some show." But he confessed that he was powerless to act further until he had certain recommendations from the Secretary of War.

Dave stayed in Washington so long that he was finally without funds. Then he appealed to his Kansas friends. On February 15 he telegraphed Secretary Blubaugh for money, but received no answer and concluded that he was "out of town." Two days later he wrote Koller, of St. Louis, "I am still here without money." But he assured Koller that he was yet confident of accomplishing the object of his mission. "I tell you we will win. The only thing is the want of money." Koller had recently written Dave about money he had borrowed from a "Mr. Quinn." The prodigal captain was unable to meet his obligation, but he asked Koller to assure his friend "not to be uneasy, for he shall have his money." If Quinn knew of Payne's past monetary delinquencies, however, he had good cause to worry.

Payne probably accomplished more in Washington than he realized. "His letter to Commissioner of Indian Affairs Price," admitted the *Indian Journal* of April 3, "has attracted attention. Some of the members of the Military Committee, and of the public lands committee of the House, think that Captain Payne's case is worthy of a thorough Congressional investigation." Still, Congress took no definite action. So in March, 1884, Payne started homeward, visiting first his relations in Indiana.

On March 13, 1884, he wired Mrs. Haines from Eudora, Kansas: "Speak here tonight. Osage City Saturday night. Home Monday." His return to Wichita was noisily acclaimed by Kansas Boomers. "Now," they said, "we shall have action," and action it was. On April 16, through the *Beacon*, Payne announced one result of his recent trip to Washington. He stated (with an air of withholding something) that the United States Army would not again be used to bolster up "the Indian department, Senate cattle rings, and land thieves." He did not tarry in Wichita, for his trial before Judge Foster in Topeka was to come up the following week. Accompanied by Stafford, he presently started for Topeka. When he arrived in the Kansas capital, however, the case was moved up to the June term of court in Leavenworth. Payne now hurried back to Arkansas City and on April 24 set up his headquarters there for a new Indian Territory invasion.

Boomers came into the new camp in ever-increasing numbers, so by the middle of May they were holding frequent night meetings. The editor of the Caldwell *Journal* (quoted by the

Indian Chieftain, May 29, 1884) slightingly referred to the results of these conferences as "resolving to do or die and die and do, or something of that sort," and stated that as long as the Boomers paid their assessments of $2.50 per head to "Cap," just so long would he stay with them.

As usual, military officers took every precaution to guard against Boomer intrusion into Oklahoma. Payne understood this and sought to circumvent them. While his colonists were encamped near Arkansas City, he and Stafford rode southward through broad, sweeping prairies of billowing bluestem grass. They stopped at a ford of the Chikaskia River on the Texas cattle trail, within the Cherokee Strip, about five miles below Hunnewell. Here they found and surveyed an ideal site for the Colony. The river ran about midway through the town plot, and could furnish excellent water power. Near the center of their survey were two falls, one of three and one of four feet, and a short distance above these were other falls, and rapids and a dam. The south bank of the river presented a bold bluff forty feet high and gradually lessening toward the lower portion of the town plot; the north bank was a gradual ascent to the highlands, stretching away towards Kansas. The clear water of the stream flowed over a solid rock bottom. Blue and gray sandstone jutted out from the banks where the cattle trail dipped down to the water's edge, thus revealing to the delighted prospectors and surveyors the possibility of rock quarries for future building needs. The surrounding country was an undulating prairie of black and mulatto loam soil, with rich uplands for wheat and a wealth of corn land in the valley.

On this site, early in June, 1884, descended an avalanche of white-topped wagons, filled with Boomer families, household effects, plows, tools, lumber, and every necessity for a permanent stay. As though by magic the thriving young settlement of Rock Falls sprang up, for which the *Oklahoma War Chief* of June 14 had words of praise. "From Arkansas City to here," Editor Harris wrote, "ground is being plowed, some minor crops growing, claims being staked, everything denoting the influx of the irrepressible pale face, who will soon give to this garden spot of the earth the impress of his enterprise and industry. . . . The town site covers two sections, with liberal avenues, the main street being 100 feet wide."

Dave moved among his followers "like a tired General," having cheering words for those fearing troop intervention, directing the work of staking claims, helping to locate other townsites, and organizing other invading parties. And like a flood breaking through a crevice, ever widening, the Boomers poured over the Kansas boundary to occupy the surrounding prairies, hills, and valleys. Payne, Stafford, and others, all old-timers who had shared the privations, dangers, and sacrifices of previous expeditions, located five or six other townsites selected and surveyed in Oklahoma (of which Payne claimed that the Strip was a part), waiting the hammer's and trowel's music to wake up this sleeping garden.

Like a prairie fire Boomer enthusiasm swept beyond the bounds of Kansas. Colonists numbering more than two thousand had launched a movement at St. Joseph, Missouri, to colonize the old Boomer grounds of the Cimarron and Canadian rivers; and still others from Missouri, Iowa, Illinois, Indiana, Kentucky, Ohio, and from the Atlantic seaboard states of Virginia, Maryland, and New York, wrote letters of inquiry to Boomer headquarters at Arkansas City.

At Rock Falls, meanwhile, the Boomers were as busy as beavers. Some began plowing and planting; some with picks and shovels built dugouts, and carpenters started the erection of a building to house the *War Chief*. Every day witnessed the arrival of new recruits, who, by the end of June, had increased the Rock Falls settlement to more than fifteen hundred people.

Green prairies, splashed profusely with fields of yellow, red, and blue flowers, were nature's joyous welcome; and a blue sky-dome, flecked with lazy cumulus clouds, smiled an assent.

But all was not harmony and good will, for on the hills to the north there appeared blue-coated mounted troopers. They had come from Colonel Edward Hatch's camp near Caldwell. They were merely on patrol and did not molest the watchful Boomers. Then they rode away, and a few hours later reported to Hatch what they had seen. The colonel was quite alarmed and decided to visit Rock Falls in person. Later, in reporting to his superiors, he said that he found Payne "disposing of claims at from $5.00 to $10.00," and that on some days the sale had amounted to twenty-five. And most alarming, he found that colonists had staked from six to ten thousand claims. Even absent Colony members were regularly assessed! Hatch was also concerned because of the hostile tone of the border editors, who counseled armed resistance to removal; he had heard, too, that the Boomers were well armed. He said that he could take no action against the colonists until he had sufficient reinforcements to comb the entire country, for settlers were widely distributed, and he urged that additional cavalry be promptly sent.

Colonel Hatch could have found border editors not friendly to the Boomer cause, had he searched long enough. The editors of the Caldwell *Commercial*, the Wichita *Eagle*, and others had repeatedly denounced the Boomer leaders and their movement. On July 5, the *Cheyenne Transporter* quoted the *Eagle* on a Boomer meeting in Wichita. "The chief speaker of the evening, as a matter of course," ran the news item, "was the aforesaid captain [Payne] and his harangue was thoroughly characteristic of the man—inconsistencies, bad grammar, blackguardisms, and profanity being its main features. After the speakers had relieved themselves of a fair amount of personal venom, the crowd dispersed, little, if any, more enlightened on Oklahoma matters."

The flood tide of Boomer enthusiasm found free rein in a Fourth-of-July celebration at Rock Falls. The *Oklahoma War Chief* of July 3 advertised, "Grand Celebration at Rock Falls, on the coming Fourth of July. Come Everybody! Bring your Baskets! Come for Fun! Come as Patriots! Come to see the Beautiful Country!" Then on July 4 the *Chief* carried an assortment of news and quips such as these: "Go to Eckert's for ice cream"—"Postage Stamps on sale at Smith and Wilson's drugstore"—"Ye editor-in-chief is in possession of a new straw hat, and it's a daisy too"—"During the past week there has been erected in this city some very nice buildings"—"Call for mail at Smith and Wilson's drugstore, and leave all mail there going out"—"Rock Falls mail arrives at 3 P.M. Thus far it has been run at the expense of our citizens"—"For real luxury go to Eckert's, sit under the trees and grape vines (a natural grove and arbor) and spend one of these moonlight evenings eating ice-cream."

Colony meetings were now frequent, Boomer songs were sung, and exuberance was unbounded. On July 28 Payne was re-elected president of the Colony by acclamation, since he had "a patent on this movement that combined forces in opposition cannot strangle or cover up." W. L. Couch was named vice-president, because he had "a cool head" and was "worthy and competent." N. T. Nix, of Emporia, was elected treasurer, because no one could "doubt his integrity." Then, in order, J. W. ("Johnnie") McGrew, "from the Hoosier State and responsible," was made secretary, and Harry Stafford, "the best surveyor south of the Mason Dixon line," was elected Colony surveyor.

Never were the troopers busier in patrolling the border, rounding up small parties of Boomers who had come into Oklahoma by twos and threes, and turning back large wagon trains. Extensive Boomer activity on every hand brought to federal officials bitter complaints from Indians, and Agent John Q. Tufts,

H. H. STAFFORD   G. F. GOODRICH   A. P. LEWIS

A. C. MCCORD   DAVID L. PAYNE   W. L. COUCH   JOE PUGSLEY

Captain Payne and His Lieutenants, 1884

of the Union Agency (for the Cherokees, Creeks, Choctaws, Chickasaws, and Seminoles) at Muskogee, sent Connell Rogers out to the Strip to investigate. Rogers arrived at Caldwell on the evening of July 25 and made hurried inquiry, and what he learned caused him to visit Rock Falls to confer with Boomer leaders. This Rogers did in company with P. N. Blackstone, but he accomplished nothing. He urged Payne and his followers to abandon the idea of occupying the Strip, since it was Indian land and not government land. But Payne replied that he proposed to remain until a federal court had settled the matter. When Rogers left Rock Falls he hurried to Colonel Edward Hatch's camp eleven miles away on the Chikaskia to ask for the expulsion of the Boomers.

14 : Thirty-two Days of Suffering

*T*HE BOOMER INVASION of the Cherokee Strip caused great excitement among the Indians, cattlemen, and Oklahoma military officers. In June, 1884, Colonel Edward Hatch, in command of the Ninth Cavalry, moved to the Chikaskia, within eleven miles of Rock Falls, and established his camp. He presently reported to the Adjutant General that settlers had fairly well occupied the region south of the Kansas line to a depth of forty-five miles, and on a front of about the same distance. Connell Rogers came to this camp shortly after his conference with the Boomers, and urged Hatch to expel the Boomers while there was still time. They were coming in ever-increasing numbers, he warned, and Rock Falls and Staffordsville, only a few miles away, promised to become populous towns. Hatch told Rogers that he was anxious to move against the settlers but that he must wait for orders from his superior at Fort Leavenworth.

It was not until Tuesday, August 5, 1884, that Hatch received a wire, "Remove intruders from Indian country under the direction of the Indian Agent." Before carrying out the order, however, he rode over to Rock Falls with a fellow officer, Lieutenant W. L. Finley, acting assistant adjutant general, District of Oklahoma, and Inspector A. R. Green, of the Department of the Interior. The three men found Dave and other Boomer leaders in the office of the *War Chief*. Without wasting words Hatch read them his orders, bluntly warning them that he meant business. The Strip was not a part of the public domain, he declared, and the settlers were intruders without any rights.

Payne listened with mounting anger. For several days past he had been drinking heavily, and he was far from prepared to receive these blunt words. Memories of past rebuffs by the soldiers and of the government's open favoritism to cattlemen seemed to flood his soul and sear his mind. In loud, angry tones he sought to argue with Hatch on the legal aspects of the Strip land problem. He said that upon his recent visit to Washington, Commissioner McFarland had advised him that the Strip was a part of the public domain and that he valued that opinion more than Hatch's, Pope's, or other military men's. Since it was a part of the public domain, he felt that under the pre-emption and homestead laws he and his Boomer friends had as much right there as did the cattlemen, and there he proposed to stay. "You had better not bring your soldiers here!" he warned the colonel.

But Hatch was obdurate. He replied calmly that he had no personal grievance against the Boomers. Indeed, he sympathized with them in their desires to acquire homesteads. He had no authority to pass on the legal aspects of the land problem; his orders were to expel intruders, and this he must do. Unless the Boomers pulled stakes and cleared out by the end of the day, he would return with his men and eject them and arrest old offenders.

Payne could no longer contain himself. Angry and abusive words burst from his lips, as he strode rapidly up and down the room, stopping occasionally to shake his finger under the imperturbable colonel's nose. He charged that all officers of the government, from the highest to the lowest, were a pack of thieves. J. B. Cooper, nominal editor of the *War Chief*, also broke in with angry "vituperations and threats." And all the while the three visitors stood tense and alert.

Soon Payne observed that Hatch was not impressed by his threats and switched his attack. He only wanted to be tried before a United States court, he said, so that the land problem could be settled once and for all. Over and over he asked for this privilege. In order to assure his visitors a case against him, he said that he would then and there sell them liquor or cigars without a license or permit. Such an offense carried a penalty of a prison sentence. "Dine with me," he angrily shouted, "and I will offer you plenty of liquor!" By this time a large crowd of grinning, approving Boomers from the tents and dugouts along the river had collected, and thus encouraged, Payne continued to lash out with verbal thrusts. Hatch finally caught Payne in a pause and ended the conference by saying that he must return to camp but that he would be back again with troops to execute his orders. According to the Geuda Springs *News* of August 14, Payne's only reply was "a torrent of abusive epithets that cannot be published."

After the visitors rode away, panic seized the Boomer camp. News of the stormy conference spread from campfire to campfire. Many settlers who had crossed the Kansas line had believed that McFarland's opinion was equal to the government's permission to occupy the Strip. Now Hatch's threat caused great unrest and confusion. Boomer leaders went from claim to claim to reassure their frightened friends, but were unsuccessful, for the latter well understood that Hatch would carry out his orders. Several campers hastily loaded their wagons and drove hurriedly toward the Kansas line, while others gathered in groups here and there and anxiously discussed their plight. Then came other exciting news. Before noon a horseman dashed into camp to announce that the "Yellow Legs" were already at work turning back settlers traveling from Kansas to the Chikaskia. So others scurried about to load their wagons, and before nightfall hardly 250 settlers were left at Rock Falls.

At 8:20 A.M. the next day (Thursday, August 6, 1884), Captain Francis Moore rode into Rock Falls with two troops (eighty-five enlisted men) of the Ninth Cavalry. With him were Connell Rogers and several cowboys who had "come along to see the fun." Moore was instructed by the Secretary of War to take orders from Rogers, who identified some of the Boomer leaders and ordered their arrest. The cowboys pointed out others whom he did not know. Women and children and first offenders, including Grant Harris, a young printer whom Payne had employed to help with the *War Chief*, were rounded up and ordered to "scoot" for the Kansas line.

Rogers' report to Agent Tufts a short time later ran: "I arrested fifty men, the women and children, I took no note of, but suppose in all there were 100 souls. With the exception of those destined to be taken to Fort Smith, I had the rest removed to the Kansas line near Hunnewell, and they were admonished under penalty of being taken to Fort Smith, not to return. A great many said that they would not, others said they would." In a roughly pencil-scrawled notebook diary Dave accused Rogers of "dictatorily giving orders," aided by cattlemen who were "hopping and telling who the men wer and pointing ones out to the Soldiers." He said that his own followers did all they could have done without being killed, and that he and five others were immediately arrested and shut up for a time in the office of the *War Chief*. Then, he said, "they commenced to work off our paper," and "with insulting words hand[ed] the paper out to cattlemen and others but refused a paper to any of our friends." Quickly and efficiently the Negro troopers addressed themselves to their tasks and presently, after the prisoners and the *War*

Chief press had been loaded in wagons, the printing office, two boardinghouses, a drugstore, a cigar store, and restaurant, and some cheap dwellings made of canvas and boards, were in flames.

In his diary Payne made no mention of his own arrest. It was alleged, however, that when the Negro troopers approached his tent, he threatened to cut the throat of the first man who attempted to arrest him. Another contemporary reported him as saying: "No damned nigger can arrest me. I will surrender to a white man, but if any of you niggers want to die just make a move in this direction." But whether he made the one statement or the other, the soldiers beat a hasty retreat in search of Lieutenant Jackson, to whom Payne finally surrendered. Then he was put under the charge of one of the offended troopers who "marched him about the camp for an hour." On August 6 a reporter of the *Indian Journal* said that Payne had been on "a drunken debauch for a week, and was too drunk last night to attend a conference of squatters after General Hatch left Rock Falls."

Payne's own account (in the *Indian Champion*, Atoka, Indian Territory) of the destruction of Rock Falls did not appear until September 6, 1884. He said that the cattlemen who accompanied the soldiers threatened to assassinate the Boomers, and that a cowboy tore down the United States flag flying from the *War Chief* building to use it for a saddle blanket, but that Captain Moore made him surrender it to a little girl, who wrapped it about her and brought it to Payne.

The Boomers arrested as old offenders were: J. B. Cooper, D. G. Greathouse, T. W. Echelberger, J. D. Ross, J. S. Clark, C. W. Holden, S. L. Mosely, and Payne. These were put in a wagon pulled by a six-mule team and guarded by soldiers until the firing of the buildings was complete, then they were started for Camp Hatch. By nightfall the last of the settlers had been

driven back across the Kansas line, and Rock Falls and Staffordsville were entirely abandoned.

Mrs. Haines and George were among those sent back across
the Kansas line. During these days of trial, Payne seemed to have
affectionate regard for Anna and George, and in letters un-
burdened his mind to them whenever the opportunity afforded.
These letters, together with diaries which he and Mosely kept,
furnish graphic details of the prisoners' grueling experiences.

Moore arrived at Camp Hatch a short time before sundown.
Payne immediately held an interview with Hatch, although the
reader will probably wonder whether he was in a better frame
of mind then than when he met the colonel at Rock Falls. He
promised that if Hatch would allow him bond, so that he could
return to Kansas to demand a hearing before the United States
District Court at Wichita, he would post fifty thousand dollars!
Certainly Payne did not have that amount. True, he had hidden
a flour sack filled with Colony money in a well when he saw
Moore approaching, the morning of the burning of Rock Falls;
but the total amount would not have exceeded two thousand dollars. Attorney Gilbert had advised Payne that under a recent
enactment of Congress this part of the Indian Territory was
placed under the jurisdiction of the Wichita court. Payne said
that he would go to Fort Smith, or any other place, however,
if he were allowed bond. But Hatch could not grant bond. He
replied that he had been ordered to send the prisoners to Fort
Smith, and to Fort Smith they must go!

The Boomers were held at Camp Hatch for three days, during which time they were visited by Anna, George, and other
Boomers. Only a few visitors were allowed to talk to them, including Gilbert, Anna, and George. Payne wrote in his diary
that Gilbert gave him "some good thought and several letters."
The "good thought" was probably an opinion that the Wichita

court had jurisdiction in the Boomer case and that he could secure Payne's release by a writ of habeas corpus. At least, such an attempt was made a short time later.

On August 11, during a violent rainstorm, Captain Gardner left Camp Hatch with his prisoners. The covered wagon in which the Boomers rode leaked badly and by the time the storm had passed they were soaked to the skin. The wagon sheet was now removed and presently the warm sun dried out the prisoners' clothing. Nevertheless, Payne suffered ill consequences. Riding in a cramped position for hours, with no exercise allowed, had brought on his old rheumatic trouble, accompanied, too, by excruciating pains in the head. All his pleading for relief, however, fell on deaf ears. Only in a few instances was the prisoners' food varied. Bacon, bread, and coffee was served, and much of the time, said Payne, it was of poor quality.

On the journey to Fort Smith, Gardner followed the road through the Nez Percé reservation to the Oto Agency, and thence to Red Rock Creek. While they were on the Oto reservation, and just as they were breaking camp on the morning of August 13, Deputy Marshal W. B. Williams for the District of Kansas served a warrant for the arrest of the Boomers. But Gardner would not recognize it. He told Williams that his orders were to take the prisoners to Fort Smith and this he must do. Mosely wrote in his diary: "I gess they was both of them Scared for both was trimbling. Williams Did Not want us aney way." Gilbert had accompanied Williams, but there was no other aid that he could render the prisoners under the circumstances, so he returned to Wichita with the marshal.

Payne now seemed to lose his courage, for the remainder of his day-by-day narrative is gloomy, as is that of Mosely. The latter wrote that Gardner feared that "P. M. Gilbert would come and Demand the Press . . . and put a gard to gard the press." He referred here to the *War Chief* press, packed in another wagon. Neither Payne nor Mosely had a high opinion of Gardner. At Baughman's ranch, Mosely said that "Bofman," Gardner, and some of the soldiers went hunting and brought in a deer and four turkeys, after which "Gardner and big Bofman drink red liker." But the prisoners were not allowed to share in either. Still later, he wrote that Jackson was a "damned Dude," and as though this were not enough, added, "that is the kind of West Point maskott he is." Payne said that Gardner was not a soldier "but a bigoted fool—full of vanity and insulting." A short time later, however, Gardner returned to his old post, leaving the prisoners in the care of Lieutenant Jackson. At Red Fork Store the new officer permitted the Boomers to purchase cabbage, apples, and other groceries, but they soon discovered that their change of masters did not materially improve their lot.

From the Oto Agency, Jackson's road led through Muskogee and Fort Gibson. The weather was sweltering hot and some of the Boomers suffered from chills and fever. At night they were forced to sleep in a small tent in front of a fire and were not allowed to come out for fresh air. When, finally, soldiers and prisoners had arrived on the banks of the Arkansas, opposite Fort Smith, all were in ill humor. Here Payne poured out his woes in letters to Anna and George. On August 19 he wrote Anna that Judge Parker would have nothing to do with the Boomers and that Jackson had recrossed to the Indian Territory side of the river for fear that Boomer sympathizers would secure a writ of habeas corpus against him, or would serve other papers. Dave said that he and his friends were closely guarded at night in two little tents and "not allowed to stick a head out and breath[e] one fresh breath of air." "Most kills me today," he grumbled. "Seems as though I can't breath[e] as I am trying to write this on my knee."

Mosely added dramatic corroboration to Payne's narrative. "Oh holy terer," he wrote. "They built a fire in front of our tents last night. My God, we could not sleep aney all night, only to lay there and die with heat. We never suffered so in our life." Mosely said that finally Payne came from the tent and told Jackson that he could shoot him if he liked, but that he would stay cooped up no longer. It was killing him by inches. Jackson then allowed all the prisoners to leave the tent and sit under a near-by tree.

On August 28 Dave wrote in a similar vein to George. "Can't stick my head out without a cock[ed] gun in my face. Never did suffer so, as many times as they have had us." He said that he had been guarded within the tent for five days and had not been allowed to be on his feet or walk any since his arrest at Rock Falls. "With a bad case of rheumatism in my legs anyhow," he complained, "and cramped up so long that my legs are almost useless to me—could hardly walk now if I had the chance." Again the prisoners were allowed to purchase food, though. They employed the Fort Gibson cook, "Frenchy" Schiller, to prepare it. Mosely said that on September 1 "we had the best meal we have had since on the road."

Next, Dave told George of an exciting camp incident. "They have tried their best to kill us all this time without doing it outright. . . . Yesterday was the first day we have been allowed to talk to anyone, not even our attorneys. Mr. Gilbert, one of them, and Mr. Cravens [representing the Associated Press], come over in the evening and we were permitted to crawl out, set outside a few moments and talk with them. Did not know before what either Gilbert or them had done. When I first seen Mr. Gilbert I called to him to come to me. [He] said they would not allow him. I said, we are in Arkansas now, come here until I shake hands with you anyhow. He ran to me and a Negro Sergt. run with cock[ed] gun, leveled it on me and yelled out, 'Payne get on that wagon again,' and I know that he wanted me to refuse so that he could shoot me. Mr. G. broke away and I of course clim[b]ed onto the wagon—about this time the lieut. found out that the civil officer would not receive us—whirled the wagon onto the boat and back to this side where we yet are." Later, he said that Gilbert was allowed to bring him many things. "I just know," Dave philosophized, "the Good Man will remember and bless him for his kin[d]ness to us prisoners."

Gilbert also brought Payne word that Wichita Boomers were planning a great reception for him when he returned to Kansas. A speaker from Chicago had been employed and many Boomers from neighboring towns invited. Yet Dave could not forget his tribulations. In closing his letter to George he said, "I must close, the sweat runs off me so that I fear it will spoil this letter."

From Fort Smith, Jackson marched his prisoners back to Fort Gibson, where they were held for several days. Then he was ordered to take them again to Fort Smith.

It was while he was in the Fort Gibson guardhouse that Payne wrote his second letter to Anna, on September 2. Gilbert had just informed him that Judge Parker had not yet made up his mind as to the proper jurisdiction of the Boomer case, but he thought that the judge would decide soon. Dave sardonically added that the soldiers would hold him anyway until it would be too late to appear before the fall term of court at Wichita. But he had cause to be thankful. He and his comrades were then held in the Fort Gibson guardhouse, in a room twenty feet wide, which gave them plenty of room to exercise their cramped legs. "I know that we will win and that victory is now near or in our grasp," he hopefully wrote. "It is ours now unless I am badly mistaken."

Payne had still another brush with Jackson. On September

7, as the prisoners were being conducted from Fort Gibson to Fort Smith by the soldiers, they came to a fine spring. The day was hot and the men had gone without water for fourteen hours. Jackson proposed to allow the horses to drink first, and when David Greathouse approached to fill his jug, the angry officer jerked him back. Payne, now furious, leaped from the wagon and rushed forward. "I am going to drink," he angrily muttered, "if a thousand bullets pass through me." Whereupon he threw himself beside the spring and began to drink thirstily. Jackson ordered his men to lead their horses over Payne's prone body; but before they could do so, the now thoroughly aroused Boomer fought them back until all his fellow prisoners had satisfied their thirst and Greathouse had filled his jug.

At last, on September 8, the Boomers were freed. The Fort Smith *Daily Tribune* reported the arrival of Jackson and his prisoners on the west bank of the river, opposite Fort Smith. Jackson then sent a trooper to inform Marshal Boles that he wished to surrender his prisoners to him. Boles, accompanied by Deputy Kell, promptly went over the river to receive them. When they were brought before Judge Parker, all the Boomers were set at liberty but were cited to appear at the next term of court. Payne, however, was promptly arrested on a charge of introducing whiskey into the Territory. His friends posted a bond of a thousand dollars and he, too, was allowed to go free. Then on Wednesday all the prisoners except Payne left Fort Smith by rail for Wichita. Payne followed the next day.

In scathing terms, the *Tribune* condemned the military for keeping the Boomers for thirty-two days under strict guard and dragging them around from one point of Indian Territory to another, when it was well known that there were no real charges against them. "If this great government had mounted Lieutenant Jackson on a trick mule," ridiculed the editor, "and encompassed his negro soldiers round about with pink dominoes, and launched out in the circus business, it could not have played the Simple Simon more completely, or pursued a course less devoid of dignity and justice."

Payne had not expected the liquor-selling charge to be lodged against him and was greatly fearful of its consequences. Forthwith he employed Attorney J. Wade McDonald, of Winfield, Kansas, to represent him. And later, on November 17, McDonald wrote to Major John F. Lyon, of Fort Gibson, adviser of the Cherokee Strip Live Stock Association, and asked if it were possible for him to secure a dismissal or nonprosecution of the whiskey case then pending at Fort Smith against Payne. If this were done, he assured Lyon, "your lands will not again be troubled in any way by the Boomers." Just how Payne could guarantee the breakup of the Boomer Movement he did not say.

There is little doubt that Payne's spirits were at a very low ebb when he returned to Wichita on September 10. Conviction on the liquor charge would certainly mean a prison sentence for him, and probably a considerable fine. His friends could raise funds for the fine, and even employ expert counsel, but they could not serve his prison sentence. Moreover, Dave was physically exhausted and ill. Terrific pains racked his body and he was intermittently prostrated with chills and fever.

Anna and George and a large throng awaited Dave at the Wichita depot, and he was so pleased that he was once more able to enjoy to its fullest his role of hero and martyr.

Meanwhile, Gilbert and other loyal friends had prepared a royal reception for him. Giant mass meetings had been staged for Wichita and Wellington, and Boomers from distant towns had been urged to attend. At Wichita, elaborate preparations had been made. A large public hall was secured to accommodate the hundreds who were expected to assemble. On the stage back of the speaker's stand was displayed a large motto, "Oklahoma Now and Forever," and at the other side of the platform was the flag which had been torn down from the *War Chief* building at Rock Falls. By eight o'clock, on the evening of September 12, the hall was thronged with an excited mass of people, all eager to see the great Boomer. W. H. Miller then came to the speaker's table and called for order; J. G. McCoy was promptly elected president, and Judge Glenn and General Eagleston, vice-presidents. Then Professor Arbuckle was introduced to sing a song, dedicated to the Boomer cause, written by William F. Gordon. Never was Arbuckle's voice so powerful and vibrant with emotion, as he sang "Give us a Home":

> We sing a song of a mighty wrong
>   Which threatens the life of the Nation;
> We're robbed by the rich, oppressed by the strong,
>   Who prostitute every high station.
> The country's life in the fearful strife
>   Is not thought of, but wholly neglected
> By those once in power, who employ every hour
>   For themselves from the time they're elected.
>
> The money and lands are clutched by foul hands,
>   Thus kept from the poor and the needy,
> While Liberty stands in fetters and bands,
>   Being outraged by officers greedy.
> The Senators come—at will they may roam
>   O'er a hundred square miles of plantation,
> While the homeless may come, be denied a small home
>   On the free public lands of the Nation.
>
> The vilest crew this world ever knew,
>   Made wealthy by bold star-route stealings,
> Flee to the West, of land take the best,
>   And are treated with tenderest feeling,

While hard working men are put in the "pen"
　　Or driven from station to station,
Denied the small farms, and by force of arms
　　Made pris'ners in the name of the Nation.

Shall these things be, while we are yet free,
　　Shall a few thus trample the many
With unholy feet, and compel them to eat
　　What is left, or go without any?
Let freemen arise, and while our flag flies
　　Let our vows be once again plighted
That we'll never rest, but with votes do our best,
　　Resolved that the wrongs shall be righted.

As the final notes of the song died away, the Boomers leaped
to their feet and literally shook the rafters of the building with
their deafening demonstrations. Then McCoy and Judge J. W.
McDonald discussed the legal aspects of the Boomer cause and
the injustices perpetrated on the homeseekers by the government
and "cattle rings." These addresses, however, were only intended to compose the setting for the speech by Payne, who
limped into the hall amidst a bedlam of shouting and cheering.

Dave was ill. He had a heavy cold, and fever and rheumatism wracked his body. McCoy presented him to the audience,
which arose as one man with noisy acclaim. Haltingly, and with
a voice trembling with emotion, Payne addressed his devoted
followers. He was disappointing in his logic and oratory, for he
was worn and tired, but what he had to say aroused the Boomers
to deep anger against a government that, at the dictates of the
cattlemen, would persecute poverty-ridden homeseekers. In terse
sentences Payne sketched his experiences from the time he was
arrested at Rock Falls until his release at Fort Smith. And before leaving the platform he warned any cowman who might be
present that the Boomers were going to return to Oklahoma to

mete out "to others some of the same medicine they had been forced to take." Attorney Cowart, of Wichita, closed the meeting by introducing resolutions roundly denouncing the government's policy and calling for a showdown on the Boomer issue.

At Wellington, too, on September 18, Payne's return was that of a conquering hero. The skating rink had been secured for an eight-o'clock engagement. Yet there were other attractions in town. The county fair was in full headway and the Union Square Comedy Company had been billed for the opera house on the same evening. But an hour before Payne was to speak the skating rink was comfortably filled and a buzz of excited conversation swept the audience. The crowd was not kept waiting. Promptly at the appointed hour the presiding officer introduced Payne to an applauding audience.

On this occasion Payne probably made the best speech of his life. Although his voice seemed fired with deep emotion, he was logical and convincing. He reminded his listeners that the Negro soldiers had destroyed the press of the *War Chief* and its building, but that the ashes of the burned houses were still smouldering and that the same had ascended to Heaven as a testimony against the vandals who had applied the torch—"a smoke that will roll on and yet open Oklahoma to its rightful owners." He was severe in condemning the army. It had been used not only to keep him out of the Territory but to keep him out of court! He said that the Constitution provided that no citizen could be deprived of his life, liberty, or property without due process of law, but that during the late raid upon the Boomers at Rock Falls the soldiers had burned their houses, burst open their trunks, opened private letters, and scattered the pictures of dead friends upon the ground! "Shall it be said," he continued bitterly, "that the Courts can give no remedy when the citizen has been deprived of his liberty, his property, and his estate seized and converted to the use of the government, simply because the President of the United States has ordered it, and his officers are in command? If such is the law of this country, it sanctions a tyranny that has no existence in the monarchies of Europe, nor in any other government which has just claims to well regulated liberty and the protection of personal rights."

When Payne had finished, his listeners broke into stormy applause. Then William F. Gordon by request read his song, which had been sung so effectively by Arbuckle at Wichita a few nights previous.

15 : "The Daylight Dawning"

*F*OLLOWING the Boomer meetings at Wichita and Wellington, Payne's Oklahoma Colony received hundreds of
members. The refusal of Lieutenant Gardner to recognize Deputy Marshal Williams's writ, and the cruel treatment accorded
the Boomer prisoners by Lieutenant Jackson while on the trip
from Camp Hatch to Fort Smith, had created great sympathy
for the Boomer cause among border people and had stimulated
Colony enlistments. To the average homesteader, here was a
clear-cut case in which arbitrary federal officers had favored
cattle kings and corporate interests at the expense of poor land
claimants. As a consequence, the fall of 1884 found Captain
David L. Payne the most popular man in southwestern Kansas
and northwestern Texas. Colony headquarters at South Haven
tacked up large lithograph posters and distributed thousands of
handbills advertising Payne's Oklahoma Colony, but Payne himself was a far greater drawing force. His oratorical power and
earnestness so impressed those who attended his Kansas meetings
that when he recounted his hardships and experiences with the
soldiers his listeners often gave way to angry imprecations and
weeping.

Payne returned to Kansas to find his secretary-treasurer generously supplied with funds as the result of the increase in Colony
membership. These funds he augmented by retrieving his flour

sack of Colony money from its cache in the well at Rock Falls. Yet his pressing needs necessitated considerable expenditures. Lawyers must be employed, traveling expenses met, and hotel bills paid. Moreover, the *War Chief* must be published and given wide circulation and posters and handbills continued. But Dave now had an undivided organization, seasoned by adversity and trial, to support him; and he felt assured that they would supply his every need.

Soon the *War Chief* had been revived at South Haven and was sending out its rallying cry; and on September 20, at the same place, an enthusiastic Colony reorganization meeting was held. Of course Dave was unanimously re-elected president, and Couch vice-president. Other officers chosen included: A. C. McCord, secretary, recorder, and treasurer; H. H. Stafford, surveyor; P. M. Gilbert, general business manager; L. Weythman, marshal; H. H. Maidt, T. W. Echelberger, Z. H. Radabaugh, W. H. Miller, William F. Gordon, members of the board of arbitration on land claims; Gilbert, Radabaugh, and Maidt, finance committee. Gordon, D. Zerger and Gilbert were named to revise the constitution of the Colony. Before the meeting was adjourned, arrangements were made to employ attorneys, and Oxford, Sumner County, Kansas, was named for the next Colony meeting, to be held October 4, 1884.

Opposition newspapers were greatly aroused by this new surge of Boomer enthusiasm. In more than one issue through September both the *Indian Chieftain* and the Wichita *Eagle* denounced Payne as an opportunist and dead beat. And the Geuda Springs *News* of October 23, 1884, likened him to Banquo's ghost, which would not down, and angrily recommended that he be put on a chain gang to crack rocks, "instead of being the drunken idol of a crowd of deluded followers." Sheridan was praised because he had ordered Colonel Hatch so to employ his troops as "to make the demagogue the object of their peculiar care."

The Boomer Movement also invaded the realm of politics. Politicians, currying public favor, took up the Oklahoma movement with avidity, some candidates proclaiming from the housetops the evils of the government's alliance with cattle rings and corporations, while others called Payne and his followers drunkards and rebels against the government. The *Oklahoma War Chief* of October 23 supported the candidacy of Judge Tipton, of Winfield, for Congress, against B. W. Perkins, a Republican, who had sought vainly the votes of the "Oklahomaites." A Democratic convention that had placed Tipton in nomination had declared: "We believe that the public lands of the government ought to be open to settlement, and that the people ought to have the right to settle upon said lands without molestation; and we denounce, in immeasurable terms, the unjust and brutal expulsion of peaceable citizens from government lands by United States soldiers in the interests of monopolies and cattle kings." This ringing declaration lined the Boomers up behind Tipton almost 100 per cent.

The *Chief* also urged the voters to examine closely the claims of John J. Ingalls, candidate for the Senate. He and Senator P. B. Plumb were thought to be enemies of the Boomer Movement. Since the next United States Senate would be called upon to study and revise the whole Indian Territory problem, the *Chief* asked its subscribers "to vote for a man for the Senate or the Legislature who you know will oppose John J. Ingalls."

Even Payne found time to take a hand in the election. In this way he could kill two birds with one stone. Not only could he help in the election of friendly legislators, but also he could get free advertising for his Colony. Under the caption, "Two Shows Under One Tent," the Geuda Springs *News* of October

23 stated that "Captain Payne and Judge Campbell spoke to a small audience in front of the Marble block, most of whom were Republicans." But, growled the editor, "Wind is a good thing and never convinces anybody." Campbell was candidate for the position of Chief Justice of the state Supreme Court. *Harper's Times* also noticed that the Oklahoma agitator was drawing larger crowds than "any of the political speakers of any party," and thought it strange that a "brazen faced fraud and sot, as Payne is well known to be, should receive so much attention." The *Times* regretted that a man who "had collected thousands of dollars for which he has given nothing in return" should be so popular. But the *Oklahoma War Chief* countered with the charge that the *Times* carried on its masthead the name of Ben S. Miller, cattleman. And thus the political war went on, while the Boomer leaders were preparing to take their case before a federal court.

During the early days of November, Payne and his Boomer friends, George F. Brown, David Blubaugh, T. W. Echelberger, M. Harris, W. L. Couch, H. H. Stafford, J. B. Cooper, John S. Koller, and P. M. Gilbert, came to Topeka and registered at the Dutton House. In September preceding these men had appeared at Wichita, at a session of the United States District Court, and had voluntarily gone before the grand jury to give evidence of their invasion of Oklahoma. This resulted in an indictment against them for conspiracy against the government as covered by Section 5440 of the *Revised Statutes* (and a subsequent amendment.) The conspiracy charge consisted of a combination between the defendants to enter upon what were known as the "Oklahoma lands" and to take possession of the same, while these lands were yet a part of the Indian Territory. This, the indictment averred, was a violation of sections 2118, 2147, and 2148 of the *Revised Statutes,* which prohibited locations or settlements on Indian lands, in the Indian country, or on lands secured by treaty with the United States to any Indian tribe. District Attorney Hallowell and J. Wade McDonald, the Boomer attorney, agreed that they would waive all technicalities in their arguments on the case and confine themselves to its essentials; namely, whether Oklahoma was a part of the public domain or still within the Indian Territory, and whether the Boomers entering therein were guilty of trespass. The case was to be decided before Judge C. G. Foster at the fall term of the district court at Topeka.

Payne now told his Boomer friends that this was the opportunity he had been seeking for several years. To Robert A. Freidrich, of Wichita, Payne expressed great hope of satisfactory results from such a hearing. "At last," Freidrich reported him as saying, "I begin to see the daylight dawning. We now have the question fairly and squarely presented to a court. I have great confidence in the fairness and good judgment of Judge Foster, and if he decides against me, I shall think I have been wrong and give it up."

Shortly after Payne and his friends had arrived at Topeka, a reporter of the *Capital* came to the Dutton House for an interview. He found Payne out at the time, but Gilbert volunteered to answer all questions. The conversation ran in part:

REPORTER: "If these cases are decided against you will the colonists give up the idea of getting possession of these lands?"

GILBERT: "No sir. [This was probably contrary to what Payne would have said.] We are determined to test the merits of this affair in every detail, and will continue to assert our right until Congress legislates upon the subject, either for or against us. About 2,000 people are now camped along the line in Kansas, and will move forward again about December 1st. We will make this move whether the courts decide against us or not."

REPORTER: "What was the result of the late ejection of 'Boomers' from the territory?"

GILBERT: "It has just made the people more determined. I was one of the 'Boomers' captured at the time. We were taken by the military in wagons from one post to another and back again to prevent us from getting a complaint into the court then in session at Wichita. As soon as court adjourned we were taken back to Wichita. This is but one instance of the abuse of justice and American citizenship in that country by Government officers."

REPORTER: "Have the military used any violent means to carry out their objects?"

GILBERT: "Very often. They went so far as to order the men to fire upon our men, but luckily no one was killed. When we go in again the Government may as well bring down a load of spades instead of guns, for they will have to bury us there. We won't ask them to board us again. The people of the colony have been camping along the line since last spring, and will continue in camp until the forward movement this winter, when they will go over the line again. One man, named Anderson, who is a 'Boomer' was allowed to remain with his family in the territory just because he had a few head of cattle. Even he has had two houses burned from over his head by orders of the military officer. . . ."

The *Capital* of November 13 also noticed that Payne had "fifteen or twenty cases" chalked up against him. "They were postponed until yesterday," continued the news item, "when four cases, charging conspiracy against the Government in attempts to settle in the Oklahoma country, were tried before Judge Foster. The balance of the cases will be subject to the decision of the Judge upon these four, which decision will be rendered during this week. The decision will virtually settle the question as to whether the Oklahoma country belongs exclusively to the Indians or not."

This summed up the situation well. The Boomers realized that they had approached a supreme crisis, and were therefore nervous and anxious during the court proceedings. But many other Boomers were present to lend moral support. The two attorneys presented their cases well, each arguing learnedly and citing other decisions bearing on the Indian land problem. Finally the arguments were in and Judge Foster took the case under advisement, and two or three days later announced his decision. "I am of the opinion," he said, "that the acts charged do not show a conspiracy to commit an offense against the United States within the meaning of the conspiracy clause of chapter 8, *Supplement, Revised Statutes,* and for this reason these indictments must be quashed" *(Federal Reporter,* XXII, 427). In arriving at this conclusion the judge made a distinction between an "indictable offense" that could not be prosecuted by criminal proceedings and an offense created by statute.

Judge Foster's decision was a triumph for the Boomers. On November 20 the *Oklahoma War Chief* exultantly headed a column: "GLORY! HALLELUYAH! OKLAHOMA AT LAST OPENED! FIRST DECISION OF THE COURTS, AND IT IS IN FAVOR OF THE COLONISTS! THE LONG WAR ENDED! JUDGE FOSTER'S DECISION, OKLAHOMA IS PUBLIC DOMAIN!" Seven days later the Payne's Oklahoma Colony was called into session at Arkansas City by Vice-President Couch. Payne was reported to have been stricken with "something like diptheria and was too ill to preside." Those present, however, voted to postpone a proposed invasion of Oklahoma until December 1, so that Judge Foster's decision might reach Washington. It was believed that the Secretary of War would speedily send instructions to all military officers to cease their expulsion of Boomers who entered Oklahoma, and thus abide by the new court ruling.

Already Boomers had prepared to take advantage of a decision of this sort. In October, 1884, E. H. Gilbert and a party of surveyors had slipped past the Kansas line and had again entered Oklahoma. Here they surveyed Nugent City, which was to be their new capital. Its location was on Section 31 and Section 32 of Township 12, North Range 4 West, or in the western suburban district of Oklahoma City. Then they returned to Kansas.

But just at the height of Boomer enthusiasm their cause was dealt a staggering blow. On Thursday night, November 26, Payne addressed a large assembly of jubilant Boomers in the Wellington courthouse. Those who heard him pronounced his speech the finest he had ever made. After the meeting, about 11 P.M., he told some of his intimate friends that he was very tired and wished to retire, and went to his room in the Hotel De Barnard. He slept soundly during the night and was up early the next morning, feeling greatly refreshed and in good spirits. He entered the dining room of the hotel with Anna, John Koller, and a few other friends, and ate a hearty breakfast. Then he ordered a glass of milk. While he was waiting, one of those present asked him what he thought the effect of Judge Foster's decision on the Oklahoma land problem would be. Payne started to reply, then quickly turned to Anna as though he was surprised, and slumped forward in his chair. Anna sprang to her feet, rushed to Payne's side, unbuttoned his collar, and began to rub his wrists vigorously. But it was to no avail. Payne's muscles became tense, those in his neck standing out like whipcords, and in a moment he was dead.

Great excitement now prevailed. One of those present ran to the office of Dr. W. O. Barnett, but by the time the physician arrived his services were not needed. Many of Payne's friends thought that he was poisoned, and M. Stone, of Wellington, wrote to the Topeka *Capital* on November 30 that the doctors who first examined Payne were in doubt as to his ailment. "Some [Boomers]," he said, "entertain the opinion that it was heart disease, others say it was from blood poison, by means of a slow and deadly drug." But a post-mortem examination a few hours later showed that death was caused by a blood clot forming in the orifice of the pulmonary artery.

Payne's body was allowed to lie in state in the hotel for the day, and hundreds of mourning friends came to view it. Then on Sunday following, the Reverend S. Price conducted Payne's funeral service at the Methodist Church in Wellington. The church was crowded and hundreds were compelled to remain outside for lack of room. And the funeral procession from the church to the graveyard was a mile in length, made up of members of the Grand Army of the Republic, the Wellington military guard, relations in carriages, then a long line of Colony members led by Couch, and finally local citizens. Payne's body, in a metal casket, was buried on a lot purchased by Anna.

At the time of his death, Payne was preparing to go to Fort Smith for his trial on the liquor charge, in which Connell Rogers and N. P. Blackstone were to be the government witnesses. The trip was also to be a honeymoon, for he and Anna had planned to be married. At Anna's request the Wichita *Eagle* printed an explanation of her relations with Dave. They had early formed an attachment for each other, and had deferred marrying until Oklahoma was opened for settlement so that each could acquire a 160-acre claim under the Homestead Act. An interesting corroboration of this statement is found in a Boomer claim ledger. Entries of June 2, 1884, are of Dave's and Anna's claims to the two 160-acre tracts forming the northern half of Section 29, Range 2 West (which today has its northeastern corner immediately east of the Oakhurst schoolhouse, about six miles north of Oklahoma City and on the Oklahoma City–Guthrie highway). But disappointments and delays caused them to decide to wait no longer. Anna was to accompany Dave to Fort Smith, where they were to be married.

Although the Boomers keenly felt the loss of their leader, in a way his death completed their victory. The Wichita *Beacon* of November 19, 1884, stated that "Payne dead will be a greater man than Payne living." Boomer factionalism was submerged in pungent grief. More than one editor who had previously condemned Payne now characterized him as a great leader, thereby creating a greater measure of sympathy for the Boomer cause.

The editor of the *Beacon* best appraised Payne's leadership. He stated that Payne had come to him seven or eight years before his death to advocate the opening of Oklahoma. But through the columns of the *Beacon* he made "an open fight against the movement, and publicly and privately denounced it as a scheme to rob the red man." After the Fort Smith trial, however, he came to regard the government's policy as "dishonest, tyrannical and infamous" and the cause of the Boomers worthy. "Through failure, through evil and good report," he continued, "I have stood by Payne and the Oklahoma movement. . . . For six years we have never doubted the justice of their cause. With us it was not a question of the personal character of the leader, nor of his private life or habits. We met every charge against Payne with the reply that he was the originator of the movement, and had done, and was doing, more to keep it before the people than any other man. . . . It was of little moment whether Dave was actuated by selfishness or by a pure public spirit. We knew there were too many cool-headed, long-headed men among the colonists to be hood-winked or bamboozled by Payne or any other man, and the fact that they recognized him as leader was guarantee enough to us that he was the right man to make the fight. . . . Dave Payne's faults will disappear and the future will recognize in him really great qualities. His name will be forever linked with the history of the state that is sure to be created in the country south of us. What Daniel Boone is to Kentucky, Dave Payne will be to Oklahoma."

These words were written on November 19, 1884. How prophetic they were! Dave had his faults, of which the opposition press, Indians, and cattlemen never ceased to proclaim; but he also had his merits. He was indefatigable, unselfish, determined, perennially optimistic, and active. After each hard experience his buoyant spirit rebounded to give new force and drive to his cause. Regardless of whether he was employed by railroads or other selfish interests, he could not have been paid for his untold suffering, exposure, and disappointments. If he took in large sums of money from needy homesteaders, he just as readily expended the entire amount on the cause he loved; and he died, as he had lived, without funds. The government at Washington regarded the Boomer Movement as an outlaw movement, and so generally the nation frowned upon it. Only a leader with a sufficient love for a cause to ignore official and popular frowns and to drive forward toward a seemingly hopeless goal could measure up to Boomer demands. And that man was David Lewis Payne!

16 : *The Last Oklahoma Raids*

*T*HE DEATH OF PAYNE does not quite conclude our story, for his dynamic personality carried on to final victory. Others might hold aloft the Oklahoma banner, but it was his spirit that yet led the way. It was indeed in this frame of mind that Couch, Goodrich, and others lifted Colony responsibilities from their dead chief's shoulders and bore them onward proudly.

At a mass meeting of the Oklahoma Colony shortly after Payne's death, Couch was elected president. The new leader had been one of Payne's most trusted friends and advisers as well as vice-president of the Colony. Physically, he did not have the commanding personality of his predecessor. He was medium in height, had pleasing blue eyes, and generally wore a long beard. He was congenial, spoke with authority, and was uncompromising. In past crises he had demonstrated a rare presence of mind; and in Colony matters, he was conservative, intelligent, and persistent. After joining the Boomer Movement he had studied assiduously all treaties, laws, and court decisions bearing on the Oklahoma land problem, and could present Boomer claims concisely and logically.

Couch lost no time in assuming leadership, even though he knew that trouble and hardship were ahead. In fact, on December 8, 1884, he again left the Kansas line at the head of three hundred Boomers bound for Oklahoma, his wagons extended along the trail making a picturesque spectacle. Four days later the invaders reached Boomer Creek, near the present site of Stillwater, and immediately set to work to prepare winter quarters. They did not propose to suffer from exposure. Dugouts were constructed, tents were stretched over wooden frames, and covered wagon boxes were removed from the running gear, placed on the ground, and banked about with earth.

The Boomers who accompanied Couch were a sober lot. They had resolved to defend their rights by force, if need be, and had come heavily armed; they had studied at least the rudiments of military maneuver and before long had dug an entrenchment about their camp. Gilbert's threat made to the *Commonwealth* reporter while he was in Topeka attending the federal court was no idle boast. Couch and other conservatives in camp hoped that the military would not challenge them, but if it did, they did not intend to withdraw.

A severe test of this resolve was not long delayed. Hardly had they crossed the Kansas line before a cavalry scout had spotted them and ridden to Hatch's Chikaskia camp with the news. Hatch had wired the Adjutant General, who in turn notified President Chester A. Arthur that an armed body of men was on the march for Oklahoma. Arthur promptly issued a proclamation, re-emphasizing his predecessor's policy and warning all prospective homesteaders not to intrude.

Pursuant to this new proclamation, Lieutenant M. W. Day and thirty troopers of the Ninth Cavalry came to the Boomers encamped on Stillwater Creek to demand their surrender. Couch had been expecting such a move and had his men on the alert, ready to resist. When he observed that the Boomers outnumbered his own men several times over, Day acted with caution. He demanded the surrender of the intruders, but Couch replied that he and his men were law-abiding American citizens and were there to establish claims under terms of the Homestead Act, in an area to which they had settler rights under Judge Foster's recent ruling. They did not court trouble, he said, but they would not surrender without a fight.

Day was wise enough not to force the issue and quietly withdrew his men to ask his superior, Colonel Hatch, for new instructions. Hatch was very much alarmed. He had been ordered to use moderation in his dealings with the invaders, for the Oklahoma issue had arrived at a critical stage. Soon he hastened to the scene of disturbance, however, with all the troops at his disposal; and later, between January 7 and 24, others joined him, so that seven companies of cavalry and one of infantry were under his command and had taken their stations before the Boomer camp.

Early Monday morning, on January 24, 1885, at the sound of the bugle, the soldiers were "at ready," with two pieces of artillery wheeled into line. Colonel Hatch then sent Captain Carroll forward to demand the surrender of the intruders. Crisply the captain executed his order, warning Couch that he must comply within five minutes or the artillery would open fire. Before leaving Fort Reno, Hatch had told the *Transporter* editor that he would not sacrifice any of his men. He intended to keep the intruders out of rifle range and to force them to surrender by training his artillery on their camp, if he were compelled to resort to such extreme measures.

But Couch was no more intimidated than he had been when confronted by Day's troopers. He told Carroll that the Boomers did not want trouble but were resolved to defend their rights. When Hatch was informed of Couch's refusal of his demand, he revealed an excellent strategy. He did not open fire, but withdrew his men a short distance northward and went into camp.

Among those who had followed Couch into Oklahoma were many hotheads. They now demanded that they be permitted to fire on the soldiers if they should again come within range. This greatly alarmed Couch. He argued with them that this would discredit the Boomer cause and would call down the full force of the army. But the radicals were hard to convince. During the day and well into the night they employed their time in making hostile preparations—casting Winchester bullets, reloading cartridges and brass shotgun shells with buckshot. Couch sought desperately to repress their hostility, but he was only partly successful and greatly feared the reappearance of the soldiers.

When daylight came next morning (January 25), Couch anxiously gazed out toward the cavalry camp. But for a time all was quiet. Minutes seemed like hours. Finally the soldiers were astir, and smoke from their breakfast fires rose lazily on the still morning air.

About an hour later, several small detachments of troopers were seen hastily leaving camp, traveling east, north, and west. What did this mean? Surely Hatch had not decided to withdraw! But a short time later, Couch had an answer to his question. He could see other Boomers and his supply wagons coming across the prairies to his camp. These the soldiers met and turned back toward the Kansas line! This, then, was Hatch's plan. The soldiers would neither permit other Boomers to re-enforce those in camp nor allow the campers to receive supplies! And if they did not receive supplies, ultimately they must abandon camp and return to Kansas.

Hastily Couch made a check of his stores and found that he could hold out only five days. Then he counseled with his men. It was decided to break camp and return to Kansas, although still there were some who clamored for a fight with the soldiers. So on January 30 the disappointed settlers reloaded their wagons,

Leader W. L. Couch and His Boomer Friends

Left to right: top row; Mrs. Wilcox, Wilcox, Mrs. Haines, Couch, Brown, Ketcham;
Bottom row; "Dad" Echelberger; Mrs. Echelberger; Mrs. Ketcham, Mrs. Brown.
The names of the two children are unknown.

The Boomer Camp at Caldwell, Kansas, in the summer of 1885: W. L. Couch in the right foreground.

hitched their teams, and drove back to Arkansas City, flanked on either side by the cavalry.

After the Boomers had returned to Kansas, Couch and twelve others who had resisted arrest were apprehended and taken before the United States District Court at Wichita on a charge of treason and lodged in jail. District Attorney Hallowell planned to use Hatch and other officers of his command as witnesses. But the colonel evidently did not wish to become involved in court action, for when the court met he and his brother officers did not appear, and the cases were dismissed.

Soon thereafter Couch went to Topeka to arrange for the sending of a Colony delegation to Washington. Grover Cleveland was to be inaugurated as the first Democratic President since the Civil War, and the Boomers believed that he would favor their cause if only they could present it properly. They also were agreed that Couch was the logical man to send to Washington, for he was better informed than any one else.

A mass meeting of the Boomers, at which Couch presided, was held at Topeka on February 4. Here the Colony reorganized and all state movements of a similar sort were integrated. Then resolutions were adopted reasserting homesteader rights in Oklahoma and denouncing President Arthur for permitting the military to continue its expulsion of settlers in opposition to Judge Foster's recent ruling. A resolution was also adopted censuring an Associated Press agent at Caldwell, Kansas, for denying that cattlemen had in the past held, or were then holding, large herds of cattle, enclosed by fences, on Oklahoma lands. Such a representation was denounced as "wilfully false and calculated to mislead the public." And before adjourning, they made plans to launch a new Oklahoma invasion on March 5.

A short time later Couch journeyed to Washington. He shaved off his long beard, laid aside his rough boots, wide hat, and blue flannel shirt, and then donned as suitable apparel as that of any other well-groomed Washington visitor.

The Boomer emissary wasted no time in sightseeing and the pursuits of pleasure, but immediately sought out federal officials. Secretary of the Interior L. Q. C. Lamar was the first visited. For Couch's reception by Lamar and the purported conversation between the two, it is helpful to turn here to the columns of the *Indian Chieftain* of April 16, 1885.

"What is your wish?" asked Lamar, following his introduction to Couch.

"I want to know what course the administration has determined to pursue with reference to Oklahoma and the settlers," bluntly replied Couch.

"Well Sir," said the other, "I will state to you the policy of this administration with regard to the Oklahoma country. It considers the Oklahoma territory on which the persons you represent are preparing to make settlement as within part of the Indian Territory. The administration regards it as not a part of the public domain open to entry and settlement and acquisition of titles under the land laws of the United States. Being Indian country, this territory is acquired and reserved for Indian occupancy. The Government is pledged to the protection of it and the security of the Indians from intruders. No white persons have the right to go there and reside without a permit, and when they do go they are intruders acting illegally and wrongfully. The policy of the President is to execute the pledge of the Government and to protect the Territory from the intrusion of white persons who claim that they have a right to enter upon it and that it was public domain subject to pre-emption and homestead settlement."

"Is that the final decision?" asked Couch.

"It is and will be enforced," snapped back the secretary.

Couch also inquired what the policy of the government was toward the cattlemen who were already in Oklahoma and who had been permitted to remain there by the previous administration.

"They will not be permitted to graze their cattle within the limits of that territory," Lamar replied with emphasis. And with this statement the conference came to an end. From Couch's later comments on his Washington visit, at least this was the substance of his interview with Lamar.

The discouraged Boomer did not tarry long in the capital. But he remained long enough to find that many members of Congress were favorably impressed with Boomer demands and to learn that soon a determined effort would be made to open Oklahoma to peaceful settlement. Sidney Clark, of Kansas, and James B. Weaver, of Iowa, were reported to be acting in behalf of the Boomer cause. Couch returned to the Boomer camp south of Caldwell, Kansas, to report the results of his trip.

Couch was correct in appraising the sentiments of members of Congress, for already, on March 3, that body had passed an act directing the President to begin negotiations with the Creeks and Seminoles looking toward a clear United States title to Oklahoma, and with the Cherokees for the Strip. Nevertheless, Boomer leaders had failed to catch the full significance of such a move. They were therefore discouraged with Couch's report. Lamar's declarations had caused their dream castles to come tumbling down around their heads, and they were hardly in a position to catch at straws in their ocean of despondency. Yet it must be recognized by the readers that this was a pronounced congressional step taken in the direction of acceding to Boomer demands.

When the watchful homesteaders saw no movement of the military to remove the cattlemen from Oklahoma, they charged

Lamar with insincerity. Both through the press and from the platform they accused federal officials of accepting bribes, and voiced angry threats against any future efforts to frustrate their invasions. Editor Samuel Crocker's verbal thrusts through the columns of the *Oklahoma War Chief* were so sharp that on July 10, 1885, he was arrested on a charge of "seditious conspiracy and inciting insurrection" and was confined in the Cowley County (Kansas) jail. But after almost a month's imprisonment, he was released on bond. When on October 12 he finally appeared before the federal court at Leavenworth, the prosecuting attorney caused the charges against him to be dismissed, evidently feeling that sufficient rebuke and punishment had already been administered.

It should be stated, too, that federal officials, civil, judicial, and military, did not care to have Boomer grievances aired in court, as the federal government might well have done under the Indian Intercourse Law. They realized that a hollow victory, as in the Payne case, would bring little credit to the federal cause, and if repeated would tend to hold up the government to ridicule. Moreover, the Boomers used such occasions to accuse government officials of persecution, as a result of which other border settlers joined their ranks.

By 1885 the Boomers had become imbued with new courage and had resumed their attacks on the Oklahoma cattlemen. Throughout Kansas, and even in neighboring states, they voiced their grievances—so much so that neither state nor national legislators could ignore them.

In the early summer of 1885 a Senate subcommittee, consisting of senators Dawes, Jones, and Morgan, was sent to the Indian Territory to investigate the whole problem of Indian rights and leasing to graziers. Couch now saw an opportunity to broadcast Boomer grievances, and on June 4, 1885, he wrote to Dawes, asking that a hearing be held at Caldwell and that he be permitted to testify. He offered to prove eight points, some of which were that a number of the leases to cattlemen were secured by bribing the Indians; that government officers had both given and received bribes; that cattlemen had been permitted to hold large parts of Oklahoma while homesteaders were denied the right to establish claims there; that the army had "inflicted inhuman outrages" on American citizens in Oklahoma contrary to the plain provisions of the *Revised Statutes*.

Among the "inhuman outrages" cited by Couch was an instance in 1883 in which a citizen of Kansas was arrested (near where Camp Russell on the Cimarron then stood), kept a prisoner ten days, then tied by troopers and dragged behind a wagon for several miles in the presence of his wife and family. His wife was so shocked with fright by this violence to her husband that she gave premature birth to a child, which resulted in her death. A year later D. J. Odell, of Duchess County, New York, was treated in the same manner by Lieutenant Stevens, being dragged a distance of about thirteen miles. Then there were other species of indignities alleged. In 1883 H. H. Stafford, W. L. Couch, M. Q. Couch, and five others were arrested in Oklahoma and taken to Fort Reno, imprisoned and "treated with great inhumanity," and finally taken to and discharged in the middle of the Red River without any charges having been preferred against them. And in 1884, John S. Wilson, Morgan Bush, Charles E. Streeter, and W. L. Couch were arrested in Oklahoma, taken to Fort Reno, jailed, and compelled to sleep on the floor for several nights without bedclothes.

Senator Dawes was evidently impressed by Couch's allegations, for two days later the subcommittee came to Caldwell and Couch was asked to appear. Couch's testimony, embraced in the questions and answers, comprises twenty-three pages of the committee's report and covers such subjects as Boomer invasions, status of the Oklahoma lands, cattlemen's leases, and bribes given and received. Senator Dawes and Morgan, conducting the hearing, were very considerate of Couch's feelings, at one point speaking of him as being "honest and intelligent." But throughout the questioning they sought to impress upon him that he had no more right in Oklahoma than thousands of other homeseekers who were patiently awaiting the action of Congress to open the country to settlement.

Next, Dawes reminded Couch of his proposal to present proof of the taking and giving of bribes in connection with cattlemen's leases. Couch replied that B. M. Campbell of the Cherokee Strip Live Stock Association had told him in Wichita that thirty-six thousand dollars had been paid the Cherokees as "corruption money" to obtain a lease on the Strip, but he said there were no other witnesses to the cattleman's story. He also stated that at the proper time he was prepared to name witnesses who would testify that officers of the government "having secured bribes have approved of leases or permits." When Senator Morgan pressed him to name the witnesses, then and there, Couch mentioned David Greathouse, of Grenola, Kansas; "Mr. Windsor," of the firm of Windsor Brothers, of Wichita, Kansas; Jacob Carter, of Garden City, Kansas, who at one time was agent of the Sac and Fox Agency; Frank Hudson, of Arkansas City, Kansas; and Dickey Brothers, of the Indian Territory.

Couch also testified as to the location of ranches within Oklahoma, in some instances naming the acreage or number of cattle ranged. Among those involved were the Wyatt Cattle Company, the main grazing range of which was in the Cherokee Strip but reached into Oklahoma between the Cimarron River and the Strip; the McClellan Cattle Company, occupying 100,000 acres of Oklahoma east of the Wyatt Company's range and north of the Cimarron; the Berry Brothers, who had 100,000 acres north of the Cimarron and adjacent to McClellan's; the Fitzgerald Brothers, located south of the McClellan range and the Cimarron; the Burt and Martin ranch, about 10,000 acres between the Cimarron and the McClellan range; a "Mr. Ewing," who was located farther west, supporting a small herd of 2,000 or 3,000 cattle; A. J. S. Anderson, who ranged a small herd on Deer Creek; a "Mr. Gilbert," of Caldwell, who had a small herd adjacent to Anderson's; the Belle Plaine Cattle Company, on Deep Fork; a "Mr. Roberts," occupying a large tract south of the Cimarron with 3,000 or 4,000 cattle; and, finally, Butler Brothers, on the North Canadian.

After the Senate committee departed from Caldwell, many Boomers decided to return to their homes and await the action of Congress. But others held on. They had spent all their resources on the invasion cause and felt that only by persistent effort could they win final success. When fall came, however, and still Congress had delayed remedial legislation, they became restless and disgruntled. Couch saw that something must be done to satisfy them or their disaffection would spread to others and thus cause the complete disintegration of the movement. So he planned a new invasion.

On October 22, 1885, the Boomers broke camp on Bluff Creek and started southward. In addition to the usual wagon train, several of the invaders rode horses; these included W. L. Couch, Abe Couch, Joe Couch, Joe Blackburn, Dr. Ross, Arch Stinson, William Renfrow, Isaac Renfrow, and Samuel Crocker. The invaders followed the old Chisholm Trail to the Cimarron crossing and then turned toward the southeast until they arrived, on the afternoon of October 28, at the military crossing on Deep Fork, where they encamped for the night. Next day the journey was resumed. They traveled southward for four miles to Round Grove (the present site of Stiles Park, in Oklahoma City). Here, between a large grove of oak trees and a fine spring (now on the campus of the Webster Junior High School), a permanent camp was set up, which Couch would ultimately make the capital of the future state of Oklahoma. What a beautiful panorama stretched out before him! In the distance rose the oak-crested hill upon which Payne had proposed to establish his "New Philadelphia," and in between was the sharply curving North Canadian, its banks lined with tall, stately trees. Then to the north could be seen Deep Fork, meandering eastward as though it were playing hide-and-seek with the Cross Timbers. From the main camp, avenues could be projected toward every point of the compass, thus laying the foundation for a city not greatly unlike the federal capital at Washington.

But Couch did not spend his time in daydreaming. The Colony surveyor, with helpers, was sent out to mark the streets and avenues and to run the lines of the surrounding settler claims. William Echelberger seemed to believe that at last the Boomers would be left in peace, for he opened a general provision store.

Once more the home-building activities of the intruders were rudely interrupted. Lieutenant James presently showed up with a considerable force of troopers, placed all the Boomers under arrest, and took them to Fort Reno. But they were held here only a short time and then conducted to the Kansas line and dismissed.

17 : "Harrison's Hoss Race"

THAT the darkest hour is just before dawn certainly proved true of the Boomer Movement during its nadir of 1885. Payne was dead; Couch, Goodrich, and other leaders were under charges of treason; cattlemen were still in Oklahoma; and several hundred Boomers had broken camp and gone home, disappointed and penniless. Many of the latter urged that no further invasion attempts be made and that the action of Congress be awaited. The low tide was reached when in the midsummer of 1885 the Boomers met at Caldwell and adopted a resolution asking the government to drop all charges against their leaders on condition that they would disband. Their attorney, J. Wade McDonald, was instructed to make such a proposal to Secretary of the Interior L. Q. C. Lamar. On August 11 of the same year, Lamar transmitted their request to the Attorney General with his endorsement, and a short time later the treason cases were dismissed.

Then came the dawn. Military officers patrolling Oklahoma began to round up and expel the cattlemen and to destroy their fences and other improvements. The Cheyenne-Arapaho leases were also voided. Disgruntled cattlemen, not parties to the leases of 1883, had joined hands with equally disgruntled Cheyennes and Arapahoes, led by Chief Stone Calf, to provoke a near-war. And on July 15, 1885, President Cleveland dispatched Sheridan to Fort Reno to inquire into the disturbance. After talking with

Agent D. B. Dyer (who had superseded Miles), the cattlemen, and the leaders of the two Indian factions, Sheridan recommended to Cleveland that the leases be canceled and that a new agent be appointed to take the place of Dyer, who had refused to accept responsibilities growing out of the dispute. The President promptly accepted Sheridan's recommendation; he ordered the leases annulled and the cattlemen expelled, and named Captain Jesse M. Lee as the new agent.

The Oklahoma movement was pitched on a less objectionable plane by Lamar's understanding with the Boomers. And this gave it great impetus. Thousands of border folk had strenuously objected to the previous invasions on the ground that they were in violation of federal law; but they now enthusiastically supported the efforts of Thomas Ryan, James B. Weaver, William M. Springer, and other Senators and Representatives in Washington, who vied with each other in seeking Boomer favors. Politicians readily sensed that now the Boomer Movement was popular. Here and there mass meetings were held and petitions and memorials were drawn up asking for the opening of the Indian Territory to settlement.

Military and Indian Service officials also approved the new movement. In his annual report of 1885, General Nelson A. Miles, commander of the Department of Missouri, referred to the Indian Territory as "a block in the pathway of civilization." He recommended that it be abolished, its Indians allotted lands in severalty, and all surplus lands disposed of to homesteaders. Miles's superior, General Phil Sheridan, was not willing to see the Indian Territory abolished, but he heartily endorsed Miles's suggestion of the allotment of lands to the Indians and of the settlement of surplus lands by homesteaders. Secretary Lamar and Commissioner J. D. C. Atkins were in accord with Sheridan's proposal, but they preferred that eastern Indian Territory be preserved intact for the Indians.

There is little doubt that these opinions influenced Cleveland. In December, 1885, he recommended to the Forty-ninth Congress the appointment of a commission to study the Indian Territory land problem with a view of condensing the reservations still further and negotiating for the surplus lands when the allotment program was completed. Congress needed little encouragement. Within the next three years various and sundry bills for Indian allotments, for revamping the Indian Territory's judicial system, for the disposal of its surplus lands to homesteaders, and for the creation of the Territory of Oklahoma were dumped into the House and Senate legislative hoppers. But it is not necessary here to follow the varying fortunes of each of these. It is enough to say that, growing out of these proposals, a signal victory was gained by the Oklahoma champions on February 8, 1887, when President Cleveland approved the Dawes Act, providing for the allotment of lands in severalty to the Indians. The bill was so drawn, however, that it included neither the lands of the Osage, Peoria, Miami, and Sac and Fox Indians nor those of the Five Civilized Tribes. Under its terms, each head of a family was entitled to 160 acres of land and each single person over eighteen years of age (as well as each orphan under that age) to 80 acres; other persons under eighteen were entitled to 40 acres. Those to whom allotments were made could not sell or mortgage their lands for twenty-five years. The President could negotiate with a tribe for any surplus lands after allotments had been completed, and these he could dispose of to settlers in tracts of 160 acres each.

Numerous petitions were now sent up to Congress by the victorious Boomers. Their unremitting efforts during the uncertain past had created great confidence among them and had led them to believe that final victory was near. On February 8, 1888, as a climax to all these efforts, Boomer delegates from all the states bordering on the Indian Territory met at Kansas City in a rousing convention. They drew up a memorial stating that only "chiefs, squawmen, and half-breeds" were in favor of retaining the Indian Territory as it was; that general lawlessness existed in the Territory because no court had jurisdiction in civil cases arising between citizens of the United States and the Indians; and that since the Territory was an obstacle to trade and commerce, at least its western half should be opened to settlement, with compensation to the Indians for all lands taken. Couch was one of the most conspicuous delegates present and was selected as one of eighteen representatives to go to Washington to present the memorial and other resolutions to Congress.

The now thoroughly alarmed Creek and Seminole leaders saw that they could claim Oklahoma no longer, and resolved to make the best possible settlement with the government. In January, 1889, a Creek delegation headed by Pleasant Porter went to Washington and offered to relinquish the tribe's claims on Oklahoma for a consideration. Secretary William F. Vilas, who had succeeded Lamar, then proposed an agreement with them whereby for the sum of $2,280,000 the Creeks would withdraw all claims to Oklahoma, and on January 31 the Creek legislature accepted the proposal. The United States Senate approved the bill on February 15, after Senator Henry L. Dawes had attached a rider stipulating that in the event that any homesteader should intrude within the region purchased prior to its opening by law, he should forfeit his right to establish a claim. The measure was passed by the House on February 23 and was signed by Cleveland three days before he went out of office.

On February 15 two Seminole delegates also came to Washington with a similar offer. But Vilas told them that their rights were only implied in the treaty of 1866, and not expressed, as were those of the Creeks. Yet he placed their proposal before Cleveland, who in turn transmitted it to Congress. Promptly a bill was introduced in the Senate to accept the Seminole offer, proposing an appropriation of $1,912,000 as an additional compensation to that paid in 1866. The bill also carried a rider similar to that in the Creek measure, penalizing those who might seek to establish claims on the relinquished lands before they were opened by law.

Since the adjournment of Congress was at hand, friends of the bill despaired of its passage. Consequently they attached it as a rider to the pending Indian appropriation bill, with additional features authorizing the President to establish two land offices within Oklahoma and to open the district to settlement under the terms of the Homestead Law. The amended appropriation bill passed the House on February 27 and was approved by the Senate and signed by the President on March 2. Twenty-one days later the new president, Benjamin Harrison, issued a proclamation throwing open the entire Oklahoma district to settlement "at and after the hour of twelve o'clock, noon, on the twenty-second day of April."

The border settlers celebrated their great victory noisily. A Wichita correspondent for the *Boulder County Herald* (Colorado) wrote on April 3 that the news of the proposed opening was received in his town by the firing of cannon and the display of bunting, and that bonfires were burning all over southern Kansas. He observed that so many people were starting for the new country that many of the towns would be depopulated. One man, he continued, had already been killed over a claim dispute, and some had sold their rights for as much as five hundred dollars. At Purcell, Indian Territory, Couch found the interest of settlers equally great. Writing on March 10, he said that every day from five to twenty wagons passed through Purcell headed for the boundary line (the South Canadian River).

Thus, after exactly a decade, the Boomers had won the long

and bitterly fought battle. And had it not been for the bulldog tenacity of Payne it is more than probable that they would have ceased their agitation long before victory finally came. Many of them had suffered from exposure, imprisonment, and numerous other hardships, and had expended their last dollars in sustained efforts during invasion after invasion. Payne and legal advisers had told them that claims thus entered would be recognized under the terms of the Pre-emption Law once the country was legally opened to settlement. But in this they were bitterly disappointed. They were now placed on the same footing as those who would enter Oklahoma for the first time on April 22. All would be well only if they could reach their claims first; if others should precede them, then the newcomers' rights would be recognized by the Land Office.

From March 23 until April 22 the Kansas and Texas roads leading toward Oklahoma were once more crowded with covered wagons, hacks, buggies, and horseback riders. Border towns—Caldwell, Arkansas City, Wichita, Hunnewell, and Wellington, in Kansas, and Denison, Gainesville, and Vernon, in Texas—were crowded with movers jostling each other good-naturedly, swapping stories and information concerning roads and trails. Hotels and railroad depots were overflowing with promoters, businessmen, land agents, and homeless men, women, and children, all bound for the "promised land." And mingling with these were the less desirable individuals—gamblers, swindlers, adventurers, and ne'er-do-wells, who sought every opportunity to fleece the unsuspecting homesteaders or to take advantage of any circumstance that might present itself. Marion T. Rock thus pictured such a motley array of people at Arkansas City: "Scenes in and about the depot on Sunday night [before the opening on the next day] reminded one of the vast, surging crowds at the Philadelphia railway station during the Centennial of 1876." And in heavily laden freight wagons on the crowded streets could be found assorted groceries, dry goods, printing presses, boxes of hardware and lumber—all to furnish new business ventures in towns soon to appear in Oklahoma.

It should be remembered that Oklahoma was separated from Kansas by the Cherokee Strip and from Texas by the Chickasaw Nation, across both of which areas homeseekers were allowed to travel to the boundary of Oklahoma before April 22. Then there were means of travel to favor those who were not fortunate enough to have conveyances of their own. The Santa Fe Railroad crossed the unoccupied lands from north to south, thus making possible transportation for hundreds of homeseekers and enormous quantities of materials that would be needed by incoming settlers and business enterprises. And a parallel stage road, along the Kingfisher-Chickasha-Duncan line, was another well-known route of travel.

Within Oklahoma were less than twelve thousand tracts of 160 acres each, and according to one contemporary authority there were a hundred thousand homeseekers, all eager to establish claims. On April 8 an observer at Gainesville, Texas, stated that throughout the Chickasaw Nation arrangements were being made among the noncitizen tenants for a general exodus to Oklahoma on the date of the opening. This move had gained such proportions that Chickasaw landholders had become alarmed, fearing that not enough noncitizen tenants would remain to till their growing crops. Over two hundred tenants on Captain Murray's Wichita Valley farm, for instance, had banded together to go to the new land. A general migratory movement was also observed throughout northern Texas.

This and other similar situations would obviously provoke a scramble for homes. To those mounted on fast horses would go the best chances of establishing choice claims. Certainly few of the needy homeseekers could expect success, for as a rule they came to border towns and camps in overloaded wagons pulled by scrawny, hidebound horses and mules. For this reason, on the day of the opening, more than one wagoner laid aside the harness and mounted the fastest horse of his team for the race.

By the morning of April 22 the northern boundary of Oklahoma was lined by thousands of prospective settlers, their far-flung line of wagons, buggies, hacks, and carts presenting a never-to-be-forgotten sight. Excited contestants milled about their camps, employing their time by greasing the axles of their vehicles, inspecting harnesses and saddles, and making last-minute preparations for the great race. They laughingly referred to the forthcoming event as "Harrison's Hoss Race." It was to be a contest for free homes. And even though only a small per cent of those present could succeed, good cheer and lively conversation were heard on every hand.

Blue-coated cavalrymen rode the boundary to keep back overly ambitious Boomers. They, too, smiled their good will toward the contestants, for their years of vigil and patrol were behind them. No longer would they be compelled to escort unwilling Boomers back to the Kansas line. Now they were umpires, to see, insofar as the law was concerned, that the race was run fairly and that one contestant did not have an advantage over another. Stationed at intervals along the boundary, they were to signal the beginning of the race and were to maintain order.

Promptly at twelve, by bugle notes or pistol shots, the signals were sounded and the race was on. Thousands of contestants surged across the line in a mad, headlong rush toward the coveted lands. The clamor and confusion of the race was like the noise of battle. The pounding of hoofs, the frightened neighing of horses, the thunderous rattle of wildly careening vehicles, the raucous shouts and curses of excited riders and teamsters, the shrill screams of terrified women and children, and the crash of overturning vehicles—all blended in a wild, deafening din never before heard on the prairies.

Several Santa Fe passenger trains had also moved southward from Arkansas City to join in the race. They had proceeded to the Oklahoma boundary where they, too, awaited the signal to carry their hundreds of passengers into the lands to be opened. Passengers sat in seats and windows, stood in aisles and on car platforms, and some clung precariously to window sills. Engineers were to regulate the speed of the trains to conform to that of horse-drawn conveyances. But presently they had gone beyond the line of racing horseback contestants and had disgorged their cargoes of human freight. In some instances excited homeseekers jumped from the cars while the train was still moving at a lively rate and were sent sprawling beside the track; but if they were not seriously hurt, they forthwith leaped to their feet and dashed away to race other contestants. And when the cars finally ground to a stop, hundreds of others poured from doors and windows as though the coaches were possessed by Satan and all his imps.

Along the South Canadian, the southern boundary of Oklahoma, the scenes were to some extent different. Purcell, on the south bank of the river, had been an assembling point for several weeks and on April 22 had a population of more than four thousand souls, three-fourths of whom were there for the "run." Here, too, a passenger train was to transport hundreds of homeseekers northward. The river bed was quite filled with muddy, swirling water, as hundreds plunged into it at the sound of the pistol shot fired by an officer on the opposite side. Some of the heavily laden wagons and hacks foundered in the quicksand, only to have the teamsters wade out, unhitch their favorite mounts, and continue the race. Others pulled through to the opposite bank. Within one hour the whole landscape on the south side of the river, near what is now Lexington, Oklahoma, was covered with riders and footmen dashing here and there seeking unoccupied tracts or engaged in angry controversy over choice claims. Still others wandered forlornly from place to place to find that more fortunate contestants had preceded them.

Similar scenes were enacted on the Canadian River below present-day Moore, Oklahoma, and near the site of the Norman bridge. Hundreds of happy settlers at last established claims and immediately began to build homes and plow fields; but there were thousands who drove back to Kansas, Arkansas, Missouri, and Texas to await the action of Congress in opening the remainder of the Indian Territory to settlement.

On the same prairies over which General Nelson A. Miles and General B. H. Grierson had conducted a campaign against the wild Comanches, Kiowas, Cheyennes, and Arapahoes in 1874–75, now within a day sprang up Oklahoma City, Guthrie, Kingfisher, and Norman. Oklahoma City was a tent town of more than seven thousand souls by the end of April, as was Guthrie also. Streets and avenues were surveyed, lots were awarded, and soon the sound of hammer and saw heralded the approach of metropolitan life. Within each town the Anglo-American's genius for organization was tested. A temporary framework of government was set up—a mayor was chosen and councilmen and a board of claims were appointed. W. L. Couch was named Oklahoma City's first mayor, and D. B. Dyer was chosen for the same position at Guthrie. Inspector Pickles of the Department of the Interior found on visiting Guthrie at this time that the municipal council assumed "grave responsibilities" but that "generally they settled them in a creditable manner." They had "ordered the survey of the town and practically cleared the streets." There were other evidences of a healthful social order: tuition schools were launched and churches were organized.

"Harrison's Hoss Race"

At the same time, there was much strife and confusion. Long before April 22 many prospective settlers had crossed the Oklahoma boundary to stake claims, in spite of Harrison's warning that they would be dispossessed of all rights if they were found guilty. They had eluded watchful soldiers, had chosen homesites, and had then hidden in timber or ravines near by until the hour of the opening. Bone fide settlers who arrived within the heart of the district well ahead of other racers were more than once chagrined to find these intruders occupying, and sometimes even plowing, choice claims. Of course they knew that their rivals had jumped the official gun, but there was no way to prove it. These individuals the new arrivals called "Sooners," because they had entered Oklahoma sooner than they were entitled to under the President's proclamation. They were well distributed throughout the district and were ready to meet in court those who had made the run.

There were others who made the run from Santa Fe construction camps. W. L. Couch was employed at this time in the construction of a segment of the Santa Fe roadbed near the North Canadian River, within what is now eastern Oklahoma City. He had engaged Mrs. Rachel Anna Haines as cook and proprietress of his dining shack. On the morning of April 22 she and George mounted a horse and crossed the river, and there where the stream bends toward the northeast she drove down her claim stake. Meanwhile, Couch located another quarter-section claim west of and including the site of the present Montgomery Ward building. But soon other contestants arrived and a bitter controversy ensued. In the months to follow, the Couch men were known as the "Seminoles" and their rivals were called the "Kickapoos." The former were better organized in the beginning, however, and thus Couch was elected the city's first mayor. Yet the first comers had increasing difficulty in maintaining their land claims. Day

after day Couch and his sons guarded their property against tres-
passers, among whom J. C. Adams was most persistent and determined. Adams's annoying efforts finally led to a gunfight with
Couch in which the Boomer leader was wounded. Couch died on
April 21, 1890, from his wounds, leaving his family to keep up
the unequal struggle.

Other Sooners encountered the same kind of opposition, and
the courts were burdened with land cases which dragged on for
many months. Finally, by the Smith vs. Townsend case (Oklahoma, No. 1173), the Supreme Court of the United States up-
held a territorial court decision that those who had made the run
of April 22, 1889, from railroad construction camps had violated
the terms of the President's proclamation and were therefore
disqualified from holding claims.

Mrs. Haines, along with Couch and others, fell under the
ban of the court decision. Anna was now penniless and heart-
broken. Since 1879 she had shared with Payne and others the
privations and hardships of pioneering and had spent, according
to her admission in later years, more than fifteen hundred dollars
on the Oklahoma cause, in addition to the insurance legacy that
Payne had left her. On her North Canadian claim she had built a
house, fenced her property, and made other improvements. And
now she must move out. Sorrowfully she and George left the Territory of Oklahoma (created in 1890) and moved to Oregon,
where she established a final residence. Here in 1912 she died in
great poverty. Before her death, the secretary of the Payne Memorial Association, T. N. Athey, sought her consent to remove the
remains of Payne to Oklahoma City, since he had been buried on
a lot owned by Mrs. Haines. But this she refused unless a home
were given her within the state. She felt that she had been un-
justly robbed of her North Canadian farm and demanded that
such a wrong be righted.

Today one who visits the sites of Payne's and Mrs. Haines's claims finds ample evidence of the irony of fate. Where Anna's house stood, a steel oil derrick now rears skyward. And standing here one may count twelve others on the 160-acre tract. Farther to the east is the 640-acre claim which Dave sought to establish in 1880 (east of High Street and south of Southeast 29th Street). It is at present the very center of Oklahoma City's great oil field. Yet both claimants died without funds. Mrs. Haines spent her last days at hard toil. She and Payne had won for others what they could not enjoy themselves.

Not many other members of Payne's Oklahoma Colony were able to enjoy the land for which they had fought, for that matter. Of more than fourteen thousand certificate-holders, only Sam Crocker, A. C. McCord, "Captain" Cooper, Dad Echelberger, and a few others who had been followers of both Payne and Couch had established homes along or near the North Canadian, and less than one thousand had found claims elsewhere in Oklahoma in 1889. Yet some of them had spent more of their own means than a 160-acre Kansas or Texas farm would have cost. But it mattered little. They had championed the rights of the poor against "greedy cattle rings" and "land-grabbers" at a time when others feared to do so. They had suffered from the rigors of winter and the blistering heat of summer and from the want of food. They had submitted to the indignities of arrest and abuse at the hands of Negro troopers. Now their crusade was vindicated. Victory had perched on their banner. Once more they were respectable citizens in the eyes of their fellows, and Payne and Couch were martyrs to a noble cause. The average Boomer felt that he had been amply repaid for his labor and expenditure, for by pluck and persistence he had caused Oklahoma to be opened to thousands of homeless people.

Bibliography

A. MANUSCRIPTS

While selecting materials for the construction of this study, I examined more than 1,000 documents, including letters, reports, petitions, memorials, affidavits, court decisions, Boomer literature; and in addition, approximately 300 newspaper articles—all contemporaneous with the Boomer Movement, but only the more important of which I shall list. In the National Archives, Washington, D.C., are the old records of the War Department, the Department of the Interior, and the Department of Justice. These contain much material relating to Boomer activities and the leasing problem during the period from 1879 to 1885, consisting of letters, reports, and miscellaneous documents from the President, departmental secretaries and officials, and army officers and Indian agents.

The Oklahoma Historical Society Library, Oklahoma City, houses three important collections: (1) the Payne papers, consisting of Payne's letters and other materials of the period, 1879–84; (2) the Indian Archives, files of the several Indian agencies of the Indian Territory; and (3) the T. N. Athey papers, comprising Athey's correspondence and numerous newspaper clippings.

Among the records of the Department of Justice and the Department of the Interior, I secured microfilms of 427 documents; 178 from the Department of Justice files, and 249 from the Department of the Interior files (a large part of which was transmitted manuscripts from the War Department). These materials are of several classes—letters, reports, petitions, maps, Boomer literature, and printed documents—and are of various lengths, ranging from short telegrams to long reports of ten or more pages. Generally they present the official point of view toward the Boomer Movement, although Boomer letters and petitions are to the contrary. A study of these documents is indispensable for a clear understanding of the Oklahoma problem.

The extended reports of army officers who arrested Payne in Oklahoma are particularly illuminating. For example, in "Records of the Department of Justice, Files of the Attorney General, re. David L. Payne, 1880–1884," are found the following (which include some miscellaneous dispatches):

Report of Lieutenant G. H. G. Gale to the Post Adjutant, Fort Reno, I.T., May 17, 1880, concerning Payne's first arrest; "Extract," sent by General John Pope to the Assistant Adjutant General, July 27, 1880, including Captain T. B. Robinson's report, dated "Pole Cat Creek, I.T., July 22, 1880"; Robinson's supplementary report to the Assistant Adjutant General, Caldwell, Kansas, July 23, 1880, sending names of Boomer prisoners; Colonel C. H. Smith's report to Pope relative to Boomer activity, Caldwell, Kansas, December 7, 1880; Payne's protest to Pope while a prisoner on Pole Cat Creek, signed by all the prisoners, August 2, 1880; Pope to Colonel W. D. Whipple, Assistant Adjutant General, Chicago, December 11, 1880; Captain F. T. Bennett to Whipple, Fort Reno, I.T., September 30, 1882, transmitting the report of Second Lieutenant C. W. Taylor, Ninth Cavalry, who conducted Payne and party to Fort Smith via Henrietta, Texas, September 30, 1882; Report of Agent C. F. Somner to Lieutenant Colonel J. D. Bingham, Deputy Quartermaster General, Arkansas City, Kansas, February 2, 1883, concerning his visit to the Boomer camp; Report of Somner to Bingham, Caldwell, Kansas, February 5, 1883; Captain G. B. Russell's report on conditions in Oklahoma to the Adjutant General, May 15, 1884, and his supplemental report on the Boomers, May 24, 1884 (a full report on the Rock Falls affair); Colonel Edward Hatch's reports to the Assistant Adjutant General, June 22 and June 26, 1884; Captain Francis Moore's report to the Adjutant at Fort Reno, I.T., "camp on the Chikaskia," August 9, 1884; Hatch's report to the Assistant Adjutant General, September 30, 1884.

Also among the extended reports are two in "Records of the Department of the Interior, Office of Indian Affairs, Incoming Correspondence, Special Case No. 111":

W. A. Phillips, Special Agent and Counsel, Cherokee Nation, to Commissioner Hiram Price, August 29, 1882; Connell Rogers' report to

Bibliography

Agent John Q. Tufts, of the Union Agency, Muskogee, I.T., August 18, 1884.

Less extended letters and reports, of a miscellaneous character, are likewise found in "Records of the Department of the Interior, Office of Indian Affairs, Special Case No. 111." Under "Incoming Correspondence" are:

A. H. Norwood to W. P. Adair, February 24, 1880; Assistant Adjutant General R. C. Drum to Lieutenant General P. H. Sheridan (telegram), May 6, 1880; Thomas D. Craddock to J. J. Ingalls, May 13, 1880; Agent John D. Miles to Price (telegram) May 17, 1880; D. W. Bushyhead, Principal Chief of the Cherokees, to Attorney General Wayne McVeagh, March 22, 1881; McVeagh to Secretary of the Interior S. J. Kirkwood, March 24, 1881.

Under "Outgoing Correspondence, Land Office Book, Vol. 43," are:

Price to L. S. Johnson, September 13, 1881; Price to C. C. Matson, September 15, 1881.

Under "Letters Received" are:

Payne to Secretary of War Robert T. Lincoln, July 17, 1882; E. W. Warfield, Superintendent, Railway Mail Service, St. Louis, to W. B. Thompson, General Superintendent, Railway Mail Service, February 11, 1883; Agent Jacob V. Carter to Price, July 8, 1883; Acting Adjutant General C. McKeever to Pope, July 12, 1883; Hatch to the Adjutant General, July 4, 1884.

Routine correspondence (but bearing on the Boomer problem) in "Records of the Department of Justice, re. Captain D. L. Payne, 1880–1884," Instruction Book I, includes:

Attorney General Charles Devens to B. T. Simpson, United States Marshal, January 26, 1880; District Attorney J. R. Hallowell to Devens, February 14, 1880; Payne to Hallowell, March 27, 1880, and March 29, 1880; Sheridan to Townsend (telegram), May 19, 1880; Townsend to Sheridan, June 3, 1880; Pope to Townsend (telegram), July 13, 1880; Payne to Lieutenant Pardee, July 16, 1880; Ramsey to Devens, July 19, 1880; Captain Thomas B. Robinson to the Assistant Adjutant General, August 3, 1880; Ramsey to Devens, August 12, 1880; Pope to Drum, November 24, 1880; Pope to Devens, November 29, 1880; Sheridan to Drum (telegram), December 14, 1880, and December 16,

1880; Ramsey to Devens, January 5, 1881; Pope to the Assistant Adjutant General (telegram), January 8, 1881; General W. T. Sherman's endorsement on Pope's letter, May 24, 1882; Sheridan to Drum (telegram), May 23, 1882; Price to Kirkwood, September 1, 1882; Captain F. A. Bennett to the Assistant Adjutant General, September 11, 1882; Secretary of War Robert T. Lincoln to Devens, October 18, 1882; Acting Attorney General S. F. Phillips to Clayton, October 19, 1882.

In Instruction Book II are:

Lincoln to Devens, February 14, 1883; Dewees to Townsend (telegram), February 14, 1883; Drum to Pope, February 16, 1883; Sheridan to Townsend (telegram), February 21, 1883; Pope to Lincoln (telegram) June 25, 1883; Brewster to Hallowell, June 26, 1883; Hallowell to Brewster, July 2, 1883; Brewster to Lincoln, July 7, 1883.

And in Letter Book M is:

D. B. Smith to Secretary of the Interior H. M. Teller, February 21, 1884.

Then in the file "Letters Received" are four letters as follows:

Captain G. B. Russell to the Assistant Inspector General, May 24, 1884; Lamar to Brewster, August 11, 1884; John Tweedale to Brewster, August 3, 1884; Price to Lamar, September 27, 1884.

Among the Payne papers in the Oklahoma Historical Society Library, Payne's part-diaries, scrawled by pencil in notebooks, are most interesting. The first covers the period from April 24 to June 1, 1880, during which time Payne made his first Oklahoma invasion. The second, from January 29 to March 15, 1882, comprises his grueling experiences in an Oklahoma dugout. The winter invasion of February, 1883, and the establishment of Camp Alice are included in his day-by-day record from February 1 to 20, 1883. And the last embraces his Rock Falls arrest and detention, from August 7 to 28, 1884. These are extremely important to use in clearing up many points not explained in other contemporary documents.

Also in the Oklahoma Historical Society Library are Payne's other papers, listed here chronologically as follows:

W. W. Bloss to Payne, January 28, 1880; Assistant Adjutant General E. R. Platt to the commanding officer, United States troops, Caldwell, Kansas, March 6, 1880; Petition to Major General John Pope signed by Payne and nineteen others, August 2, 1880 (copy); "Consti-

Bibliography

tution and By Laws of the Southwestern Colonization Society," August 27, 1880; Payne to the *Indian Journal,* September 3, 1880; G. A. Beidler to Thomas D. Craddock, September 27, 1880; An agent's application form, Payne's Oklahoma Colony, October 8, 1880; M. A. Lester to Payne, October 31, 1880; John J. Anderson to J. M. Steele, November 9, 1880; "Bills and Receipts," March 26, 1881; J. W. Buel to Payne, April 17, 1881, and May 20, 1881; T. D. Price to Payne, August 29, 1881; Judge George W. McCrary to Senator George T. Hoar, March 25, 1882; Ben Lower to Payne, April 24, 1882; Payne to President Waldren, Kansas City Oklahoma Colony, December 16, 1882; Lower to Payne, December 17, 1882; Payne to "My Dear Sir," December 18, 1882; George W. Ohular(?) to W. H. Osburn, December 20, 1882; *To Our Oklahoma Colonists, Those Who Wish Homes in That Beautiful Country* (pamphlet), signed by D. L. Payne, 1882; Payne to Dewees, February 10, 1883; "Constitution and By Laws of Payne's Oklahoma Colony and Minutes," February 27, 1883; S. N. Wood to A. W. Harris, February 27, 1883; Wood to Payne, March 20, 1883; Payne to "My Dear Sir," March 21, 1883; A. B. Calvert to "Friend Garrison," April 11, 1883; Payne to the editor of the Wichita *Eagle,* April 13, 1883 (his reply to Nugent); Payne to Calvert, April 19, 1883; C. C. Parker, conductor on the Chicago, Rock Island and Pacific Railroad, to other conductors, May 1, 1883; John Hufbauer to Payne, August 31, 1883; "Friends" to Payne, September 20, 1883, relative to the employment of expert legal counsel; Claims Ledger, 1884; Payne to Mrs. R. A. Haines (telegram), no month given, 1884, and February 2, 1884; Unsigned letter to Payne, February 4, 1884; Payne to W. S. Rosecrans, chairman of the House Committee on Military Affairs, not dated, but in the spring of 1884; Rosecrans to Payne, April 5, 1884; Payne to "the Congress of the United States," 1884; Payne to General Ben Simpson, February 2, 1884; Alfred Tyrrell to Payne, February 26, 1884; N. T. Nix to Payne, February 29, 1884; Extract from the *National Republican,* March 22, 1884, on a 20 per cent dividend declared by the Dominion Cattle Company; Payne to "My Dear Annie," (Mrs. R. A. Haines), August 8, 1884; Payne to "My Dear Boy George" (his son), August 28, 1884; Payne to "Dear Annie," September 2, 1884; Payne to "The Judge of Election of South Haven Precinct, County of Sumner," November 4, 1884; J. B. Cooper to Payne, November 11, 1884; Payne to "Friend Jones," November 27, 1884; J. Wade McDonald to Major Lyon, November 17, 1884, in regard to dropping whiskey charge against Payne; "Constitution and By Laws of Payne's Oklahoma Colony," signed by W. L. Couch, April 2, 1885; Assessment notice on Mrs. R. A. Haines's life insurance policy, No. 5134, and findings of physicians with regard to the cause of Payne's death on November 28, 1884.

The Indian Archives contain miscellaneous materials bearing on the Boomer problem. Items worthy of mention are *Indian Affairs, No. 7070* (pamphlet), May 2, 1881, in "Chickasaw Federal Relations"; and another pamphlet, *Acts and Resolutions Passed by the Regular Term of the General Council of the Choctaw Nation, October, 1880* (Denison, Texas, 1880). Letters revealing the Indian leaders' anxiety about the Boomer Movement, in "Creek Foreign Relations," include:

D. W. Bushyhead to Samuel Checote, September 10, 1880; G. W. Grayson's report on progress made by the "prosecution committee" to the Creek National Council, October, 1881; Bushyhead to Checote, October 5, 1880; Resolution of the convention of the Five Civilized Tribes relative to the prosecution of Payne, October 20, 1880; Grayson to Checote, October 22, 1880; Secretary of the Interior S. J. Kirkwood to Checote, April 23, 1881; Joint letter from the "prosecution committee" to Samuel Checote, May 2, 1881, in *Indian Affairs, No. 7070;* Manuscript copy of Judge Isaac C. Parker's decision, 1881; Checote to B. E. Porter, October 20, 1881; Porter to M. Berryman, October 20, 1881; Agent D. B. Dyer to Price, August 19, 1882, in Press Copy Book H (July 25, 1882, to January 5, 1883), Quapaw Agency Files; Agent John D. Miles to Price (telegram), May 12, 1882, in Press Copy Book C, p. 436; Miles to Price, March 1, 1883, Press Copy Book A-4, p. 436; Cheyenne Agency Files; Agent Jacob V. Carter to Price, July 3, 1883, in Press Copy Book, Sac and Fox Files.

The T. N. Athey Collection consists of numerous newspaper clippings and an extensive body of correspondence (generally after 1900). In this depository are six letters written by Rachel Anna Haines to Athey while he was secretary of the Payne Memorial Association; they are dated February 21 and March 17, 1902, and April 29, May 4, May 25, and November 15, 1903. All are in regard to the removal of Payne's remains from Wellington, Kansas, to Oklahoma City. Other letters of the Athey Collection consulted are:

Bibliography

Mrs. J. E. Brewer to Athey, August 26, 1901; Mrs. Brewer's "Biography of David L. Payne"; Mrs. Brewer to Athey, March 14, 1902; W. D. Brewer to Athey, January 4, 1883; Samuel Crocker (for a time editor of the *War Chief*) to Athey, March 3, 1902.

I used still other manuscripts and records of a miscellaneous nature. Miss Mary Thoburn furnished me with William W. Bloss's unpublished "David L. Payne," a narrative continuing down to 1881. Bloss's manuscript was approved for publication by Payne before his death, but for some unknown reason it never appeared in print. It is generally dependable, but occasionally it deviates from other reliable contemporary evidence. Judge John Nicholson, of Newton, Kansas, furnished me with two photostat copies of deed records of Payne's Sedgwick County homestead, listed as "Southeast ¼ of Section 6, Township 23, South of Range 1 East." Then in the Kansas State Historical Society Library is a large manuscript volume entitled "Corporation Charters," which in Volume III, page 375, lists the names of the Newton townsite stockholders of the early 1870's. Here also are the S. J. Crawford papers, of which I examined three (a letter and two telegrams, respectively) relating to Payne's Indian campaign of 1868. They are: Crawford to J. S. Beard, February 20, 1868; Payne to Crawford, October 22, 1868, in "Telegrams (copies), 1864–1868"; and Payne to Crawford, October 26, 1869.

B. PRINTED GOVERNMENT DOCUMENTS

The annual printed reports of the Secretary of War and the Commissioner of Indian Affairs, 1879–89, with accompanying documents, cover various aspects of the Boomer Movement. Of the House and Senate documents, I found the following of considerable use:

Sen. Ex. Docs., No. 20, 46 Cong., 1 sess., 1–34 (on Boomer activity during 1879).

Sen. Ex. Docs., No. 10, 46 Cong., 2 sess. (Sheridan's proposal to counteract the Boomer Movement).

H. Ex. Docs., No. 1, 46 Cong., 3 sess., Part 5 ("Invasion of Indian Territory," 1880), and Part 2 ("Indian Territory").

H. Ex. Docs., No. 145, 47 Cong., 1 sess. (on Boomer invasions).

Sen. Reports, No. 1278, 49 Cong., 1 sess. ("Testimony Taken by the Committee on Indian Affairs of the Senate in Relation to Leases of

Land in the Indian Territory and Other Reservations"), Vol. VIII, Part 1, 3–770; Part 2, 437–63 (Couch's testimony before the committee at Caldwell, Kansas); Appendix, 18–19 (Couch to Dawes, June 4, 1885), and 27–36 ("Brief of papers showing action taken by the War Department in connection with the invasion of the Indian Territory by D. L. Payne and others since April, 1879").

The legal problems incident to Payne's two trials before Judge Parker and Judge Foster are treated in *Federal Reporter;* the first, "United States *v.* David L. Payne," in Volume VIII, pages 883–96, and the second, "United States *v.* Payne and Others," in Volume XXII, pages 426–27. Another legal document used was a pamphlet listed as follows: *In the Circuit Court of the United States, District of Kansas. David L. Payne Complaintant vs. Robert T. Lincoln and John Pope, Defendants, in Equity, No. 3868. Brief of Defendant John Pope, Resisting the Application for a Temporary Injunction* (J. R. Hallowell, United States Attorney, and Charles B. Smith, Assistant United States Attorney).

The annual printed reports of the Adjutant General of Kansas for the period 1868–70 give details relative to Indian raids and the operations of the Eighteenth and Nineteenth Kansas Volunteers.

C. NEWSPAPERS

Both metropolitan and small border-town newspapers were examined in connection with this study. In the former class are the *National Monitor,* the Kansas City *Evening Star,* the Kansas City *Times,* the St. Louis *Globe-Democrat,* the St. Louis *Republican,* the Topeka *Capital,* the Topeka *Commonwealth,* the Little Rock *Daily Republican,* and the Chicago *Times.* Some of these furnished only one item or certain facts bearing on a particular episode. Those used more extensively, with dates and (where possible) captions of articles, are as follows:

Kansas City (Mo.) *Evening Star:* "Missouri and Kansas," December 11, 1880; "Oklahoma," December 14, 1880; "The 'Best Dug-Out' in the World," January 8, 1881; January 15, 1881; February 9, 1882; "Oklahoma Payne," May 22, 1882; "Oklahoma Tourists," February 24, 1883; "Another Invasion," November 26, 1884; and "Death of Oklahoma Payne," November 29, 1884.

Kansas City (Mo.) *Times:* "The Indian Territory," April 23,

Bibliography

1879; "Indian Territory," April 24, 1879; "Hayes Has It," April 26, 1879; "The Indian Territory," April 29, 1879; "On to Oklahoma!" April 29, 1879; "Oklahoma," May 1, 1879; "The Indian Territory," May 2, 1879; "The Oklahoma Raid," May 2, 1879; "The Raid of Raids," May 3, 1879; "On to Oklahoma!" May 4, 1879; "National Notes," May 6, 1879; "The Oklahoma Raid," May 6, 1879; "Washington Letter," May 7, 1879; "Oklahoma Hash," May 7, 1879; "The Oklahoma Raid," May 8, 1879; "On to Oklahoma!" May 8, 1879; "The Rush to Oklahoma," May 8, 1879; "The Oklahoma Raid," May 9, 1879; "On to Oklahoma!" May 9, 1879; "Oklahoma," May 10, 1879; "Oklahoma Stew," May 13, 1879; "Vox Populi, Vox Dei," May 15, 1879; "The Booming Boom," May 16, 1879; "On to Oklahoma!" May 16, 1879; "Backbone," May 20, 1879; "The Oklahoma Veto," May 31, 1879; "Indian Territory," June 4, 1879; "Oklahoma," June 7, 1879; "Indian Territory," June 14, 1879; "On to Oklahoma!" January 3, 1882; "The Promised Land," January 12, 1882; "The Raider's Revenge," January 28, 1882; "Suit Against General John Pope," August 6, 1883; "Affairs in Oklahoma," June 12, 1884; Payne's Predicament," August 18, 1884; "A Changed Tone," December 1, 1884; and "The Facts as They Are," December 4, 1884.

National Monitor (Washington, D.C.): "A Trip to Oklahoma," June 10, 1879; "Oklahoma Colonial Proclamation," February 7, 1880; "Payne," August 4, 1880; "Payne," September 22, 1880; and September 22, 1880.

St. Louis (Mo.) *Globe-Democrat:* "Payne's Plight," July 20, 1880; "The Indian Territory," August 8, 1880; "Indian Territory," August 9, 1880; "On to Oklahoma!" September 9, 1880; "Topeka Topics. Payne's Proclamation," November 8, 1880; and "Indian Territory Lands Leased," January 6, 1883.

St. Louis (Mo.) *Republican:* "Indian Territory," February 3, 1880; "Indian Territory," February 21, 1880; "Indian Territory," March 5, 1880; "In the Wilderness," April 10, 1880; "Oklahoma," July 10, 1880; "The Indian Territory," July 25, 1880; "Payne Protest," August 9, 1880; "Captain Payne," September 1, 1880; "Oklahoma," November 25, 1880; "The Oklahoma Colony," December 5, 1880; "On to Oklahoma!" December 12, 1880; "Cooler Counsels for Oklahoma Settlers," December 16, 1880; "Dr. Wilson in Washington," December 19, 1880; "On the Border," December 29, 1880; "Indian Territory,"

January 4, 1881; "Cattlemen," March 19, 1881; editorial, April 21, 1881; "Mr. Wilson's Position on Oklahoma," August 26, 1881; "Boudinot's Opinion on Indian Affairs," October 17, 1881; "A Letter of Instruction," January 5, 1882; "Payne's Pleadings," March 8, 1882; "Railroad Bills," January 8, 1883; "The Indians and Cattlemen," May 11, 1883; "Indian Lands Leased," November 5, 1883; "Oklahoma Payne," January 17, 1884; "Oklahoma Colony," March 9, 1884; "Leased Lands," July 25, 1884; and "Sudden Death of Captain of the Colonists," November 29, 1884.

Topeka (Kan.) *Commonwealth:* "Boomers," March 6, 1880; "D. L. Payne," May 13, 1880; September 3, 1884; "Death of Captain Dave Payne," November 29, 1884; "Open to Settlement," December 9, 1884; "Indian Leases," December 26, 1884.

The migratory *Oklahoma War Chief* (see page 227) was the official organ of the Boomers and is quoted extensively; and the Wichita *Beacon,* although not under the control of the Boomers, also championed the Oklahoma cause. Indian Territory newspapers, such as the *Cherokee Advocate,* the *Cheyenne Transporter,* the *Indian Champion,* the *Indian Chieftain,* and the *Indian Journal,* were opposition publications, as might be supposed. And actively aligned with them were the Caldwell *Commercial,* the *Sumner County Press,* and the Wichita *Eagle,* particularly after 1883. The neutral press was represented by the *Bates County Record,* the St. Joseph *Herald,* the Sedalia *Daily Democrat,* the Emporia *News,* and other Kansas papers farther from the border. A selected list of items carried by these is as follows:

Bates County Record (Butler, Mo.): July 17, 1880; "Second Arrest of D. L. Payne," July 24, 1880; "Estimated Number of Boomers," November 13, 1880; November 27, 1880; December 18, 1880; "Caldwell Citizens Pledge Boomers Support," December 25, 1880; January 1, 1881; proclamation signed by Payne, January 8, 1881; "Boomers Break Camp," January 29, 1881; "Negro Boomers," April 30, 1881; "Kirkwood on Negro Colonization," May 7, 1881; "Secretary Teller on Boomer Invasion," February 3, 1883; and "On to Oklahoma!" February 7, 1885.

Caldwell (Kan.) *Commercial:* "The Oklahoma Boom," May 13, 1880; "Oklahoma by Rail," January 5, 1882; "General John Pope Sued," February 2, 1882; "Bouncing the Boomers," February 16, 1882; "The Oklahoma Boom," May 25, 1882; "D. L. Payne Interviews H.

Bibliography

M. Teller," July 20, 1882; "The Oklahoma Business," July 27, 1882; "Payne's Side of the Story," October 5, 1882; "Payne's Projects," October 12, 1882; "Payne's Last Raid," December 14, 1882; "The Boomers Abroad," February 1, 1883; "Threat Against D. L. Payne," February 8, 1883; "The Boomers," February 15, 1883; "The Oklahomaites," February 22, 1883; and "Agent Tufts' Report on Wire Fences," March 15, 1883.

Caldwell (Kan.) *Post:* "The Oklahoma Meeting," March 11, 1880; "Busted Oklahomaites," May 20, 1880; "Meeting of Boomers," December 9, 1880; "Mr. Wilson, The Oklahoma Ambassador, Meets With Much Discouragement," December 23, 1880; "The Oklahomians," December 23, 1880; "Oklahoma," December 30, 1880; "Status of Oklahoma," January 13, 1881; "D. L. Payne Fined," May 12, 1881; "Booming Again," July 21, 1881; "Oklahoma Notes," March 1, 1883; and "Gath on Indian Territory," March 8, 1883.

Cherokee Advocate (Tahlequah, I.T.): "Payne, a Dime Novel Reader," May 19, 1880; "Payne Captured at Fort Reno," May 26, 1880; "Payne's Raid," June 2, 1880; "Oklahoma Again," July 13, 1880; "Payne's Capture," July 21, 1880; "Payne and His Comrades Held as Prisoners," August 11, 1880; "Payne, Ft. Smith for Trial," August 18, 1880; "The Indian Territory. Shall it be Opened?" August 18, 1880; "Payne's Bayonet Rule," August 25, 1880; "Payne, Reception at Wichita," September 8, 1880; "The Indian Territory Trials," September 8, 1880; "Payne, Unscrupulous Man," October 13, 1880; "Defense of the Five Civilized Tribes," October 27, 1880; "Payne's Invasion," January 5, 1881; January 12, 1881; "Oklahoma Boomers Turned Government Freighters," January 26, 1881; "Life of Land-Grabbing Payne," February 2, 1881; "Cherokee Opinion of D. L. Payne," February 2, 1881; "David L. Payne's Trial," March 16, 1881; "Letter to Hon. S. J. Kirkwood," April 20, 1881; "Parker's Decision," June 1, 1881; December 2, 1881; December 9, 1881; January 27, 1882; February 10, 1882; "Payne to Bring Suit," March 3, 1882; "Skirmish," April 14, 1882; "Oklahoma Tactics," May 5, 1882; "Payne and Followers," May 26, 1882; "Payne, The Irrepressible," June 2, 1882; "Payne Captured," June 16, 1882; "Payne to be Put Out of I.T.," July 14, 1882; "Payne in Oklahoma Again," September 1, 1882; "Payne in Prison," September 8, 1882; "Payne Trial," September 15, 1882; "Payne and Followers Released," September 29, 1882; "Payne, His

Side of the Story," October 13, 1882; "On to Oklahoma," February 16, 1883; "Advice to Payne," February 16, 1883; "Oklahoma Boomers Arrested," September 13, 1883; "Payne and Followers to be Taken to Ft. Scott, Kansas, for Trial," August 29, 1884; and September 19, 1884; "Intruders Ejected," September 19, 1884.

Cheyenne Transporter (Darlington, I.T.): August 30, 1880; "Invasion of Oklahoma," November 26, 1880; "Boomers Fired Out," November 26, 1880; "Payne to Cross the Line," November 26, 1880; "The Oklahoma Boom," December 24, 1880; "The Sad Story of One of Payne's 'Dupes'," December 24, 1880; "Fort Reno News," December 24, 1880; "The Oklahoma Craze," December 24, 1880; "The Last Wail of the Boomer," December 24, 1880; "Intruders Prevented," January 1, 1881; "Troops Watch Payne's Town Site," January 10, 1881; "Arrest of Boomers," February 10, 1881; "Payne Paralyzed," May 10, 1881; "Catching at Straws," May 10, 1881; "Decline of the Boom," May 10, 1881; "Judge Parker's Decision, the Oklahoma Version," May 25, 1881; "Another Boomer," October 25, 1881; "Stockmen in Oklahoma," November 25, 1881; "Instructions to Agents," January 10, 1882; "The Big Captain," January 25, 1882; "D. L. Payne Postpones Oklahoma Invasion," January 25, 1882; "Payne on Canadian," April 10, 1882; May 25, 1882; "Ousting of Boomers," June 10, 1882; "Payne Advised by Secretary of the Interior Teller Not to Move to Oklahoma," July 25, 1882; September 11, 1882; "Oklahoma Notes," February 26, 1883; "Obliged to Capitulate," August 28, 1883; July 5, 1884; "The Boomers Removed," August 15, 1884; "Oklahoma Payne Dead," December 5, 1884; and "The Oklahomaites Capitulate," January 30, 1885.

Indian Champion (Atoka, I.T.): "Arrest of D. L. Payne," July 19, 1884; "Payne Has Taken His Case to Brewster," September 6, 1884; "Intruder's Arrest," September 6, 1884; and "Death of Oklahoma Payne," December 6, 1884.

Indian Chieftain (Vinita, I.T.): "Saint Louis and San Francisco Railroad Company," September 29, 1882; "Payne Arrested Again and to be Tried," September 21, 1883; "Couch's Colony," January 8, 1884; "Payne's Pretext," May 22, 1884; "Troublesome Boomers," May 29, 1884; "Payne and His Followers Holding Meeting at Arkansas City," May 29, 1884; "Payne and Followers to be Turned Over for Trial," August 28, 1884; "Grand Jury Returns an Indictment Against Payne,"

Bibliography

September 18, 1884; September 25, 1884; "A Little History," October 2, 1884; "Payne Preparing to Locate in Oklahoma," October 30, 1884; "Another Invasion," November 13, 1884; "Miss Anna E. Haynes," December 18, 1884; January 27, 1885; April 16, 1885; and June 10, 1901.

Indian Journal (Muskogee, I.T.): "Trial of Captain D. L. Payne," March 3, 1881; "Land Titles," March 5, 1884; "Payne in Washington," April 3, 1884; "Payne Notified to Go," July 31, 1884; "Payne's Raid Ended," August 14, 1884; "Captain Payne Reaches His Oklahoma," December 4, 1884; February 19, 1885; March 5, 1885; and April 30, 1885.

Oklahoma War Chief (various points along the Kansas border): "The Indian Territory," January 12, 1883; "On to Oklahoma," January 12, 1883; "Capt. Payne in the Courts," January 19, 1883; "Colony Meeting," January 19, 1883; "Oklahoma Payne," January 19, 1883; "Payne *vs.* Pope," January 26, 1883; February 2, 1883; "Oklahoma," March 2, 1883; "Payne at Wichita," March 2, 1883; "Payne's Oklahoma Colony," March 2, 1883; "Solid Facts," March 9, 1883; "Entering Oklahoma," March 9, 1883; "The Gallant Five Hundred," March 9, 1883; "Oklahoma Again," March 9, 1883; "March of the Five Hundred," March 9, 1883; "Mr. Osburn's Letter," March 9, 1883; "Reply to Mr. Osburn," March 23, 1883; "Payne's Opinion of Geuda Springs, Kansas," March 30, 1883; "To the Oklahoma Colony," May 17, 1883; "A Letter From Payne," May 17, 1883; "Petitioning Congress," May 17, 1883; "Payne's Headquarters," June 7, 1883; "W. L. Couch, Injunction Fund," June 7, 1883; editorial, June 7, 1883; "Letter from W. L. Couch," June 28, 1883; "Payne Wants an Injunction," June 28, 1883; "The Fourth at Geuda," July 12, 1883; editorial, August 30, 1883; "Members of Payne's Colony," August 30, 1883; "Mail Carrier for Oklahoma Colony," August 30, 1883; November 27, 1883; "Why It Is Not Opened," April 26, 1884; "The Letter," May 3, 1884; "Oklahoma News," May 3, 1884; "A Flagrant Violation of Law," May 10, 1884; "Oklahoma Interest of Senator P. B. Plumb," May 20, 1884; "Oklahoma Boomers," May 20, 1884; "Oklahoma News," May 20, 1884; editorial, May 20, 1884; "Oklahoma Colonists," May 20, 1884; "The New Oklahoma City," June 14, 1884; "Cattlemen in Oklahoma," July 4, 1884; "Celebration at Rock Falls," July 4, 1884; "Activities at Rock Falls, I.T.," July 4, 1884; July 13, 1884; "Election of Officers of Oklahoma Colony," July 31, 1884; "A Letter," July 31, 1884; "Payne Notified He Must Leave Oklahoma Territory," August 7, 1884; "Election of Payne's Oklahoma Colony," August 24, 1884; "The Payne Capture," September 11, 1884; "Cattlemen Prosecute D. L. Payne," September 11, 1884; "Oklahoma Payne," September 25, 1884; "The Oklahoma Boomers Turned Loose," September 25, 1884; "Waking Up," October 2, 1884; "The Oklahoma Vote," October 23, 1884; October 30, 1884; "Oklahoma at Last Opened," November 20, 1884; "Death of Payne," December 4, 1884; and "Payne Succeeded by Couch," December 4, 1884.

St. Joseph (Mo.) *Herald:* "The Oklahomaites," March 5, 1880; "Payne's Invasion," July 11, 1880; "On to Oklahoma," December 11, 1880; "The Indian Territory Drive," August 26, 1881; "On to Oklahoma. Payne's Enterprise," May 13, 1882; "The Oklahoma Colony Settlement Being Made," May 23, 1882; "Payne in Oklahoma," August 29, 1882; "The Indians Excited Over Capt. Payne's Invasion," February 7, 1883; "Prisoners Will Be Taken to Fort Scott," August 27, 1884; and "Sudden Death of Capt. Payne, the Oklahoma Boomer," November 29, 1884.

Sedalia (Mo.) *Daily Democrat:* "Open the Territory," January 1, 1880; "The Indian Territory," January 23, 1880; "Gould's Territory Scheme," January 29, 1880; "In Regard to the Indian Territory," January 30, 1880; "Facts and Figures," February 5, 1880; "Oklahoma," February 14, 1880; "The Drive," May 29, 1880; "On to Oklahoma," July 10, 1880; "What Payne Proposes," September 4, 1880; "Payne and I. T.," September 17, 1880; "Will Payne Pause," November 21, 1880; "That Oklahoma Payne Boom," May 5, 1881; "Facts at the Fort," December 23, 1881; "Oklahoma," January 13, 1882; June 6, 1882; "Oklahoma," February 8, 1883; "Oklahoma Boomers Arrested," September 13, 1883; and "Payne's Successor," November 29, 1884.

Sumner County Press (Wellington, Kan): "The Right of Way Through the Indian Territory," February 19, 1880; "The Territory Invaded," May 6, 1880; "After Payne," May 20, 1880; "A New Philadelphia," June 3, 1880; "The Oklahoma Question," July 15, 1880; "Fort Reno News," November 18, 1880; "Fort Reno News," November 25, 1880; "A Geographical Hint," December 2, 1880; "Fort Reno News," December 2, 1880; "The Oklahoma Boom," December 2,

Bibliography

1880; "Fort Reno News," December 16, 1880; "The Great Raid," December 16, 1880; "Fort Reno News," December 23, 1880; "Thou Shalt Not Steal," December 23, 1880; "Another Oklahoma Fraud," December 23, 1880; "The Oklahoma Farce," December 23, 1880; "The Oklahoma Outrage," December 30, 1880; "Border Notes from Hunnewell, Kansas," April 19, 1881; "The Oklahoma Fraud," May 5, 1881; "Capt. Dave Payne," May 19, 1881; "Booming Again," July 28, 1881; and December 15, 1881.

Sumner County Standard (Wellington, Kan.): "Grand Rally at Wellington," September 27, 1884; "Oklahoma," September 27, 1884; "G. W. Glick and Oklahoma," October 11, 1884; October 25, 1884; "Oklahoma Public Domain," November 29, 1884; and "Oklahoma's Chief Fallen," November 29, 1884.

Wichita (Kan.) *Beacon:* May 12, 1880; June 23, 1880; a Payne letter, July 14, 1880; August 11, 1880; "Oklahoma," September 8, 1880; "Proclamation by Captain Payne," November 3, 1880; "Boomers in Camp," December 29, 1880; January 26, 1881; August 3, 1881; D. L. Payne to the *Beacon,* October 9, 1881; April 26, 1882; May 10, 1882; "Oklahoma," June 28, 1882; October 3, 1883; April 16, 1884; "Oklahoma," April 30, 1884; May 7, 1884; "Oklahoma," May 14, 1884; "Reliable from the Front," May 21, 1884; "The Real Question Involved," September 17, 1884; "Waking Up," September 17, 1884; November 19, 1884; "Oklahoma and Captain Payne," December 3, 1884; "To Honor Payne," September 20, 1900; "He Knew Him Well," December 23, 1900; "Brief History of Oklahoma Movement and the Martyrdom of Capt. David Payne," February 11, 1905; and "Payne's Proclamation," February 10, 1929.

Wichita (Kan.) *Eagle:* "Opening of the Indian Territory," February 13, 1879; "Sedgwick *vs.* Harvey," February 27, 1879; "The Indian Territory Question," May 8, 1879; "Raid on the Territory," February 5, 1880; "Indian Territory," March 18, 1880; "Invasion of the Indian Territory," July 15, 1880; "On to Oklahoma!" July 22, 1880; "The Oklahoma Question," December 2, 1880; "Judge Campbell and the Oklahoma Boomers," December 2, 1880; "The Oklahoma Scheme," December 16, 1880; "On to Oklahoma!" December 23, 1880; "The Oklahoma Question," December 30, 1880; "Oklahoma Payne's Arrest," May 25, 1882; "The Boomers," January 18, 1883; "Oklahoma," February 1, 1883; "On to Oklahoma!" February 8, 1883; "Payne's

Paradise," March 15, 1883; "The Inside of the Oklahoma Boom," March 29, 1883; "Nugent on Oklahoma," April 12, 1883; "Petitioning Congress," May 17, 1883; "Oklahoma Lands," January 9, 1884; "A Conflict of Authority," August 22, 1884; "The Real Question Involved," September 17, 1884; "Waking Up," September 17, 1884; November 19, 1884; and "Opening Oklahoma," December 19, 1884.

Other newspapers from which one or only a few items were used include: *Arkansas Valley Democrat* (Arkansas City, Kan.), January 23, 1883; Blackwell (Okla.) *Times Record*, November 15, 1900; *Boulder County Herald* (Boulder, Colo.), "Oklahoma Boomers," March 20, 1889, "On to Oklahoma," April 3, 1889, "The Rush to Oklahoma," April 17, 1889, and "The Oklahoma Metropolis, Guthrie, Oklahoma," June 5, 1889; Chicago (Ill.) *Times*, February 17, 1879; *Cowley County Telegram* (Winfield, Kan.), "Proclamation by Capt. Payne," November 3, 1880, "Another on to Oklahoma!" November 3, 1880, "The Oklahoma Boomers," December 22, 1880, and "Oklahoma," June 8, 1881; *Daily Oklahoman* (Oklahoma City, Okla.), December 6, 1903, and August 10, 1913; the Emporia, (Kan.) *News*, "D. L. Payne in Emporia," August 13, 1880; Geuda Springs (Kan.) *News*, "Boomers Expelled," August 14, 1884, October 23, 1884, and "Two Shows Under One Tent," October 23, 1884; Little Rock (Ark.) *Daily Republican*, February 16, 1873, and March 27, 1874; Shawnee (Okla.) *Herald*, May 26, 1904; Topeka (Kan.) *Daily Capital*, "The Boomers," November 13, 1884, "The Oklahomist," November 29, 1884, "Capt. Payne Dead," November 30, 1884, and "Captain David L. Payne," December 21, 1884; *Weekly Kansas Chief* (Troy, Kan.), "Dave Payne Dead," December 4, 1884, and "Dave Payne," April 25, 1889; Winfield (Kan.) *Courier*, May 12, 1881.

D. PERIODICALS

Buck, Solon J., "The Settlement of Oklahoma," in Wisconsin Academy of Science, Arts, and Letters, *Transactions*, XV, 325–80.

Dallas, E. J., "Early Day Post-Offices in Kansas," in Kansas State Historical Society, *Transactions*, VII (1901–1902), 441–46.

Dawes, Anna Laurens, "An Unknown Nation," *Harper's New Monthly Magazine*, Vol. LXXVI, No. 454 (March, 1888), 598–605.

Bibliography

"End of the Kansas Fight," *Kansas State Historical Collections*, XI, (1909–10), 592–93.

Gordon, William F., "Oklahoma," *Southern Bivouac*, New Series, June, 1886–May, 1887.

Hadley, James A., "The Nineteenth Kansas Cavalry and the Conquest of the Plains Indians," in Kansas State Historical Society, *Transactions*, X (1907–1908), 428–56.

Jenness, George B., "Personal Recollections of David L. Payne," *Sturm's Oklahoma Magazine*, Vol. VI, No. 2 (April, 1908), 15–20.

————, "Flight of Payne and the Boomers," *Sturm's Oklahoma Magazine*, Vol. VIII, No. 2 (April, 1909), 19–26.

Jenness, Theodora R., "The Indian Territory," *The Atlantic Monthly*, Vol. XLIII, No. 258 (April, 1879), 444–52.

King, Henry, "The Indian Country," *Century Magazine*, Vol. XXX, No. 4 (August, 1885), 599–606.

Osburn, W. H., "Tribute to Captain D. L. Payne," *Chronicles of Oklahoma*, Vol. VII, No. 3 (September, 1929), 266–77; Vol. VII, No. 4 (December, 1929), 375–87; and Vol. VIII, No. 1 (March, 1930), 13–34.

Payne items in *Historia:* Lon Whorton, "Payne Day Reminiscence," Vol. I, No. 2 (December 15, 1909), 7–8; "Mother Haines Dead," Vol. VI, No. 1 (January 1, 1916), 205; "Captain Payne's Old Trunk," Vol. VI, No. 2 (April 1, 1916), 207–208; Payne's letters to Anna and George, Vol. VIII, No. 4 (July 1, 1920), 361–62; T. E. Beck, "Grant Harris on Payne," Vol. VIII, No. 7 (April 1, 1921), 409–10; "A Few Payne Siftings," Vol. VIII, No. 8; (July 1, 1921), 433; and "Col. David L. Payne Monuments," Vol. XIII, No. 1 (April 1, 1922), 477–78.

Peery, Dan W., "Colonel Crocker and the Boomer Movement," *Chronicles of Oklahoma*, Vol. XIII, No. 3 (September, 1935), 273–96.
————, "Captain David L. Payne," *Chronicles of Oklahoma*, Vol. XIII, No. 4 (December, 1935), 438–56.

"The Story of Oklahoma," *The Nation*, Vol. XLVIII, No. 1240 (April 4, 1889) 279–80.

Wicks, Hamilton S., "The Opening of Oklahoma," *Chronicles of Oklahoma*, Vol. IV, No. 2 (June, 1926), 129–42.

E. MISCELLANEOUS

Alley, John, *City Beginnings in Oklahoma Territory*. Norman, 1939.

Barnard, Evan G., *Rider of the Cherokee Strip* (E. E. Dale, editor), Boston and New York, 1936.

Buel, J. W., *Heroes of the Plains*, 498–571. St. Louis and Philadelphia, n.d.

Couch, Eugene, "A Pioneer Family" (manuscript). Narrative of the Couch family's experiences on the Kansas and Oklahoma frontiers.

Coyne, Marjorie Aikman, "David L. Payne, The Father of Oklahoma," (manuscript). Master's thesis, University of Wichita, Wichita, Kansas, May 30, 1930.

Crawford, Samuel J., *Kansas in the Sixties*. Chicago, 1911.

Dale, E. E., *The Range Cattle Industry*. Norman, 1930.

———, *Cow Country*. Norman, 1942.

Dale, E. E., and Rader, J. L., *Readings in Oklahoma History*. New York, 1930.

Edwards, John P., *Historical Atlas of Harvey County, Kansas*. Philadelphia, 1882.

Foreman, Carolyn Thomas, *Oklahoma Imprints, 1835–1907*. Norman, 1936.

Gittinger, Roy, *The Formation of the State of Oklahoma, 1803–1906*. Norman, 1939.

Hill, Luther B., *A History of Oklahoma*. 2 vols., Chicago and New York, 1909.

Jackson, A. P., and Cole, E. C., *Oklahoma, Politically and Topographically Described. History and Guide to the Indian Territory*. Kansas City, 1885.

Jefferson, O. E., *Oklahoma, the Beautiful Land*. Chicago, 1889.

Bibliography

Matthews, W. B., *Matthews' Guide for Settlers upon the Public Land.* Washington, 1889.

Proceedings of the Convention to Consider the Opening of the Indian Territory Held at Kansas City, Missouri, February 8, 1888 (pamphlet).

Rister, Carl Coke, *Southern Plainsmen.* Norman, 1938.

Rock, Marion T., *Illustrated History of Oklahoma.* Topeka, 1890.

Thoburn, Joseph B., and Wright, Muriel, *Oklahoma, a History of the State and Its People.* 4 vols., New York, 1929.

Wardell, Morris L., *A Political History of the Cherokee Nation, 1838–1907.* Norman, 1938.

Wood, S. N., *The Boomer. The True Story of Oklahoma.* Topeka, 1885.

Index

Boles, Thomas, United States Marshal: 112

Boomer: average, 46–47

Boomer Movement: Payne organizes, 51; supported by five firms of lawyers, 54; height of popularity, 77–78; St. Louis and Kansas City businessmen back, 90; cattlemen alarmed at, 117; *War Chief* aids, 135; dissension, 135 ff; at supreme crisis (1884), 183–84; federal government regards, 188; reorganized (February, 1885), 193; effected by Lamar's policy, 202; final victory, 205 ff

Boone, Daniel: carves Wilderness Trail, 3

Boudinot, E. C.: sponors opening of Indian Territory to settlement, 41, 52; works for Missouri, Kansas and Texas Railroad, 42; activities, 42; meets D. L. Payne, 50; addresses Boomers at Kansas City, 55; chides Payne, 97

Boyd, John J., captain of Company F, Tenth Kansas Volunteers: 11

Boyd, J. R.: purported Oklahoma settlement of, 43

Brewster, Attorney General Benjamin H.: Payne challenges, 155

Bridger, Jim: mountain man, 4

Brown, George F.: 181

Buffalo Bill: shares in Payne's Oklahoma Colony, 107; seeks to employ Payne, 154

Bush, Morgan: 197

Bushyhead, D. W.: moves to thwart Boomers, 72; plans Payne prosecution, 90

Butler Brothers, Oklahoma: ranch, 199

Caldwell, Kansas: Boomers at, 55; troops at, to thwart Boomers, 56; as Boomer outfitting town, 43, 65; Boomer camp near, 85, 86, 87; *War Chief* published at, 135; in 1885, 195; in 1889, 206

Caldwell *Commercial:* quoted, 99, 119

Caldwell *Journal:* quoted, 157

California: gold rush to, 36

"California Joe," scout: 21

Calvert, A. B.: Boomer organizer, 139;

conspiracy charge against, 142

Cameron, R. A.: 121

Camp Alice, Indian Territory: location of, 125; excitement at, 128

Camp Russell, Indian Territory: 197

Camp Supply, Indian Territory: troops at, 49

Carpenter, C. C.: Boomer movement of, 41, 45; criticized, 45–46; boasts of, 47–48; McNeal warns, 49; end of movement of, 49

Carroll, Captain: arrests Boomer leader (1883), 125–26; opposes Boomers, 197

Carter, Jacob V., Sac and Fox agent: 141, 198

Cattlemen: alarmed at Boomer Movement, 117; Texas, drive herds northward, 130; lease Indian reservations, 130–32; in Old Greer County, 131; Kansas, practices of, 132; fence properties in Cherokee Strip, 133; Washington lobby of, 133; Secretary Teller permits to range herds in Oklahoma, 149–50; Nugent's charges against, 150–51; Senate Committee investigates activity in Oklahoma (1885), 196–99; alleged Oklahoma interests (1885), 198–99; Cheyenne-Arapaho leases voided, 201

Checote, Samuel, Creek chief: 72

Cherokee Advocate: quoted, 75, 89, 93, 98

Cherokee Indians: renounce support of Confederacy, 37; asked to open reservation for settlement, 42; Washington agents of, 47

Cherokee Strip: definition of, 37, 117; cattlemen lease, 130; President authorized to negotiate for, 195

Cherokee Strip Live Stock Association: 132–33

Chessman, L. E.: 119

Chetopa, Kansas: Boomers in, 43, 48, 55

Cheyenne Indians: depredations of, 19–20, 38; lease ranges to cattlemen, 130, 131–32

Cheyenne Transporter (Darlington, Indian Territory): quoted, 98, 99, 105, 129, 159

236

Index

Index

Index

Payne, William: 5

"Payne's Ranch": 25–27; "toughs" at, 26

Peoria Cattle Company: 151

Perkins, B. W.: 180

Phillips, William A.: 108

Pike's Peak: region of Payne visits, 36

Pioneer school, in Indiana: 6

Plumb, Preston B.: 34; on ranging cattle in Oklahoma, 150; enemy of Boomers, 180

Pole Cat Creek, Indian Territory: Payne held at, 64, 65; Payne ill at, 64; Payne held at a second time, 73

Polk, J. W.: 35

Ponca Trail: Boomers travel over (1880), 58

Pope, Major General John: D. L. Payne protests to, 64, 73, 99, 116

Porter, Pleasant: 204

Potter, James D.: 93

Prairie Grove, Arkansas: battle of, 12

Pre-emption Law (1841): 9

Price, Captain Nathan, Company F, Tenth Kansas Volunteers: 11

Price, Commissioner Hiram: on Oklahoma, 96, 108, 116

Price, General Sterling: invasion of Missouri, 13

Price, Reverend S.: 186

Quapaw Reservation: purported Boomer invasion of, 45

Radabaugh, Z. H., Boomer official (1884): 179

Randall, Captain G. W.: commandant of Fort Reno, 64, 85; Payne a prisoner of, 100

Red Fork Store, Indian Territory: 169

Red River Crossing, Texas: 122, 130

Red Rock Creek, Indian Territory: Boomers cross (1880), 58; Boomers camp on, 68, 123

Reiman, E. A.: silver discovery of, 140; Plumb's letter to, 150

Renfrow, Isaac: 199

Renfrow, William: 199

Republican River, settlements along: 24

Richardson, W. F.: 69

Robertson, James: at Watonga, 3

Robinson, Captain T. B.: troopers of, at Caldwell (1880), 67; Payne's story to, 70–71; on Boomer Movement, 78

Rock Falls, Indian Territory: establishment of, 157; *War Chief* published at, 158; growth, 157–58; destruction of, 164–66

Rock, Marion T.: describes Arkansas City, Kansas (1889), 206

Rogers, Connell: helps to expel Boomers from Cherokee Strip, 161 ff; witness in Payne case, 186

Rogers, J. K.: 121

Rosecrans, W. S.: favors Payne's plea, 155

Ross, Daniel H.: 47

Ross, Dr.: 199

Ross, J. D.: 166

Round Grove (Stiles Park, Oklahoma City): Boomer camp at (October, 1885), 200

Ruder, William A., Indiana school teacher: 6

Ruggles, H. G., attorney: enters suit against Major General Pope, 99

Russell, Captain G. B.: condemns federal policy toward cattlemen in Oklahoma, 150

Ryan, Thomas: 202

Sac and Fox Agency: Boomer trail to, 48

St. Louis, Missouri: as border outpost, 4; businessmen of, support Boomers, 42, 78, 90, 93; Payne in (1880), 74

St. Louis *Republican:* quoted, 74

Salt Fork of the Arkansas: Boomers cross (1880), 58, 66

San Francisco, California: as Spanish town, 4

San Jacinto: battle of, 3

Santa Fe Trail: caravans on, 4; caravans on, plundered (1868), 15

Sawyer, M. W.: 146

Schiller, "Frenchy": 170

Sears, Judge T. C., Missouri, Kansas and Texas Railroad attorney: 42

Sedgwick County, Kansas: pioneer politics of, 28; Boomers in, 43

243

Index

Western Cattle Trail: route of, 130

Westport, Missouri: battle of, 13

Weythman, L.: as Boomer official (1884), 179

Whitman, Marcus: on Oregon Trail, 3

Wichita and Southwestern Railroad: 28

Wichita *Beacon:* quoted, 51, 77, 104, 105–106

Wichita *Eagle:* quoted, 28, 29, 34, 69, 83

Wichita, Kansas: D. L. Payne's claim near, 25; Boomers in, 43; Boomer headquarters in, 51; scout Harry L. Hill brings Boomer success story to, 59; Boomer throngs at (1880), 65; merchants of, accept Oklahoma Town Company stock, 80; Boomer meeting in, 174–75; Boomers at (in 1889), 206

Wichita Mountains: Payne explores, 97; purported silver discovery in, 140

Wickmiller, C. P.: describes D. L. Payne,

51; with winter expedition of 1883, 125

Wilcox, E. S.: 146

"Wild Bill": scout, 21

Williams, Marshal W. B.: seeks Payne's arrest, 168

Williams Brothers (cattlemen): 149

Williamson, Commissioner W. A.: denies Negroes rights in Oklahoma, 92

Wilson, Dr. Robert: Boomer agent to Washington, 85; colony surgeon, 86

Wilson, John S.: 197

Windsor Brothers: 198

Winter campaign (1868): against hostile Indians, 20–21

Wyeth Cattle Company: 150, 198–99

Yellow Bear, Nez Percé chief: 66

"Yellow Legs": 111

Zerger, D.: 179

245

This story of *Land Hunger* has been set

in Linotype Caslon Old Face

and printed upon wove

antique paper

UNIVERSITY OF OKLAHOMA PRESS

NORMAN

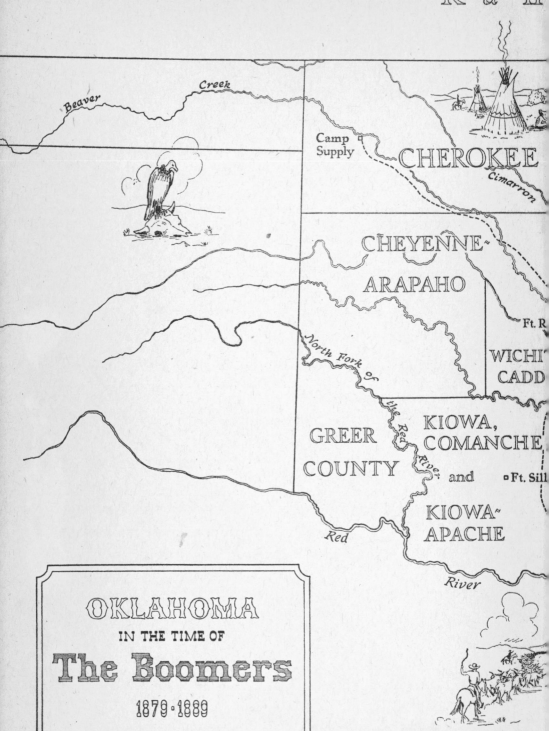

K a n

Beaver   Creek

Camp
Supply   CHEROKEE

Cimarron

CHEYENNE~

ARAPAHO

Ft. R

WICHIT
CADD

North Fork of

KIOWA,
COMANCHE

GREER   the Red River
COUNTY   and   □ Ft. Sill

KIOWA~
APACHE

Red

River

OKLAHOMA
IN THE TIME OF
The Boomers
1879·1889